CHARLES LUDLAM LIVES!

TRIANGULATIONS
Lesbian/Gay/Queer ▲ Theater/Drama/Performance

Series Editors
Jill Dolan, Princeton University
David Román, University of Southern California

Associate Editors
Ramón H. Rivera-Servera, Northwestern University
Sara Warner, Cornell University

CHARLES LUDLAM LIVES!

Charles Busch, Bradford Louryk,
Taylor Mac, and the Queer Legacy
of the Ridiculous Theatrical Company

Sean F. Edgecomb

UNIVERSITY OF MICHIGAN PRESS

Ann Arbor

Published in the United States of America by
The University of Michigan Press
Printed and bound by CPI Group (UK) Ltd, Croydon, CR0 4YY

2020   2019   2018   2017   4   3   2   1

A CIP catalog record for this book is available from the British Library.

ISBN 978-0-472-07355-9 (hardcover : alk. paper)
ISBN 978-0-472-05355-1 (paper : alk. paper)
ISBN 978-0-472-12295-0 (e-book)

~for my mom and dad
&
in memory of

Stanley Almodovar III, Amanda Alvear, Oscar A. Aracena-Montero, Rodolfo Ayala- Ayala, Antonio Davon Brown, Darryl Roman Burt II, Angel L. Candelario-Padro, Juan Chevez-Martinez, Luis Daniel Conde, Cory James Connell, Tevin Eugene Crosby, Deonka Deidra Drayton, Simon Adrian Carrillo Fernandez, Leroy Valentin Fernandez, Mercedez Marisol Flores, Peter O. Gonzalez-Cruz, Juan Ramon Guerrero, Paul Terrell Henry, Frank Hernandez, Miguel Angel Honorato, Javier Jorge-Reyes, Jason Benjamin Josaphat, Eddie Jamoldroy Justice, Anthony Luis Laureanodisla, Christopher Andrew Leinonen, Alejandro Barrios Martinez, Brenda Lee Marquez McCool, Gilberto Ramon Silva Menendez, Kimberly Morris, Akyra Monet Murray, Luis Omar Ocasio-Capo, Geraldo A. Ortiz-Jimenez, Eric Ivan Ortiz-Rivera, Joel Rayon Paniagua, Jean Carlos Mendez Perez, Enrique L. Rios Jr., Jean C. Nives Rodriguez, Xavier Emmanuel Serrano Rosado, Christopher Joseph Sanfeliz, Yilmary Rodriguez Solivan, Edward Sotomayor Jr., Shane Evan Tomlinson, Martin Benitez Torres, Jonathan Antonio Camuy Vega, Franky Jimmy Dejesus Velazquez, Juan P. Rivera Velazquez, Luis S. Vielma, Luis Daniel Wilson-Leon, and Jerald Arthur Wright.

R.I.P.

Acknowledgments

Writing *Charles Ludlam Lives!* has been an incredible journey that coincided with my own understanding of what it means to me to identify as queer in the United States today and subsequently the responsibility of carrying this legacy. Although I am sad that I never had the opportunity to see Charles Ludlam in all of his stage glory, I am so grateful to Charles Busch, Bradford Louryk, and Taylor Mac for their generosity and passion and for the friendships that I was able to develop as part of this process. In context to this book, I think it's essential to express my gratitude to the generation of LGBTQ artists and radicals who forged liberation—though many have been lost to us. These brave individuals, like Ludlam, broke ground for my own generation to have community and visibility, more autonomy and less shame.

So many mentors, colleagues, friends, and family members have guided me along the path to the completion of *Charles Ludlam Lives!.* First and foremost, Laurence Senelick inspired this entire project, and his invaluable guidance as my adviser and now dear friend is something for which I will always be grateful. The members of my dissertation committee, Claire Conceison, Downing Cless, and Gabrielle Cody, were incredibly helpful in giving sage advice on submission and publication. I'm also grateful to Barbara Grossman for her support. My Tufts University classmates Virginia Anderson, Helen Lewis, Kevin Landis, Jenna Kubly, and Callie Oppedisano were a fantastic cohort and sounding board for ideas. Fiona Coffey, Paul Halferty, Carrie Preston, Mark Gordon, and Tom Fish continue to be incredible friends, supporters, and readers of early drafts. I am also thankful for a Dr. Alfred Tauber Dissertation Fellowship and a Phil Zwickler Grant from Cornell University.

I made many wonderful friends and colleagues during my first academic appointment at the University of Queensland, Australia, where much of the writing of this book took place. Thanks to Joann Tompkins, who spearheaded my appointment at UQ and read many drafts. I particularly want to extend my gratitude to Tim Keenan and Abigail Loxham, who were incredible confidants and colleagues, Elizabeth Stephens, who so generously offered guidance and encouragement, and Morgan Richards, who was a constant cheerleader. I would be remiss not to mention Jason Staines and Alana Tierney, who were and continue to be such wonderful friends on the other side of the world.

My new colleagues at the City University of New York have been incredibly welcoming and supportive, including Maurya Wickstrom, George Sanchez, and Kevin Judge at the College of Staten Island and Jean Graham-Jones, Peter Eckersall, David Savran, and Marvin Carlson at the CUNY Graduate Center. I was given the amazing opportunity to teach a queer theory and performance seminar at the GC during the fall semester of 2015 as I was finishing this project, and I want to extend my appreciation to my students for wonderful conversations that helped my own work to develop. At CUNY I continue to serve on the board of CLAGS, the Center for LGBTQ Studies, and I want to thank all of my colleagues and particularly Kevin Nadal for his excellent leadership of a unique organization that provides support for and the dissemination of this kind of project.

Many conferences presentations, panels, and lectures helped to shape and subsequently finesse the chapters in this book. These include the American Society for Theatre Research Conference in Boston and Baltimore, the Association for Theatre in Higher Education Conference in Chicago and New Orleans, the International Federation for Theatre Research Conference in Helsinki and Osaka, the Popular Entertainment Studies Conference in Boston, the Modern Language Association Conference in Boston and Chicago, the Australasian Association for Theatre, Drama and Performance Studies Conference in Brisbane, and invited guest lectures at Emerson College, the Center for the Humanities at CUNY Graduate Center, the Prologue Series at the University of Colorado, Colorado Springs, and La MaMa in Manhattan.

David Román has been hugely supportive since I first proposed this book, and I want to thank him along with Jill Dolan for being incredible series editors of Triangulations. My anonymous readers provided invaluable feedback and insightful comments. At the University of Michigan Press, LeAnn Fields has been a dedicated editor who so carefully helped me to shape the book. I want to thank her for her patience and advice. Also thanks must be given to Christopher Dreyer, an excellent guide through the editing process.

I want to thank publishers for the permission to print early versions that inspired chapters 3 and 4: "Not Just Any Woman: Bradford Louryk, a Legacy of Charles Ludlam and the Ridiculous Theatre for the Twenty-First Century," in *We Will Be Citizens: New Essays on Gay and Lesbian Theatre*, edited by James Fisher (Jefferson, NC: McFarland, 2008), 56–78, and "The Ridiculous Performance of Taylor Mac," *Theatre Journal* 64, no. 4, edited by Penny Farfan (2012): 549–63. Also thanks to the photographers and collections credited throughout the book for the permission to use their work or holdings.

I must thank my close-knit family, the best support from the beginning in allowing me to dream beyond the potato fields of northern Maine where I grew up. Finally, a huge thank you to the Riley clan but especially Cullan, my partner in crime, who makes life happier, more exciting, more colorful, and delightfully ridiculous.

Contents

Contents

Prologue

Becoming Ridiculous

Instructions for use:
This is farce, not Sunday school. Illustrate hedonistic calculus.
Test out a dangerous idea, a theme that threatens to destroy one's
whole value system. Treat the material in a mildly farcical manner
without losing the seriousness of the theme. Show how paradoxes
arrest the mind. Scare yourself a bit along the way.
—Charles Ludlam

This is an accidental book, or perhaps, more romantically, an instance of
queer kismet. I first discovered playwright Charles Braun Ludlam (1943–
1987) in Laurence Senelick's class Lesbian and Gay Theatre during my doc-
toral work at Tufts University. I found Ludlam's plays, written in a style
called the Ridiculous, crass and raucous and esoteric. Plays like *Turds in
Hell*, *Bluebeard*, *Camille*, and *The Mystery of Irma Vep* were confusing and
brilliant, like nothing I had ever read or experienced in live performance.
As I would come to find out, these characteristics are the very hallmark
of the Ridiculous style. My classmates largely disliked and then dismissed
his work as incoherent and the humor as base, but I was hooked. Soon
after I voraciously devoured Ludlam's twenty-nine extant plays from a tattered volume I found in the basement of a used bookstore.[1] Sadly, I was
only eight when Ludlam passed away, and growing up on a potato farm in
northern Maine, I never had the opportunity to see him perform live, let
alone access to any professional theaters (not to pretend that I would have
understood the nuances of Ludlam's plays as a child). Soon after reading the plays as well as David Kaufman's excellent Ludlam biography *Ridiculous!*, I knew that as a scholar, an artist, and a self-identifying queer,

Figure 1: Charles Ludlam after a performance of *Camille* with Douglas Fairbanks Jr. and Lotte Lenya (c. 1976). Photographer unknown. Author's collection.

I longed to become a part of what I realized was a secret, elusive, and exclusive club—the Ridiculous tradition. I was even more surprised to find that so little scholarly work was available on Ludlam and his plays, but also understood how his work could be difficult to access and understand. Thus, my relationship with Ludlam required a certain queer approach to move through time critically, necessitating queer methods to figure out how my present might be linked to Ludlam's past.

This book is the product of a particular goal that I set out to achieve, inspired by the many incredible performers who have continued to chase Ludlam's queer dream and expand his unique vision. It is also an exercise in excavating performance(s) from archives, individuals, and the remnants of Ludlam that continue to flow through the ancillary neo-Ridiculous performers that I examine herein: Charles Busch, Bradford Louryk, and Taylor Mac, as well as many of their contemporaries, friends, and even their adversaries.

As an account of a specific gay history inspired by Ludlam and his work, this book introduces the concept of queer legacy as a larger framework to help understand the connection between nonnormative or queer sexualities, resultant cultural production(s), and their continuance. It applies queer*ness*, or the being and doing of queer, as a mode of ambivalent agency. My approach to queerness is defined by an unwillingness to be singularly labeled, backed into a discursive corner, or pinned down. The sort of queerness to which I refer lies hidden between the normative and antinormative and eschews the notion of these binaries as opposite identities. To paint a simpler picture, think of queerness as a fluid and ever-changing river that wends between the immovable mountains of identity (I'm certain that Ludlam would insert a sexually charged innuendo here). These mountains are formed by the psychoanalytic trifecta of sexuality, gender, and desire, traditionally represented by the gay/straight divide. The river, ever moving, ever changing, slowly and surely will, in time, erode the mighty rocks. My version of queerness refuses to be dismissed or discarded by subjective disagreements among historians and theorists and the seeming disparity between lived experience and reflective critical analysis. As Ludlam might have said with a twinkle in his eye, this is a history, a herstory, a mystory, and now a *queerstory*.

In order to produce this book, I combined archival research with performance ethnography around Ludlam's Ridiculous theater to provide an alternative narrative on the phenomenon of legacy through the process of queering and the resultant theoretical discourse. As corroborative evidence of queer legacy in action, this book is intended as both a physical record and as a springboard for new scholarship around theater and the next wave of queer theory—another opportunity to *submerge* oneself into queerness as a mode of expression through performance.

I've chosen to organize this book chronologically from past to present, an admittedly traditional and perhaps surprisingly linear structure, but an example of my intervention, a desire not to be cornered by a notion of queerness that lacks history or tradition. In my opinion, queerness has always existed; it is neither the product of 1990s umbrella theory nor a harbinger of a utopic future. To continue the watery metaphor, I believe that queerness has always run rampant beneath the landscape of normative cultural production, sometimes exploding into a geyser that seismically reshapes a changing world. I see the queer radicalism of the American 1960s as one of these geyser moments, an initial eruption set in motion by a fiery passion that eventually transformed into a roaring river, carving away layers of tradition, superstition, and oppression. As this book demonstrates, Ludlam's theater was a product of such a moment, and his heirs continue to carve new and unique tributaries, using neo-Ridiculous performance as an agent of queer progress.

The book is divided into two thematic sections. Act I, "Charles Ludlam's Queer Legacy," is a new history and critical analysis of Ludlam's work and how queer theory in a contemporary, post-millennial context may be used to better understand to the formation of queer legacies. Act II, "The Post-Ludlam/Neo-Ridiculous," applies my original theory, as inspired and developed by my research on Ludlam, through new histories of individuals I have marked as Ludlam's legatees in three case studies. Each of the chapters is preceded by a prologue, which in addition to serving as a précis, explicitly links the queer theories discussed in chapter 1 to the case studies of Busch, Louryk, and Mac. As each prologue demonstrates, the case studies inherently represent the theoretical formula of queer theory in action, thereby better to understand each selected artist. While performances of these artists and many of their contemporaries are critically analyzed, it was important to me to retain the narrative structure of each piece in an effort to preserve distinct and individual voices and as examples of previously unwritten and nuanced queer histories.

Because of its queer nature and my own queer perspective as an author, the order in which the book is read, however, is at your discretion as reader. I would encourage you to approach the book with a sense of sporadic queerness, dipping in and out of the chapters to form new constellations of queer genealogy in order to expose and plumb even more queer gaps and absences. For example, I would encourage historians to approach the case studies in Act II before returning to Act I. If you are particularly interested in a new interpretation of Camp (you'll understand the capitalization soon enough), flip to the index and commence midway through the introduction. If you are curious about how queer legacy connects to the rich web of queer theory, immerse yourself in chapter 1. In other words, choose your *own* queer adventure.

Ludlam's career lasted approximately twenty years (1967–1987) from his initial discovery of the Ridiculous theater until his death, so I've consciously decided to maintain the same period of time to structure the three case studies dedicated to the legatees herein (1987–2007), though each study is extended with an epilogue that carries the selected neo-Ridiculous artist's career to the present. In part, this is in an effort to avoid the inane though not uncommon "What would Ludlam have done if he had lived?" narrative. Because this book presents queerness as a fluid entity, I've attempted to weave a metaphoric net through my construct of queer legacy to catch what lurks deep below the surface. My decision to include acts, epilogues, and prologues, as opposed to the more common scholarly monograph parts, introductions, and conclusions, was inspired by traditional play structures as well as the essays penned by Ludlam throughout his career that took on not only the theater as its primary topic but also a distinctly theatrical tone and writing style.[2]

Because ephemeral performance is, in essence, an embodiment of liveness, the tracing of Ludlam's legacy through performance attempts to make a tangible intervention in the way we think about queer historiography as a living, growing, and ever-developing entity. My methodology is inspired by performance studies scholar Diana Taylor's work on performance as a *form* of history, arguing that "performed, embodied practices make the past available as a political resource in the present by simultaneously enabling several complicated and multilayered processes."[3] Taylor's formula for layering not only allows a better understanding of how contemporary performers continue the post-Ludlam Ridiculous tradition, but also invites an alternative reading of Ludlam's original work, using the present to better understand the past without the limitations of linear temporal frames or biological reproduction. I'm referring to the Abrahamic "begat" formula for understanding reproductive history that has marked Western approaches to historiography for millennia. My approach to layering is constructed around new and previously unwritten histories of Busch, Louryk, and Mac as an extension of the original Ludlamesque. The legacy traced herein is admittedly selective (a primarily gay male history), deeply focused on only one strand of Ludlam's widespread influence, but I hope that it might act as the catalyst to open up the possibility for more diverse studies from other scholars of queer theater and performance in the near future.

This book is not a hagiography of Ludlam (though I personally like his work very much), nor does it attempt to tie up loose ends in order to neaten the history of the Ridiculous, which, like its aesthetic, is inherently messy. Accordingly, it brings memory and nostalgic reminiscence recorded as oral histories into conversation with empirical hard evidence and preexisting narratives, manifesting not only an alternative legacy but also a legacy of alternatives. As part of this, I have taken an unorthodox approach in retaining sizable fragments of both performance texts and original quotes drawn from interviews that I completed over a five-year period—constituting an archive shaped by first-person feelings and then my own critical reflection on those emotional responses. This methodology also demands tangential exploration into lateral secondary narratives that serve to queerly intersect with, disrupt, and comment on the primary case study on which each chapter is based: I deem this approach *lateral historiography*, which is further unpacked in chapter 1. My method is also directed by queer scholar Ann Pellegrini's predictive suggestion that studies of "affective relations are part of the process [of] forging alternative histories, alternative values, queer communities"[4] and follows artist Martha Fleming's lyrical notion that queer archives are collectively made from "fragile rumors composed of flicker and smoke." [5] I apply this approach to take into consideration suspicious readings of previously recorded histories while also reading through responses rife with gossip, hearsay, and exaggeration. In early gay rights advocate Arthur Evans's little-read and sometimes-mocked book *Witchcraft and the Gay Counterculture* (1978), the author paves the way for my own resurrection of queer historiography:

> This book is as true as any other historical work. It is true because *all* historical works are one-sided, subjective and arbitrary. Every historian works this way. The real falsehood occurs when historians hide their values, emotions, and choices under a veneer of objectivity. A work of history cannot be assessed apart from the values of the person who wrote it.[6]

While Evans is speaking about his own admittedly amateur and sometimes self-indulgent work, I like that his testament corroborates that affect-driven, gay-themed histories existed long before the advent of queer theory in the 1990s. Furthermore, it was works like this one, published by small independent presses and disseminated through a network of small gay bookstores in the 1970s, that Ludlam and his contemporaries would have read, exchanged, and considered, particularly because the original Ridiculous displaced and reenvisioned history and repurposed historical icons through a queer lens via performance.

Ludlam's Ridiculous theater provides an ideal model to demonstrate the recuperative analysis of queer legacy in action, because as scholars Billy J. Harbin, Kim Marra, and Robert A. Schanke remind us in *The Gay and Lesbian Theatrical Legacy*, the preservation of such a legacy relies on "the protection of theatrical masking [and] the titillations of communicating in code."[7] This coded nature of queer legacy is made distinct through its strategic archness fueled by a distinct Camp sensibility. I have intentionally decided to capitalize the term *Camp* throughout the book to set my interpretation (drawn from Ludlam) apart from the many other preexisting definitions of the term.

Although *Charles Ludlam Lives!* is primarily engaged in tracing an autonomous lineage of gay men, it, in the words of Jennifer Moon, aspires to "provide a compelling model for other queer identities because it makes clearly visible the inconsistencies, contradictions and inadequacies that are central to *all* identities, especially those marked by sexual deviance and shame."[8] The Ridiculous was central to the battle for gay liberation, maintaining close ties if not a direct connection to the feminist movements of roughly the same period. The strategic intervention of the Ridiculous extends beyond the gay community in which it is based and employs Camp humor to transform rather than cover up—a transformation toward a united front composed of distinct disenfranchised communities. This book pursues a reparative and minoritarian tracing of Ludlam's distinct legacy through the performance of Busch, Louryk, and Mac, three queer individuals who have continued and developed the Camp tradition in Ludlam's old stomping grounds of New York City. My individual focus and particular curiosity, however, does not intend to foreclose the possibility of others to extend the Ludlamesque in alternative directions across a variety of communities and cultures. This book is just a starting point. So please, read on, or through, or back, or beyond, but always queerly. End scene.

ACT I

Charles Ludlam's Queer Legacy

Introduction

History "Mystory": Charles Ludlam's Ridiculous Theater

Camp is a form of historicism viewed histrionically.
—Phillip Core

Setting the Stage

Imagine that you have the queer power to travel through and across time.
Backward, forward, side to side. You close your eyes and click your ruby
slippers, no, your pony-hair cha-cha heels, no, patent leather fuck-me
pumps, well, whatever makes *you* feel f-a-b-u-l-o-u-s, one, two, three
times . . .[1]

In a flash, you are transported to the West Village of Manhattan in
April 1970, where Charles Ludlam and his new Ridiculous Theatrical
Company are about to perform their play *Bluebeard* at a gay bar called
Christopher's End. This dive is so named for its location at the far end of
Christopher Street, though the double entendre is quickly evident. The bar
is filthy, raucous, and exciting. It may seem like an unusual place to see a
play, but Ludlam has recently been kicked out of the La MaMa theater,
run by its doyenne Ellen Stewart, after a disagreement about royalties and
profits earned by the original production. Ludlam refers to Stewart openly
as a "bureaucratic bitch."[2] The playing space at Christopher's End is simply
an amalgam of rickety boards laid across the bar with a painted drop of
beakers and vessels suggesting a mad scientist's lair. You are packed tightly
into a crowd of young, handsome men, some in leather and all in dunga-
rees. The men openly flirt and cling to each other lustfully. The spirit of
the Stonewall Riots hangs in the thick spring air and the sparkle of disco is

only taking shape on a distant, red bandana-hued horizon. Disregarding any kind of union rules—for this is Off-Off-*Off*-Broadway, the play begins very, very, *very* late. The plot quickly descends into a depraved tale that unapologetically hurls gothic horror against B movies, wrapped around the core of Charles Perrault's fairy tale with Béla Bartók's opera *Bluebeard's Castle*, H. G. Wells's *Island of Doctor Moreau*, and a dash of Christopher Marlowe's *Faustus* thrown in. This production collages sources liberally and sometimes violently into an exciting new work. As the titular character, Baron Khanazar von Bluebeard, Ludlam leads the company, intensely committed to his dream of creating a third, gentler genital (a clear metaphor for homosexuality). He is brash and charismatic, boldly displaying an electric blue beard and eventually a nest of pubic hair dyed cobalt to match. The audience is enchanted, whooping at all the inside queer jokes and unafraid to break the fourth wall with a game of call-and-response, spurred on by a spirit of drunken revelry and Ludlam's occasional winks to the crowd. Although his troupe has gained a cult following over the past three years, this is just the beginning. Tripping over a bar stool, your heels accidentally click.

Now you are at Vassar College in a darkened auditorium called Avery Hall, surrounded by twenty-something students, many in trendy, thick-framed glasses and fleece hoodies. You have traveled thirty years to the first spring of the new millennium. Some of the same clothes worn at Christopher's End remain, a fringed vest here, a worn T-shirt there, though they have been purchased on weekend day trips to trendy vintage stores in a now gentrified East Village. A tall, slim actor, Bradford Louryk, stands on stage, dressed as Klytaemnestra, Aeschylus's matricidal heroine. The play is *Klytaemnestra's Unmentionables*, Louryk's senior project that pastiches text from Charles Ludlam and his contemporaries as channeled through the most iconic heroines of Greek tragedies. Though a program dropped on the floor reveals that Louryk identifies as male, the performative gender of this character is unclear, transforming his masculine body before your eyes with a tightly laced corset and harsh makeup. Louryk circles a raised porcelain claw-foot tub at the center of the stage, once, twice, three times before plunging into the water, sending a torrent onto the stage, metaphoric, in part, for Phaedra's suicide. As you stretch to get a better look at the puddle slowly pooling across the boards like molasses, Louryk emerges with a gasp, garments made transparent and clinging to his frame. Your heels accidentally click.

It is early summer, 1984, and you have returned to the Big Apple. A

Figure 2: Charles Ludlam probably in the mid-1970s. Photographer unknown. Author's collection.

heady potpourri of cigarettes, cologne, and earth permeates your nostrils. Settled into a gallery and performance space called the Limbo Lounge that makes Christopher's End look high rent, you realize that you are in the East Village during its so-called renaissance. You are vaguely familiar with this period through your appreciation of artists like Keith Haring, Jean-Michel Basquiat, and a young Madonna, but this is a tad more down-at-heel than you expected. People are congregated, drinking piss beer, focused on a very narrow stage where Charles Busch is performing in his play *Vampire Lesbians of Sodom*. The audience is engaged and excited, but not without an air of sadness. You think you can see an aging Ludlam watching from a corner of the room, but your eyes are probably playing tricks in the veil of New York haze on a hot night. The play is wild and crass, and a very pretty and lithe Busch is nearly naked, costumed provocatively as an adolescent girl, with a headpiece more reminiscent of John R. Neill's art nouveau illustrations of Oz than the ancient Near East. Two gym-fit boys posing in loincloths pull Busch, portraying a virgin sacrifice for a succubus, across the stage while trading knife-sharp dialogue that drips with gay innuendo. This reminds you of Ludlam's *Bluebeard*; it is somehow different, but you can't quite put your finger on it. As you look at the enraptured audience, you can't help but notice several young men looking gaunt, their cheeks dotted with wine-dark lesions. As the tightly packed, standing-room crowd shifts, a glass falls to the floor and shatters. Time stands still, you lose your balance, and your heels click.

As you open your eyes, you find yourself initially blinded by the sting of bright theatrical lights. You are sitting, cross-legged, among a sea of other audience members on a stage. As your focus settles, you see Taylor Mac in your midst, dressed in a gown of paper coins and a powder-white face awash in messy glitter. His head is shaved and unadorned and his dimples are charming. The humidity makes his dress stick to his lissome frame. You have landed gently on the other side of the globe at the Powerhouse in Brisbane, Australia, during the balmy winter of 2013. Mac is closing a performance of his abridged *20th Century Concert*, a cabaret show that mixes hit songs from all ten decades of the last century. Embodying a self-professed stage-worthy representation of himself, Mac discards his male gender to become judy (always lowercase and borrowed from *the* Judy Garland), a chanteuse who performs in the genre of pastiche, a notion drawn directly from the plays of Ludlam.[3] Mac begins to sing Irving Berlin's 1924 song "All Alone," which judy delivers as a comment on Berlin's childhood in New York City's Jewish tenements. Through this lens, the song becomes an ironic statement on the crowded conditions of this neighborhood in the first decade of the twentieth century. You and the other audience members have been called to the stage and then separated by judy into various community groups that populated the tenements: babies, kids, parents, grandparents, teenagers, and neighbors. The audience is admittedly small, as the show was bizarrely billed as a drag act, but those in attendance are enchanted. Each group is assigned a sound to perform, and you have been deemed a wailing baby. As Mac points to your group, you follow the cue and begin to mimic an infant yowl. This is fun. judy continues to croon Berlin's "Just for a moment you were mine, and then / You seemed to vanish like a dream." Your heels click once, twice, three times and you disappear, returning to a room of your own. Now, slip off those *Ridiculous* heels.

Aside from a penchant for queer performance, you might ask, what do these four diverse performers, Ludlam, Busch, Louryk, and Mac, have in common? This brief "historical" narrative, written in an attempt to evoke the Ridiculous theater style, is structured to give you a taste of the four artists who are profiled in this book. Ludlam, the very root of this study, begins a distinct approach to the Ridiculous in the late 1960s setting off a tradition and subsequent legacy that is extended through the performance work of Busch, Louryk, and Mac until the present day. All three of these legatees of Ludlam rely on Ridiculous tenets, including Camp, drag, pastiche, and traditional theater skills—which were all at the core of Ludlam's original plays—to reinvent the Ridiculous genre as a reflection of their own time(s) and place(s). In the decades since Ludlam's 1987 death, gay life, culture, and politics in America have changed rapidly. From AIDS, to hate crime, to "Don't ask, don't tell," to the legalization of gay marriage in 2015, as a "gay theater," the Ridiculous has kept pace with the times by juxtaposing contemporary social issues with pop culture and extant literature. While the tradition of the Ludlamesque Ridiculous is kept alive, it is transformed and manipulated to fit the missions and talents of individual performers. Examining Ludlam's life and work help us to see what it was like to synonymously be a gay person and a gay artist from the 1960s to the 1980s, as well as how such work and identity-making built a foundation for those who followed in his footsteps as a queer legacy. But how did Ludlam's Ridiculous differ from his predecessors and peers; and how, where, and why did this particular queer legacy take shape? Let's start at the beginning; I hear it's a very good place to start.

Just Plain Ridiculous

The seeds of the Ridiculous theater movement are apparent in the underground films that were a staple of the mid-twentieth-century American subversive art movement. The Ridiculous did not evolve in a vacuum. The West Village of the period was a hotbed of counterculture, producing experimental theater and film. Iconic theaters of the period such as theater giant Richard Schechner's Performing Garage, Joe Papp's Public Theater, and Joe Cino's Caffe Cino produced and sponsored innovative, irreverent, and often queer works that are deeply woven into the distinct antiauthoritarian culture of the period. In 1964 Cino opened his stage for the premieres of Lanford Wilson's *The Madness of Lady Bright* and Robert Patrick's *The Haunted Host*, both plays with gay themes. Although Ludlam would eventually become aware of Cino, it had little to do with his own legacy and pursuits, and as a senior at Hofstra University, he was not present for, and was unlikely to be aware of, these productions. So while the Ridiculous was, admittedly, only one facet of queer cultural production of this time and place, it is a crucial one with a distinct genealogy. Whereas Ludlam's contemporaries like Cino and their legatees have received due critical attention in books like theater historians James M. Harding and Cindy Rosenthal's *Restaging the Sixties: Radical Theaters and Their Legacies*; the Ridiculous and its heirs still remain largely absent.[4] So where and why did the Ridiculous develop in this cradle of queer creativity?

Jack Smith, filmmaker and founder of the Plaster Foundation, is often credited as the creative force behind the distinct Ridiculous aesthetic.[5] Though Charles Ludlam referred to Smith as the "daddy of us all,"[6] he acknowledged Ron Rice as his original inspiration, citing his films as being "very orgiastic with lush costuming" in an unpublished interview from 1981.[7] Rice's short *The Flower Thief* was shot in 1960, two years before Smith's notorious cult classic *Flaming Creatures* in 1962–63. Rice began to work as an assistant for Smith at his loft in the Lower East Side, producing and performing in midnight theatricals that were dependent on excessively gaudy sets and costumes, with equally bizarre titles such as *Withdrawal from Orchid Lagoon* and *Rehearsal for the Destruction of Atlantis*.[8] Often Smith and his ever-changing ensemble of performers would do little more than don outrageous clinquant costumes and move around a mass of recycled trash and objets d'art they had collected on the Manhattan streets. Although obscure and cryptic, these midnight revels were one of the first sites of a distinctly gay mode of performance in 1960s New York City and what José Esteban Muñoz refers to as a "queer fairy-tale world," where the weird and wonderful could circumvent the sectarian norms of a conservative society and magical transformations could take place.[9] Smith, sans explanation, advertised these performances on handmade flyers and in the *Village Voice* as being presented by the "Reptilian Theatrical Company." Smith was also responsible for helping to introduce the aesthetic of *genderfuck* drag as a seminal Ridiculous trait. Genderfuck drag, which unapologetically hyperbolizes expressions of gendered artificiality (both aesthetic and gestural) to "fuck" with gender perceptions, was central to Smith's exotic characters, blending socially marked male and female garments and accessories (often Salvation Army vintage, costume shop refuse or ethnic) with untrimmed body hair, drugstore cosmetics, and copious amounts of glitter.[10] Smith's approach was grounded in an effort to "exaggerate his marginalization through his flamboyance."[11] Regardless of whether Rice or Smith came first, their film and theater work is undoubtedly the first example of what would eventually be defined as "Ridiculous."

It was via Smith and his relationship with Mario Montez, drag queen and *Flaming Creatures'* subversive lead, that Ronald Tavel came into the Ridiculous fold. Tavel and Smith shared an adoration of 1940s B-picture queen Maria Montez (from whom Mario borrowed his own sobriquet). Tavel, who had been working collaboratively with Andy Warhol at the Factory making short films, was put off when Warhol's protégée Edie Sedgwick refused to participate in Tavel's perverse new script *Shower*. Tavel reacted by severing all ties with Warhol in 1965. The split fortuitously led to Tavel's introduction to a young director named John Vaccaro. Vaccaro would step in to direct the original production of *Shower* and would also cofound the Playhouse of the Ridiculous (PHR) with Tavel the same year.

While the origin of the appellation "Ridiculous" is debatable, it was at this point that a new genre in American theater solidified. Together, Vaccaro and Tavel would produce the plays *The Life of Lady Godiva, Indira Gandhi's Daring Device*, and *Screen Test* in several Manhattan galleries and theaters in 1966. It was in the original production of *The Life of Lady Godiva* that a young Ludlam, fresh from the Theatre Department of Hofstra University, played the role of Peeping Tom. Ludlam began working regularly with the PHR, and it was during the original production of *Screen Test* that he spontaneously mounted the stage in a charismatic interpretation of old Hollywood siren Norma Desmond (without the permission of Tavel or Vaccaro). He was an immediate success. While Tavel and Vaccaro's pastiched plays set the stage for Ludlam's forthcoming literary refinement of the Ridiculous genre, they were primarily haphazard entertainments for drunk and stoned audiences of the West Village seeking a venue in which to party and solicit casual sex. A young and eager Ludlam saw the Ridiculous as the catalyst for more.

As Ludlam gained prominence and popularity in the PHR troupe, visions differed and egos clashed, causing a rift to open between Tavel and Ludlam and prompting Ludlam to try his own hand at playwriting for the troupe (Ludlam had been writing plays since college). His original scripts for *Big Hotel* (1966) and *Conquest of the Universe* (1967) were performed to an eager, cultish, and mostly gay male audience by the PHR, directed by Vaccaro, and featuring Ludlam in prominent scene-stealing roles. Eventually, Ludlam's relationship with Vaccaro also became strained and Ludlam independently founded the Ridiculous Theatrical Company (RTC) in 1967 with a mutinous majority of the PHR company in tow.

Over the next twenty years, Ludlam built his reputation and refined the Ridiculous genre as his own as the RTC's resident playwright, director, and featured performer.[12] The early plays followed the same epic format that Ludlam had originated in *Big Hotel* and *Conquest of the Universe*. They were grand in scope and unconcerned with plot, as were the next two plays (both written and produced in 1969), *Turds in Hell* and *The Grand Tarot*. Ludlam's plays were recycled chaos, juxtaposing great literature, the golden age of Hollywood, and contemporary culture draped in the mantle of pastiche.

After attracting critical praise and a popular following with these initial productions, Ludlam left the epic style behind and attempted to create his own classic repertory to reflect the rapidly changing world outside as well as a more sophisticated approach to theater-making. To this end, he adopted the format of the French *pièce bien faite* as popularized by playwright Eugène Scribe over a century earlier. In the decade between 1970 and 1980 Ludlam reinvented the classics and created some of his most memorable roles. The first of these, *Bluebeard* (1970), drew from several works, including Bela Bartók's opera *Bluebeard's Castle* and H. G. Wells's novel *The Island of Dr. Moreau*. Also during this period, Ludlam created what is arguably his most infamous role, of Marguerite Gautier in his *Camille* (1973). He donned a period gown with low décolletage that exposed his hirsute chest while playing his version of Dumas *fils'* tragic heroine. He even tried his hand at Shakespeare, reworking *Hamlet* into a meta-metatheatrical romp in *Stage Blood* (1975). Successful domestic and international tours began to give the RTC some cultural cachet and improved financial stability. This allowed the troupe to sign a ten-year lease on a permanent performance space at One Sheridan Square in Greenwich Village, in 1978.

The final phase of Ludlam's playwriting and performance saw him changing his focus to concentrate on farcical situations in primarily American settings, still juxtaposing literary allusions with pop culture. He wrote and starred in *Le Bourgeois Avant-Garde* (1983) in homage to his predecessor and comic idol Molière's *Le Bourgeois Gentilhomme* (1670) and as a tongue-in-cheek reaction to what he considered the aloof and condescending silliness of performance art, which was garnering critical acclaim at the time. Ludlam differentiated his own work from the avant-garde when he stated in *Performing Arts Journal* that "a handy definition for avant-garde is that it's beige-black-white-and-gray. Ridiculous Theatre is in color."[13] Nowhere is this self-proclaimed vibrancy more apparent than in Ludlam's greatest critical success, *The Mystery of Irma Vep* (1984), a tour de force of quick change, as he and his lover Everett Quinton hilariously played all characters in a tightly structured plot. The play was based in part on Victorian melodrama and scavenged everything from Daphne du Maurier's novel *Rebecca* to the monster movies of the 1930s and 1940s that Ludlam had adored in his youth.

Having finally gained fame through the RTC and years of hard work, Ludlam began to receive calls to appear in television and film, and even the offer to take a production to Broadway. However, these possibilities were cut short when Ludlam succumbed to AIDS-related pneumonia in 1987 at the age of forty-four. David Kaufman in his biography of Ludlam writes, "Those who knew and worked with Ludlam speak eloquently of the aura of destiny surrounding him . . . [his] charisma instantly held sway over anyone who entered his orbit."[14] His death was mourned fully and openly, culminating in a lengthy obituary on the front page of the *New York Times*, an honor usually reserved for nationally celebrated figures.

Ludlam's untimely exit did not end the hopes of the RTC and its traditions; he had secured a ten-year lease on his Manhattan theater, and the complete collection of his plays was published by Harper & Row two years later. In sharp contrast to this, RTC members, when asked during a National Public Radio broadcast whether the company could continue after Ludlam's passing, earnestly responded with a communal no. But soon RTC member Steven Samuels found a typed document left by the playwright for Everett Quinton, offering instructions on how to continue the company. In it, Ludlam metaphorically stated that "the art of playwriting can be passed on from father to son."[15] Quinton attempted to keep the RTC alive by reviving productions such as *Camille* with himself in the title role and adding new works to the repertoire, including *Medea*, which Ludlam had penned but did not have the opportunity to produce before his death. Mismanagement and a growing spirit of disillusionment within the troupe caused the RTC to shut down, bankrupt by the mid-1990s. Quinton continued to perform in solo shows such as his new version of *A Tale of Two Cities* (1989) and *Twisted Olivia* (2003) (a Ridiculous spin of Dickens's *Oliver Twist*). Although Quinton was literally the next step in the Ridiculous theater after Ludlam's death, his work is more a continu-ation of the Ludlamesque sans Ludlam's charisma, rather than an artistic legacy. Because the primary intention of Ludlam's mission was to reflect the events of the contemporary world in which the playwright was living, Quinton's continuation of the Ridiculous is more of a historic re-creation than innovative Ridiculous work. In order for the Ridiculous to retain its social importance it must draw upon trends introduced by gay youth culture, and Quinton has chosen to preserve the Ridiculous of Ludlam's life and times. In 2014 Quinton helped to organize a public reading of Ludlam's *Der Ring Gott Farblonjet* (1976) as part of New York City Pride's "Yesterday's Struggle is Today's Heritage" themed celebration. The same year he directed a revival of *The Mystery of Irma Vep* at the Lucille Lor-tel Theatre in Manhattan. An attempt to present the play as Ludlam had over two decades ago, the production seemed dated and less relevant, with *New Yorker* reviewer Hilton Als commenting that "Ludlam's plays [like *Irma Vep*] are the faded flowers of his legacies."[16] Quinton's is an invaluable contribution when we attempt to better understand Ludlam's original aes-thetic, but the themes and contemporary satire of the 1970s and 1980s are often lost on a generation too distanced from the period of gay liberation to comprehend their meaning.

Camping Out with Charles Ludlam

Ludlam explained why the Ridiculous is inherently gay: "Gay people have always found refuge in the arts, and the Ridiculous is notable for admit-ting it. The people in it—and it is a very sophisticated theater, culturally—never dream of hiding anything about themselves that they feel is hon-est and true and the best part of themselves. *Nothing* is concealed in the Ridiculous."[17] In all of the previous studies that have been published on Ludlam and the Ridiculous theater, the genre has been defined by a set of characteristics that when applied independently or in combination format a Ridiculous style of performance. For example, in her preface to the 1979 edition of *Theatre of the Ridiculous*, Bonnie Marranca provides such tenets as part of a "definition" of the Ridiculous as

an anarchic undermining of political, sexual, psychological, and cul-tural categories, frequently in dramatic structures that parody classical literary forms or re-function American popular entertainments, and always allude to themselves as "performances." A highly self-conscious style, the Ridiculous tends towards camp, kitsch, transvestitism, the grotesque, flamboyant visuals, and literary dandyism. It is comedy beyond the absurd because it is less intellectual, more earthy, primal, liberated. Not tragicomedy but metaphysical burlesque, the Ridiculous offers a new version of the "clown." Its dependency on the icons, artifacts, and entertainment of mass culture in America—the "stars," old movies, popular songs, television, and advertising—makes the Ridiculous a truly indigenous American approach to making theatre.[18]

While Marranca's observations are a good place to start in understanding the Ridiculous as a genre, they fail to acknowledge Ludlam's unique contribution, which transformed the Ridiculous into the Ludlamesque. Most importantly, Marranca overlooks Ludlam's reliance on an encoded language that promotes a dialogue for the marginalized through Camp (in this case gay men) and is communicated on a subtextual level at the core of Ridiculous performances, instead favoring a list of bullet points based primarily on theatrical conventions and aesthetics. As Leon Katz, theater professor and Ludlam's personal friend, pointed out, critics often didn't understand Ludlam's work because his approach to Camp was presented through a series of "passwords,"[19] and was very different from the stereotypes that they were used to.[20] While Ludlam's Camp drew from tackiness, obsolescence, and lowbrow humor (like other Camp-based performances of the period), it also maintained an agenda that was equally phrenic and esoteric. In his memoirs Ludlam declares Camp "great," but he also goes on to perplexingly assert, "Camp is motivated by rage."[21] This overlap between frivolity and anger, and what Jordan Schildcrout deems the intersection of the "sublime and the vulgar," is incredibly important because it speaks to the unwieldy ambivalence of Ludlam's theater as a queer entity based on a queer sensibility.[22] It liberates itself from normative expectations while clinging to the traditions of the Western theatrical canon—perhaps best summed up in Ludlam's paradoxical confession, "I want to be taken seriously as an actress."[23]

Although the Ridiculous movement found its footing in the mid-1960s with works of other early practitioners like Smith, Vaccaro, and Tavel, Ludlam's approach to the Ridiculous was distinct, creating a unique sensibility that allowed the radical world of the period to coexist within the escapist world of theatrical performance, in turn building a united gay community and *communitas* that encouraged public visibility on the street and in the media. Jill Dolan points to anthropologist Victor Turner to unpack the concept of the participatory public, noting that "communitas . . . describes the moments in a theatre event in which audiences feel themselves become part of the whole . . . [toward] a feeling of belonging." It is this physical togetherness paired with being "moved" communally that "allows us to realize that such a [transformative] feeling is possible elsewhere," such as in the public sphere.[24] This causality for change is echoed in Lee Edelman's sentiment that queerness must insist on "disturbing social organizations," as an "embodiment" rather than an identity.[25] In the case of the Ridiculous, queerness embodies a sense of hope and is thus performed as a "doing for and toward the future."[26]

Although Ludlam adamantly denied that his work was intended to be grassroots, his voice is too often overlooked, considering that it has helped to inspire progressive changes for the gay community in America for more than forty years. In Ludlam's theater, movement toward social change and political progress was directed by a sophisticated exchange of exclusive codes driven by the playwright's interpretation of Camp.[27] This resulted in a unique approach to a communal and dialogue-provoking reception between the actors and audience. In forging his own definition of Camp, Ludlam was inspired by fin de siècle novelist Marcel Proust's work to move Camp beyond aesthetics to become a guiding principle, or more specifically a "special view of things" upon which his tactic to both forcibly and ambivalently "throw the audience" between worlds of reality and fantasy is based.[28] As Cynthia Morrill suggests, "Camp results from the uncanny experience of looking into a non-reflective mirror and falling outside of the essentialized ontology of heterosexuality."[29] Morrill's use of "uncanny" intimates the Freudian definition of the term to include "omnipotence of thoughts," or in this case the animistic power of Camp to transform and affectively move its participants (both actors and audience) into a queer collective.[30] In Ludlam's theater, it was hoped that this method would result in the consuming audience comprehending the signs and then responding with Robert Davidoff's inquiry: "What if whoever made this was gay too?"—inspired by Phillip Core's suggestion that "camp is in the eye of the beholder."[31] To this end, Ludlam's specialized approach to Camp encouraged the RTC's primarily gay audience to build a community toward political liberation without blatantly politicizing dramatic texts and performance with agitprop, in turn foreshadowing Eve Sedgwick's suggestion that Camp is the root of a contemporary gay identity.[32] Ludlam's vision and application for Camp as a Ridiculous cornerstone inadvertently stems from Christopher Isherwood's prophetic novel *The World in the Evening* (1954), perhaps the first work to reveal Camp to the public as an expression of what is serious to homosexuals communicated through "fun, artifice and elegance."[33]

Janet Staiger suggests that, through such queer underground cultural gathering places in 1960s New York City as bathhouses and underground theaters (featuring some of the earliest gay films and plays), "assertive rhetorical strategies" that became the base of gay liberation as an organized movement were produced, debated, consumed, and disseminated in these self-created enclaves.[34] From this queer geographical perspective the Ridiculous theater is evidenced as part of a larger network that maps queer desire and associative sites for queer exchanges and consumption. Martin Levine referred to this network in the 1970s as the four Ds: "disco, drugs, dish and dick."[35] Scholars of sexual geography including Joe Binnie, Jason Lim, Gavin Brown, and Kath Browne convincingly argue that such a mapping of lived experience as geography can reveal how and where Camp (or other modes of queer identity-making) was deployed and then made available to the general public. As Muñoz suggests, "Camp [could] work as an index to a shared aesthetic and communal structure of feeling[s]."[36] Suddenly gay was good.[37]

Ludlam saw his theater as a catalyst for communality, encouraging "those who may not have the strength to stand alone against cultural traditions which seek to denigrate and trivialize profound human needs."[38] His practical concept of an active gay theater was primarily influenced by a deep appreciation for Proust, which was in turn the catalyst for Ludlam endorsing a Proustian reading of his own work. Although several of Ludlam's close friends and lovers recall his discovery of and fondness for the father of French high modernism, it is impossible to know how deeply and critically Ludlam engaged with the text of *À la recherche du temps perdu* (though in his papers he confirms reading C. K. Scott Moncrieff's English translation [1922]). Thus, inspired by Kevin Kopelson, I suggest that Ludlam's engagement and reception of Proust's oeuvre is, in part, an imagined one. Provoked by Jean Cocteau's inquiry whether "'Proustians' read line by line or skip," Kopelson juxtaposes Harold Bloom's theory on the anxiety of influence with what he terms Barthes's "fantasy of influence," suggesting that daunting works (such as Proust) that are often started and left unfinished by casual readers are as well known in popular culture for their assumed content as for their literal text.[39] In an attempt to better understand the complex cultural position of Proust, Margaret E. Gray proposes a model of a "vernacular, popularized simulacrum," which embodies all of the myths, clichés, and "mass-cultural appropriation" that have consumed the *Recherche* since its initial publication.[40] In other words, Ludlam's understanding of Proust appears to be more of an emotional reaction based on cultural cachet than a critical analysis, but as the catalyst for his understanding of a gay sensibility, I suggest that it is an equally valuable interpretation, namely an affective mode of Camp. It is not, however, the purpose of this project to introduce a redemptive analysis of Proust's work or to present a Ludlamesque analysis of Proust. In defining a "Proustian reading," it is essential to first consider Ludlam's exposure to and reception of Proust's writing as an "optical instrument," a process endorsed by Proust himself as a mode of self-discovery.[41] Gray reminds us that "Proust insists that his project is not simply to write a magisterial book, but rather to create an instrument whereby a reader can read himself."[42] Ludlam's understanding of Proust is the seed for his personal reinterpretation of the Ridiculous with Camp as it modus operandi. In his essay entitled "Camp," Ludlam clarified his vision:

> Camp had a homosexual usage. . . . Proust explains it very clearly. In *Remembrance of Things Past* there's a long section where Proust describes camp as an outsider's view of things other people take totally for granted. Because of the inversion, everything that everyone else has taken for granted isn't true for you. Suddenly things become funny because you're seeing it through a mirror, a reverse image. Camp became a sly or secret sense of humor that could only exist to a group that had been through something together; in this case, the gay world.[43]

Gautam Dasgupta touched on Ludlam's concept of the Ridiculous as a mode of communication: "The Ridiculous remained within the realm of art as a force, a 'language,' still bound by the belief in art as a conveyor of significance in and of itself." However, it is necessary further to analyze the Ridiculous as a forum structured around a gay coded dialogue/language that serves to create an exclusive space promoting self-awareness.[44] The theory of a gay-encoded language is clarified by Proust's account of a gay sensibility, where homosexuality is seen and communicated as a system of codes; a secret language, as originally suggested by literary critic George Steiner. In her essay "Fe/male Impersonation: The Discourse of Camp," Kate Davy picks up on this and explicates the theory of encoded symbols in Ludlam's practice, suggesting that through the process of playing out canonical heterosexual romances on stage with the aid of cross-dressing, Ludlam and his company were actually "flaunt[ing] their sexuality [and making] their desire for each other" visible.[45] Though Marguerite and Armand fall deeply in love onstage in Ludlam's *Camille*, the performative actuality is that two men unabashedly demonstrate their sexual relationship for a viewing public. The contradiction inherent in this formula ties back to the concept of queer performance as an ambivalent force, what Jodie Taylor refers to as a juxtaposition of "seriousness and paradox to reveal something that is often real or essential."[46] In this regard, Ludlam's approach to the Ridiculous sensibility manifests itself as a binary: (a) as an external ideologically pseudo-Brechtian didactic genre that uses satire and reflection to speak with sincerity and anarchic civil concern to the community at large in response to heteronormative hegemony, and (b) as an internal (Proustian) codified system that formats a language to incite a subjective dialogue between marginalized "Others"—in this case gay men.[47] Though recent scholarship is rife with the Brecht/Ludlam connection, the application of a Proustian sensibility has been heretofore overlooked. Thus, no matter how you approach it, and regardless of what statistics reveal about the sexual preferences of Ludlam's audiences, the Ridiculous theater of Ludlam was the for us / by us (FUBU) interpretation of a newly visible and proud gay community in the West Village during the time of the sexual revolution.[48]

Although the RTC provided a theater for gays with gay themes (both blatant and subtextual), Ludlam did not intend for his theater to be exclusively for a gay audience. All those who were willing to queer themselves and lower their inhibitions were welcome into the Ridiculous fold. For this reason, the theater gained popularity with the avant-garde, theater, hippie, and civil rights communities. Although its inherent message was gay, its overriding discourse was one of acceptance and *communitas* for any marginalized community. The theater critics of the New York press, who adored Ludlam, revealed the RTC to a larger audience, but in their veneration also tried to co-opt him and his work for the mainstream. This act was paradoxical because it gave the RTC a much-needed financial boost with heightened ticket sales, but it also meant larger percentages of audiences who were disconnected from the gay subtext at the core of the plays. As Kenneth Yates Elliot writes, "For Ludlam, camp was a system of queer reception. As such, it could account for the radically divergent, or 'specialized' reading of his plays."[49] The Proustian connection to Ridiculous theater becomes apparent in Ludlam's description of its inherent gayness as promulgating its satirical intention and comedic form:

> I think our homosexuality gives us a certain kind of view of the world, and therefore affected our work. All our lives we're taught that certain institutions are sacred—marriage, child rearing, and the family unit. Once we've rejected all that, it's very hard to behave in a serious manner and make these things important to ourselves. These institutions can never be meaningful to us the way they are to the straight world. . . . I think we are intellectual in our view of things. We cut off feelings, probably because we have a tremendous amount of pain in growing up. We look at life cerebrally, then we become satiric. If you are very serious, on the other hand, you're bathing in the emotions of it, and allowing for these feelings. I don't think we are people who have allowed for these feelings. We have protected ourselves in a way with humor.[50]

Ludlam's musings foreshadow Judith (now Jack) Halberstam's war cry to "exploit potential for a difference in form," where heterosexual life narratives are cleverly queered through satire, inversion, and deconstruction, creating an accessible "model of contestation."[51] Thus, Ludlam's Ridiculous becomes a shared cathartic communion for both the acting company and those in the audience who can speak and comprehend the symbols and subtext of the encoded homosexual language. To this end, Stefan Brecht (son of Bertolt), who worked closely with Ludlam and the RTC, acknowledged the social/spiritual role of Ludlam's Ridiculous in descriptive terms verging on the hagiographic:

> Their play-acting was like the make-believe of children, who with a few gestures and rags of costumes, skate as it were over sunlit ice, a ground of infinite possibility; with this difference of course: that the grown-up actors had chosen a ground of the impossible, one would say the *eternal impossible*. . . . In the biblical sense, they enacted the scapegoat. Their method, too, for all its wildness, was a spiritual method: to be true to impulse and delight, to be true to yearning.[52]

The younger Brecht's description of Ludlam's Ridiculous theater points to the creation of a community and artistic forum of acceptance and understanding, elevating and celebrating the marginalized for their sexuality, and to the resulting decision to publicly acknowledge it through the creation of a newly visible culture.

Core ties Camp specifically to a childlike outlook of open possibilities, describing it as "first of all a second childhood."[53] The reference to children's make-believe is also echoed in Halberstam's belief that queer failure (epitomized by the amateur and naive nature of Ludlam's performances, as recorded by Brecht) is a sacred spot where "the wondrous anarchy of childhood" is preserved.[54] Ludlam saw his theater as a space that embodied limitless opportunities for childlike expression without fear of judgment or oppression. He also believed that such a liberated space could work "to make people more tolerant," necessitating the medium of a language to communicate his message.[55]

For Ludlam, the encoded language/dialogue is communicated through the medium of Camp. Michael Bronski noted in *Culture Clash* that "gays have hidden from oppressive straight society through circumlocution—camp—and defended themselves through wit . . . homosexual life and culture undermine patriarchal and heterosexist social assumptions."[56] George Chauncey stated his perception of Camp as a medium-cum-cultural strategy, and Moe Meyer extends this to define Camp as a "queer cultural critique" that is often appropriated and misunderstood by mainstream communities.[57]

In this vein, the term Camp has often been misidentified or misused in academic study to trivialize what is subversive, misunderstood, or "queer." Susan Sontag (in)famously manipulated the term in her pop-cultural essay "Notes on 'Camp,'" where she used it as an aesthetic judgment extending beyond the gay community to evaluate everything from Tiffany lamps to flapper dresses. In order to counter Sontag's theory it is essential to refer to Jack Babuscio's 1977 essay "The Cinema of Camp," where he unknowingly supports my Proustian language theory:

> Camp, as the product of the gay sensibility, has always existed on the same socio-cultural level as the sub-culture from which it has issued. In other words, camp, its sources and associations, have remained secret in their most fundamental aspects, just as the inner life of gays remains a secret, still, in the arts, throughout the media, and in the consciousness of non-gays generally.[58]

Unknowingly supporting Babuscio's interpretation of Camp, Ludlam states his irreverence for a heterosexual bias that misunderstands the

coded language delivered through the medium of Camp in a fairy tale entitled "Mr. T or El Pato in the Gilded Summer Palace of Czarina-Tatlina"
(1970). He revolts against the "straightness" of the patriarchy, stating in the
voice of his alter ego Mr. T: "To have a new idea is as gauche as being seen
in a new suit. Heresy is for heterosexuals. . . . Heterosexuals can't understand camp because everything they do is camp."[59] It is the total reversal of
values and evacuation of value from heterosexual affinity and sensibility
that spurs the Ridiculous theater's subtextuality. James Bidgood, underground filmmaker of *Pink Narcissus* (1973), in which Ludlam appeared,
provides a contemporary firsthand observation of Ludlam's use of Camp
when referring to a late-night performance of *Turds in Hell* that he saw
in a drug-sodden West Village apartment sometime after 1969. Of this
experience and of Ludlam's other works he recollected, "They were very
strange plays . . . if you were really straight and watching them you would
have trouble following them."[60] Bidgood's statement corroborates Camp
as the impetus behind the communal gay dialogue that takes place within
the theater and thereafter the streets. David Román notes that this Camp
and drag "of a lost era" may not be apparent to a mainstream audience but
as a remnant of what performer Lypsinka (né John Epperson) refers to as
a "secret world."[61] It was, after all, on June 28 of the same year that *Turds in
Hell* was originally produced that a bevy of decked-out black and Latino
transgender women and drag queens took to the streets, leading an angry
mob and singing, "We are the Stonewall girls . . . we wear our hair in curls,"
projecting a Ridiculous anthem and image that marked the watershed of
the gay rights movement just steps from where Charles Ludlam would
set up the long-term home of his Ridiculous Theatrical Company at One
Sheridan Square in 1978.

Although it is my goal to create an accessible legend with which to
read Ludlam's Ridiculous map as a distinct form of Camp, I am perhaps
most in line with Fabio Cleto's argument, introduced in this very series,
that it is Camp's instability (and I add ambivalence) that keeps it fresh and
poignant, regardless of changes in the social climate.[62] I cling to the idea
of Camp as a mode of expression that is off its axis, misaligned from the
normative, spinning within and taking the shape of the gap between the
normative and the queer, the universal and minoritarian.

Richard Schechner notes in *Public Domain* that "the greatest playwrights of the Western tradition (and it would seem of every civilization)
stole from each other, from the public domain, from the existing work,
from other cultures, from history. They worked as craftsmen, not 'poets.'

They organized events, performers, and things."[63] After deciphering the encoded language of Camp that Ludlam used to achieve this sensibility, it is essential to provide specific examples of this in action. Ludlam reclaimed and individualized Camp by layering meaningful references and pastiche that speak directly to the marginalized homosexual audience member, in a method that Laurence Senelick refers to as "palimpsest as performance."[64] It is a twofold palimpsest, first, for the layering and recycling of preexisting texts and comic business, and, second, as a layering of meaning, some obvious and universal, some coded and exclusive. It was through the media and juxtaposition of high and low culture that Ludlam manipulated his own version of Camp, characterized by a keen sophistication beneath an often crass and pedestrian exterior. This combination created a safe place for the encoded messages that Ludlam delivered to his gay audience through the Ridiculous theater. As Calvin Tompkins explained in his profile in the *New Yorker*, "Although the audience was not exclusively homosexual, the gay element was conspicuously present on most nights, and this element interpreted the work in its own, rather specialized way."[65]

To understand Ludlam's use of Camp in the Proustian sense it is essential to analyze critically two different examples from his plays both textually and in conjunction with the original production. The first, *Bluebeard* (1970), sees Ludlam in the role of a heterosexual man, whereas the second, *Camille* (1973), plays on genderfuck transvestitism with Ludlam in the title role.

Bluebeard

In *Bluebeard*, a mad scientist attempts to evade Darwinian science in the manipulation of human biology and the process of evolution. The title character has dedicated his life to the creation of a third genital. This bizarre and Campy plot device is a prime example of Ludlam's encoded communication to the gay community. As Rick Roemer analyzes,

> Thematically [*Bluebeard*] works on a number of levels. First, the very need to create a third sexual being indicates Ludlam's frustration with the level of bigotry against homosexuality. A gay man is not sexually attracted to women, and if society makes it difficult, if not torturous and impossible, to be true to one's homosexual desires, then that society has forced the logical, if not absurd, solution of a third type of

genital organ onto the homosexual community. As ludicrous as this may sound, it must have seemed equally ludicrous to Ludlam, and to many other gay men as well, to feel so maligned by the straight world for merely being sexually attracted to other men. Indeed, how difficult it is to develop and maintain a "normal" relationship in a society that constantly tells you how abnormal you are.[66]

It is the exclusion from "normality" imposed by the dominant hegemony of the period that Ludlam is combating through satire in *Bluebeard* (and all of his plays for that matter). The character of Sheemish points to this, with a tongue-in-cheek conservatism when he remarks on Bluebeard (played by Ludlam):

> SHEEMISH: I have been a servant on this island nineteen years and I will say this—just between us—that in my master, Baron Khana-zar, the Bluebeard, you see the vilest scoundrel that ever cumbered the earth, a madman, a cur, a devil, a Turk, a heretic, who believes in neither Heaven, Hell, nor werewolf; he lives like an animal, like a swinish gourmet, a veritable vermin infesting his environs and shuttering his ears to every Christian remonstrance, and turning to ridicule everything we believe in.[67]

Sheemish's monologue is a prime example of Ludlam's coded language in action. Bluebeard, as the metaphoric personification of the contemporary homosexual, is criminalized and rendered insane for his desires and beliefs. He is villainized as a heretic against the teachings of the church, a personal dig for Ludlam, whose conservative Catholic (and antihomosexual) upbringing is a central theme in many of his works. While the critical reception of the original production of *Bluebeard* was positive, it largely ignored (or missed) the gay subtext and symbolism so inherent in the title character and the plot. The *New York Times'* Mel Gussow took the production as simply a satirical play on Hollywood B horror films. Richard Schechner also showered the RTC and *Bluebeard* with praise in a review for the *Village Voice*, seeing the production as "exemplary of the continuation of the grand tradition of theatre."[68] While Schechner's analytical eye also homed in on Ludlam's chosen theatrical devices and "cultural recycling," he was unwilling to delve deeper and acknowledge the inherent gay message in the exercise, instead promoting a catholic appeal for the RTC, writing, "The company is straight, gay, drag—a perfectly *tra-*

ditional theater company that feasts on *acting* and *impersonation,* delights in *costuming* and *masking.*"[69] While Ludlam surely took great pride in being considered a traditional theater company, Schechner's compliments are limiting, placing Ludlam's pursuits in a historic, essentialist, and linear chronology that is traditional and not inclusive of subversion. In fact, Ludlam's use of theater as a mirror to reflect the nature of the social and political climate is more in line with the theories of the avant-garde, experimental, or epic theaters, even though Ludlam was adamant that his theater was not avant-garde because he was not ahead of his time but "of the perfect moment."[70] The importance of "timeliness" becomes apparent when Gregory W. Bredbeck brings this cause to the surface in his analysis of the play: "[Ludlam's plays] ask that they be read as specific engagements of the styles, languages, and politics of the New York gay community in the late 60s and early 70s."[71] Bredbeck also foreshadows the concept of a Proustian coded gay humor and language as used by Ludlam in writing that many of his jokes and *lazzi* "play solely to the urban gay men populating the some thirty [sic] blocks that make up Ludlam's world, the West Village of Manhattan."[72]

Bluebeard is the prime work with which to consider Ludlam's antieroticism of the nude body and ridicule of heterosexual intercourse, contrasting with the very different action of gay body worship. In act 2, scene 3 Bluebeard manipulates the character of Miss Cubbidge by seducing her; there "follows a scene of unprecedented eroticism in which Miss Cubbidge gives herself voluptuously to Baron Von Bluebeard."[73] The utter ridiculousness of the scene relied on Lola Pashalinski, the actress playing Mrs. Cubbidge, whose obese body ran counter to modern ideals of the female form.[74] Additionally, Ludlam added comic bits such as his pubic wig of bright blue hair, and a *lazzo* that involved a postcoital retrieval of his turban from Cubbidge's vagina. The success of this scene of seduction and sheer pornographic spoof was reliant on pushing the audience outside of its comfort zone as far as possible, resulting in the final product, which drew from Lotte Lenya the response, "I've never seen anything like it. It was very pure."[75] On the flip side of the coin, Ludlam used this completely unerotic and desexualized scene to display his large endowment in an effort to attract lovers from the mostly gay audience that was verging on cultish obsession. As one of his lovers from the *Bluebeard* period, John Heys, recounted, "We had a lot of fun together. But he had his sadistic tendencies too. As the public knows [since he appeared naked so many times onstage], Charles was enormously well endowed . . . he was very aggressive."[76] Thus, *Bluebeard* is a theatrical paradigm in which Ludlam used sex and sexuality to debunk socially imposed restrictions while also satiating his personal (and nonprofessional) desires in a generation of free love and promiscuity (as embraced by the newly liberated gay community).[77]

In *Bluebeard*, Ludlam's metatheatrics form a juxtaposition of life and art, both imitating and satirizing the other. The "gayness" of the performance is aesthetic in its outward Campy appearance and Proustian subtext, but it is also pragmatically erotic in its attempt to arouse the audience sexually as well as socially. Ludlam's nude body is presented as an object of desire for a portion of the audience, while also snidely debunking precepts about universal beauty. It was his egocentric desire to in turn be desired that excites a sense of pleasure in the audience and himself. Although he was short, hairy, and elfin, it was Ludlam's larger-than-life stage presence and intoxicating charisma that gave him command of his company, the stage, and often his pick of sexual partners. Ludlam's overt presentation of sexuality was misogynistic, narcissistic, frivolous, and lacking in any concrete gendered position; however, it was also liberating in its appropriation of oppressive ideologies and resultant disregard for the politically correct. Ludlam notes that he "refused to take on any role."[78] In this sense Ludlam's Ridiculous is both the "queerest" for its radical position, and beyond queer for its refusal to be labeled or confined by discourses controlled by heteronormative politics or the academy. I stress that the Ridiculous theater is inherently gay in spirit, although the original company included both heterosexual and lesbian women as leading players, namely Black-Eyed Susan (née Carlson) as the troupe's leading lady and Lola Pashalinski as its Rubenesque character actress. In fact, it was the very lack of interest in radical feminism and the refusal to take gender construction or sexual identification seriously in Ludlam's plays that prompted new feminist/lesbian women and groups, including Peggy Shaw and Lois Weaver of Split Britches, the WOW Cafe, and Moe Angelos, to break away from the original movement and form their own post-Ridiculous genre of performance. All of these performers cite Ludlam as a major influence (Split Britches, for example, opens its 1986 play *Beauty and the Beast* with the line "An Absurd Drama of Ridiculous People").[79] I hope that this study will inspire future scholarship to uncover more distinct manifestations of the Ridiculous as historiographic strands of queer legacy.

Ludlam's theater successfully operated on several levels to build a visible gay community and communality: as a liberating forum where gays and their supporters could openly express ideas (that could potentially incite political actions), as a festive atmosphere that promoted exclusivity and gay pride (long before the term existed), as practical space that further developed and spread a gay lingo, and as meeting place for casual sexual encounters without the threat of the police or the dangers of city parks, public restrooms, and other spaces used for the solicitation of illicit sex.

Camille

The second of Ludlam's plays with which to examine the nature of a Proustian coded language as gay subtext is his gender-bending version of *Camille*. In the original production of *Camille*, the doomed romantic relationship between courtesan Marguerite (as portrayed by Ludlam) and Armand Duval (as played by RTC member Bill Vehr) exemplifies Ludlam's technique of playing out gay relationships in the guise of heteronormative romances drawn from canonical texts. The relationship, though portrayed by two gay men, is approached with complete sincerity and dedication in an effort to produce what Ludlam referred to as "believ[ing] in the character beyond the gender of the actor."[80] Even though Ludlam featured his hirsute chest in his low-cut, nineteenth-century-style gown, he trusted in his innate talent to lure the audience into the story enough to forget the intentional artificiality, Camp, and anarchic disregard for verisimilitude in the production. As Marguerite, Ludlam proudly displayed his chest hair because it was an essential element to the hypermasculine "clone" style and physical aesthetic that was considered highly desirable in 1973, and might potentially attract would-be lovers. Of this he said, "I invite the audience to laugh at me from the first moment by showing my chest, I'm not tricking them like those female impersonators who take off the wig at the end of the act. Yes, I want the audience to laugh, but they should also get the impact of forbidden love—it is really tragic and shocking."[81] Misha Berson commented on the effectiveness of this unique characterization, writing, "Ludlam's Marguerite is both terribly funny and terrifically moving, both ethereally beautiful and grotesque, both real and artificial, both a man in a dress and a woman."[82] It is this artificiality that Ludlam was ridiculing, defying the hegemonic majority judgment that homosexual love is a myth and then performatively embracing it. Although Ludlam did not intend to have a reformist agenda in his work, it was in part the bicameral space in which his work was produced that encouraged community building and the resultant gay liberation front.

Camille also featured the most frequently written about and comic bit/play-on-words from all of Ludlam's plays, specifically delivered in celebration of his gay audience. In the final scene, as Marguerite convulses on her deathbed, the following lines are delivered between Marguerite and her maid:

MARGUERITE: I'm cold. Nanine, throw another faggot on the fire!
NANINE: There are no more faggots in the house.
MARGUERITE: No faggots in the house? Open the window, Nanine.
    See if there are any on the street.[83]

Senelick refers to this comic bit as a "wink," but beyond this, Ludlam is unapologetically exposing himself as a gay man onstage regardless of his feminine attire. He is reclaiming the word "faggot" with a satirical affection, as if to say, "We're in the theatre and we're on the streets of the West Village, deal with it!"[84]

Second, the choice to stage *Camille* in an homage to both Dumas *fils* and Garbo centers on a character who is shunned and marginalized for her choices, whether sexual habits or otherwise. Roemer suggests that Ludlam's attraction to this character was "steeped in his homosexuality," Ludlam having experienced intolerance for his gay lifestyle comparable to that which the courtesan had experienced for her alternative way of life.[85] Beyond this, I suggest that Ludlam's decision to portray *Camille* is a form of diva worship for all strong and no-nonsense women—honoring those characters who paved the way for gay liberation in novels and plays decades before a heroic gay figure appeared in prose, poetry, or performance. The idea of the "strong woman" and what she represents is arguably more important than the act of drag or making up. Thus, for Ludlam (who vehemently argued that he was not a drag queen) the act of dragging out to play Camille was drawn from figures in classic literature—namely women who were villainized for promiscuity and/or independent thinking. In this vein, Patricia Julian Smith suggests that such diva worship is central to the development of gay culture:

The worship of idols—of "false" gods—is, I would suggest, an integral part of queer culture, particularly in times when homosexuality is most severely proscribed. Although there are notable exceptions, organized religion has, in most instances, treated homosexuals as absolute and irredeemable pariahs. Shunned by mainstream religious devotees and—by implied extension—their "true" deity, queers (often with an ample dose of self-parodic irony) have developed their own counter-deities, who function either as the singular object of devotion or as part of an eclectic pantheon.[86]

Thus Proustian encoding is at the very core of *Camille* and all of Ludlam's plays, with one of the best examples of this exclusive encoded language being the constant reference to B-movie queen Maria Montez. She was, in many ways the reason that the early founders of the Ridiculous movement bonded. As Bidgood stated, "Every little fag in the 40's was enamored with Maria Montez!"[87] In channeling the iconic heroines of his own childhood, Ludlam hoped, in turn, to become the recipient of the very hero worship that he propagated in his drag impersonations. Montez as diva is further unpacked as a queer icon by gay historian and memoirist Daniel Harris:

> [For] gay men growing up in small-town America, film provided a vehicle for expressing alienation from our surroundings and linking up with the utopic homosexual community of our dreams. . . . At the very heart of gay diva worship . . . is not the diva but the almost universal homosexual experience of ostracism and insecurity which led to what might be called the aestheticism of maladjustment, the gay man's exploitation of cinematic versions of Hollywood grandeur to elevate himself above his antagonistic surroundings and simultaneously express membership in a hedonistic demimonde.[88]

Although Harris's broad and sweeping generalization may not apply to all gay men of a certain generation, the notion of fantastical "elevation" as a commonality is particularly relevant to Ludlam's coterie. The diva (and more specifically, for the Ridiculous subset, Montez) became a patron saint to their cause. Montez, who was notorious for her terrible acting in less than sophisticated films, became a symbol of perseverance, a beautiful spirit of truth in an otherwise ugly and rigid world. She was transformed into a figure symbolically sacrificed to the evils of heteronormative desire and its values as a packaged product for capitalist consumption. The culmination of Montez worship was the providence of a particular time and moment. Championed initially by Smith, then boosted through Ridiculous acolytes (Tavel, Vaccaro, Ludlam, and even Warhol) and their cultish fans, the inclusion of references to silver screen divas became a standard in the formula of Ridiculous plays and productions, one of many expressions of encoded Camp intended specifically for their idiosyncratic audience. This tradition continues in the work of neo-Ridiculous artists such as Busch in *Red Scare on Sunset*, Louryk in *Christine Jorgensen Reveals*, and Mac in *A 24-Decade History of Popular Music*. Though many of the original references to divas of Ludlam's Ridiculous may have been lost to a younger generation of queers, I would like to think that his plays represent another link of legacy between the past and the present: revealing a hidden past of queer divas to this generation while inspiring a formulaic veneration of new divas that continues to explode across queer art and culture today.

Although Ludlam did not invent the Ridiculous theater, by formatting his approach around an interpretation of Camp inspired by Proust, Ludlam made the form distinctly his own. It was through the development of a sensibility that was distinctly "Ludlamesque" that the playwright paved the way for his heirs to extend his original vision (made clear in both his plays and essays) into new forms that maintained relevancy into the twenty-first century.

Between 1968 and 1987 Ludlam ruled the underground theater scene in New York City with his repertory troupe, the Ridiculous Theatrical Company, a remarkable achievement, lasting two decades in the fickle and ever-changing theater world of the Empire City. At the height of his career Ludlam became a darling of the theater critics and wrote twenty-nine plays. In the decades that have passed since the playwright's death his place in the chronicle of postmodern American theater has remained constant, but his influence has changed.[89] Ludlam's career was spotlighted and even magnified immediately after his passing through acts of public mourning. These included memorial performances, obituaries, the renaming of a small street in the West Village to "Charles Ludlam Lane," and the publication of *The Complete Plays of Charles Ludlam* (which went out of print after only a year in 1989). As the Ridiculous Theatrical Company failed and shut its doors a few years later, Ludlam also began to fade into anecdote and memory. Although Ludlam as a personality retains a cultish notoriety in the theater world, he has been largely ignored in the pantheon of twentieth-century American gay male playwrights (such as Williams, Albee, McNally, and Kushner). Ludlam's absence from this fraternity is in part due to the fact that his name never lit a marquee on Broadway and thus was never nominated for a Tony Award. However, the Ludlamesque Ridiculous has continued to thrive and remain a groundbreaking genre in the twenty years following his death. It has maintained its relevance and potency by metamorphosing along with cultural changes that have occurred, particularly regarding gay identity in America.

Ludlam's unique career and influence combine to create the perfect model with which delve further into the mapping of queer legacies, moving toward a new theoretical model to assist in the resurrection and composition of previously absent queer histories.

CHAPTER ONE

Still Ridiculous

Queering Legacy

Je suis un mensonge qui dit toujours la vérité.
—Jean Cocteau, *Opéra* (1927)

Reviving Charles Ludlam

Charles Ludlam was queer—a queer. He was a playwright, actor, director, designer, painter, and essayist, as well as a control-freak, diva, liberator, homeopath, inventor, rebel, visionary, and iconoclast. As this list conveys, Ludlam thrived on enigmatic contradiction. He is best known for refining the Ridiculous theater, a distinct genre that is one of the earliest forms of gay theater in the United States. The Ridiculous originated in the 1960s in the filmic and theatrical works of Jack Smith, Ronald Tavel, and John Vaccaro. It carried with it a ubiquitous spirit of midcentury gay liberation that was both enterprising and irreverent.[1] Tavel claims to have coined the appellation "Ridiculous" to define a genre that he saw moving beyond the absurd to the "absolutely preposterous."[2] As a distinctly American form, it unapologetically juxtaposes high culture (canonical literature, grand theatrical traditions, and icons of Western history) and low pop culture (American popular entertainments, B movies, television, and icons of celebrity) with homage, travesty and Camp. Ludlam took the early conventions of the Ridiculous, introduced by his predecessors, and perfected them, creating a sophisticated theater that perfectly represented the spirit of the times. Though Ludlam was a force to be reckoned with in the downtown New York City theater of the mid-twentieth century, today startlingly few people outside of the theater community have ever heard his name.

Figure 3: Charles Ludlam as Marguerite Gautier in *Camille* with Bill Vehr as Armand. (1976). Photographer: John Stern. Author's collection.

Though Ludlam and his Ridiculous Theatrical Company were hugely popular with audiences and critics, artists and scholars have largely undervalued his posthumous influence on the genre. Following Ludlam's death, a *Theatre Week* article reduced his unique praxis and rich body of work to a mere drag act, and the genre risked being neglected evermore, but the irrepressible spirit of the Ridiculous theater has survived.[3] Ludlam saw his work as a sphere of influence. Of this he wrote, "The world outside of theatre is changing and you reflect it. One does act upon the world when the work has an incredible impact on the lives of the people who see the play."[4] The decades that have passed since Ludlam's death have been filled with fundamental cultural shifts, political developments, and global events that have radically altered the position of gay identity in American culture. Although theater scholars such as Rick Roemer, Gautam Dasgupta, Bonnie Marranca, and John Clum and biographer David Kaufman have provided excellent analyses of the playwright and his work under the banner of the countercultural, Ludlam is more accurately a gay phenomenon. In an effort to combat homophobic readings by "rescuing" Ludlam from the categorization as a practitioner of gay theater, such anti-identitarian work has inadvertently diluted the original intention behind the Ridiculous—to create experimental secret spaces that were exclusive to the gay community, but also capable of extending gay identity into the public sphere toward liberation. This formula generates a pastiche that reflects and ridicules contemporary societal hegemony in support of a distinctly queer sensibility, communality, and a cohesive identity with respect to public visibility; an alternative view from the queer side of the looking glass. This formula is inherently paradoxical, pulling in opposite directions that seemingly render social constructs of gayness/queerness contradictory and potentially futile. If Ludlam was only speaking to a minority within a protected space, how did his theater generate any kind of effective and lasting political message? On the other hand, if his theater was truly universalizing, how did it employ queerness as a mode of autonomous individualism that wasn't diluted by its widespread breadth? The answer lies within queer theorist Eve Kosofsky Sedgwick's dissentient theory built around the deadlock between "minoritizing" and "universalizing" definitions of homosexuality—simply stated, it's both.[5] From a queer perspective, it is the gap between the minoritarian and universal that acts as a fecund breeding ground for queer legacies to propagate and mature. The seemingly inimical components that make up this construct need not be assumed counterproductive when read as points of a theoretical strategy that reveal hidden paths when read in context. In this sense, the ambivalence created by the tension between the minoritarian and universal acts as a springboard for queer identity-making (in both a collective and individual sense) and its resultant legacies. The still emerging (and, I hope, potentially fundamental) concept of queer ambivalence stems from Freud's psychoanalytic (and undeniably patriarchal) notion of ambivalence, where one side tries to overcome the other through an act of repression. Sociologist Deborah B. Gould extends the Freudian notion of ambivalence to explore the line between LGBTQ radical activism and the avoidance of confrontational politics. I would add, however, that queerness renders ambivalence as a powerful force that refutes the Freudian binary and allows both side of queer contradiction to coexist, intervene in, and formulate an alternative sense of being that belies the notion of a concrete, singular choice.[6]

Ludlam's Ridiculous was created in an alternate, ambivalent gap that eschewed normative hierarchies and values for a "queer collectivity"—a queered version of the world that demonstrated its live-and-let-live creed through live performance.[7] This practice of queer cultural production seeks to "build" and "do" in response to the status of "nothing assigned to [queers] by the heteronormative world."[8] From these performances social bonds were formed that assisted in recruiting the numbers that would make the gay liberation movement a highly visible and united front—a force to be reckoned with. In short, the Ridiculous helped to bring gay culture into the public eye. It was the sense of productive ambivalence, a refusal to be pinned down and labeled into half of a concrete binary that allowed Ludlam's Ridiculous to thrive both in the theater and beyond, and admittedly in very different ways.

Ludlam used his distinct interpretation of Camp to metamorphose the Ridiculous genre into his own unique form. Ludlam's Camp was not merely an aesthetic, but a secret language, an argot that he used to communicate exclusive codes to his gay audience. This self-protective approach allowed for subjugated cultural production and dissemination among his particular subculture, in this case the urban gay community at the watershed of an organized liberation movement. Ludlam drew inspiration for this mode of Camp language from French novelist Marcel Proust (an influence that is traced and unpacked in the introduction of this book), distinctly setting his work apart from other Ridiculous artists of the period. Ludlam's cultural significance rests not only in twenty-nine distinct plays that he left behind after his death in 1987, but also in his queer legacy through neo-Ridiculous performers who have found inspiration in Ludlam and his plays via personal relationships (whether amicable, competitive, professional, or sexual), academic study, or aesthetic contexts. The Ludlamesque Ridiculous theater may be read not only as an ongoing cultural event but also a viable alternative account with which to trace a specific gay social history of late twentieth- and early twenty-first-century urban America, a queer legacy.

Queer legacy can be best summed up in queer performance scholar David Román's concept of "provisional collectives," where "*certain* artists mark themselves as historical subjects whose genealogies might be found outside of traditional systems of identification and belonging."[9] In this sense, Ludlam's collective genealogy was self-constructed and intricately developed through various kinds of performance: his knowledge and passion for theater history as well as his sexual identity, challenging the traditional systems to which Román refers. This self-made queer genealogy continues to inspire Ludlam's legacy through his heirs.

When mapping the terms "gay" and "queer" onto a specific period (in this case NYC from the period just before gay liberation until the advent of the AIDS crisis) it is key to note the complex and oftentimes forgotten relevance of the applied concepts in specific relation to time and space. As queer scholar Annamarie Jagose suggests, queerness moves "simultaneously forward and backwards as not only the evolutionary extension of a more conventional lesbian and gay studies but also its bent progenitor."[10] Perhaps unknowingly, Jagose has rather poetically set up a formula for queer legacy, wherein time runs amok with a Ridiculous spirit. Though in an institutional context queerness as a theoretical model implies a post-1990s "zone of possibilities," it seems too easy to be overcome with an anti-identitarian politics-driven amnesia that cancels out modes of queer self-awareness that existed two decades before the introduction of queer theory as a discipline.[11] I strategically use "gay" to refer specifically to the insular network of men who have sex with and openly engage in romantic relationships with other men. In midcentury New York City a particularly exclusive community of gay men developed, creating a self-constructed figural ghettoization and the resultant culture. Examples of this may be seen in other contemporary works such as Mart Crowley's play *The Boys in the Band* (1968), Andrew Holleran's novel *Dancer from the Dance* (1978), and Donald Vining's memoir *A Gay Diary: 1967-1975*.[12] When using "queer" I strategically refer to a collective body including all members of society that are outside the boundaries of the cultural mainstream, a mainstream defined by heteronormative constructs of time and space that are ruled by biological reproduction. While my application of "gay" is intended to bracket and unpack a specific community at a given time, my use of "queer" is also inclusive of this group and allows for a certain amount of slippage and what Sedgwick refers to as a "crisscrossing of the lines of identification."[13] This approach allows for queer theater scholar Jill Dolan's rich and complex theory of "multiplicity" to manifest itself into what gender and sexuality scholar Robin Bernstein propagates as a sort of actively harmonious disagreement (one again, queerly ambivalent).[14] Halberstam speaks to the diversity of people within such a contemporary queer construct, stating that "all kinds of people, especially in postmodernity, will do and opt to live outside of reproductive and family time [and] perhaps such people could be productively called 'queer subjects.'"[15] The neo-Ludlamesque is demonstrative of Halberstam's theory as a form of performative evidence that seeks to include all self-professed queers, while also advocating for disenfranchised communities with less representation such as the transsexual, transgendered, or disabled. Thus, the queer legacy of Ludlam is one of distinct transformation—one where artists can reject faithful interpretations in order to move in new interpretive directions. Admittedly the concept of gayness that I employ for this close reading is narrowly focused, speaking to a distinct time (the period of gay liberation), place (NYC), and group (gay men)—an identity that is shaped from the inside out as a self-mediated projection of positionality and location. In a historical context, the gay theater community of the West Village in the 1960s and 1970s was primarily composed of poor, bohemian communists who had been shunned from American society. They found solace in the Village, escaping from a hegemonic pathology of taboo and shame where and when homosexuals were largely seen a social pariahs, deviants, or sexual predators—black marks on any respectable family or community. This dichotomy is clarified by the relocation from rural areas to the urban, a commonplace migration by gay men of the period. Before queer was a theory, it was common ground on which the disenfranchised could build community on the margins of society.

Because queer theory emerged from the work of feminist scholars[16] dedicated to post-Foucauldian radical dissections of socially constructed genders and identities, narrative strands of queer legacy (such as this one) inherently take into account a critical restructuring of historiography drawn from a feminist perspective.[17] My suggestion for a reconsideration of legacy in a queer context is directly inspired by James Harding and Cindy Rosenthal's "feminist orientation" of legacy in context to radical theater of the 1960s. In this mode legacy becomes a "site of conceptual evolution rather than of uncritical repetitious presentation."[18]

Ludlam's particular genealogy and legacy is situated at an intersection of queer theory and queer lives, arguing for honest examples that are practically driven and honor queer individuals for their differences as much as their similarities, putting an end to the accusatory, feckless, and divisive hierarchy of "I'm more oppressed than you" rhetoric that so often accompanied identity politics in the 1970s. Dolan inadvertently supports this stance, warning: "The insistent anti-hegemonic pose of 'queer' can be a ruse for not taking responsibility for the vagaries of a movement, a style, a life."[19] I'm moved by Dolan's caveat that seems to stand in opposition to a homogenization that renders queerness apathetic. By extending queer theory and honoring it for its diverse and even contradictory strands (what Sedgwick originally theorized as "an open mesh of possibilities, gaps, overlaps, dissonances and resonances"), I hope that we may begin to recognize and deconstruct the very identity politics that shaped queerness in context to their diverse origins without resorting to them as finite signifiers.[20] Moreover, I propose fighting against the dilution of queer theory as a catchall that loses relevance and denies its roots in gay/lesbian histories and feminist discourse.

In the climate of its origin, Ludlam's theater was a catalyst for change, but in using a codified language to speak exclusively to a gay audience in an ontologically queer space, his work was also separatist and esoteric. Since Ludlam's death, advancements in civil rights paired with community visibility have forever altered marginalized gay identity in America and beyond. Ludlam was an inheritor *and* transmitter of classical theatrical traditions as he created original work through a pastiche of queer themes and culture. Although largely forgotten to time, the style of work that Ludlam created has continued in the work of new artists who honor his work through metamorphosis and subversion: queer legacy.

Toward (a) Queer Legacy

In order to focus on the post-Ludlam Ridiculous as a critical strand of alternative history, it is essential to reposition the concept of legacy as a queer discourse.[21] French philosopher Michel Foucault presents the notion of genealogy as both a search for origins and a deconstruction of truths. This approach is a solid foundation for the formulation of queer legacy as a viable paradigm with which to examine systematically subversive practices and disseminate sociocultural traditions that are passed from generation to generation through the medium of performance, without buying into ideological narratives of normative biological continuity. I'm intentionally using "generation" to help frame different temporal shifts in the development of post-Stonewall LGBT identity, rather than as a marker of biological reproduction. Simply stated, queer generations are created, not born. While it has been a historical tendency to laud legacy as the transmission of prescriptive traditions that are bound to the past with nostalgic reverence, a queer legacy is different. It rejects the act of Aristotelian mimesis and comparison as a form of violence, instead favoring subversive actions, which are creative and productive.[22] In other words, a queer legacy is liberated from traditionalist approval-seeking, such as a son attempting to ape his biological father as a sign of respect/affection. When queered, a conservative act such as this is replaced with ridicule, where the son honors his queer father by reinventing himself in an act of courage, autonomy, and independence; virtues at the core of gay liberation philosophy. This act of mimicry lies close to literature scholar Homi Bhabha's postcolonial interpretation of the term as a "complex strategy of reform" but is made queer through its liberal application of Camp as a defense mechanism.[23] Queer legacies may appear to borrow traits and formulas of patriarchal and essentialist constructs at first glance (such as the father/son model), but the queer version of this model is antiprototypical and taboo (the "father" may be romantically/sexually/incestuously linked to his "son"). Busch's Ridiculous legacy perhaps resembles this model the closest, as his origins with Ludlam were directly interpersonal (as when he briefly played the role of Hecate in Ludlam's *Bluebeard*), but Louryk and Mac also queer normative family models in their works, notably in Louryk's cutting and pasting of Ludlam's essays in *Klytaemnestra's Unmentionables* and Mac's autobiographical monologues like "Mornings" in *The Be(a)st of Taylor Mac*. All of these performers converge to create a larger legacy of queer performance that operates through mimicry and ridicule.

Ludlam's lasting cultural impact on contemporary Ridiculous theater in New York City is the prime example of a queer legacy in action, because Ludlam's unique take on the Ridiculous generated a largely untouched legacy that is rife for excavation. The idea of a queer legacy is inscribed in Ludlam's own account of his work and practice. Ludlam spoke to this implicitly in his essay "Envoi" when asked about the future of the Ridiculous on his deathbed, stating, "You must continue the theatre . . . the art of playwriting can be passed on from father to son . . . it's not genetic, it's technology."[24] For Ludlam "technology" means innovation: a catalyst for social change. The continuance of the Ludlamesque Ridiculous thrives not on reverence and revivalism, but rather anarchic reinventionist approaches that synonymously honor and deconstruct the original intentions and characteristics of Ludlam's theater of the era of post-gay liberation. This subversive practice allows the Ridiculous genre to transform as a medium that is a direct reflection of and reaction to shifts in contemporary queer culture.

Traditionally legacy is defined as an act of bequeathing or an object given to another by will. The notion of this objective passing down of history suggests a static account of the past that belies progress—an attempt to maintain what *was* as what *is*. Halberstam equates this practice of the traditional-in-action with Foucauldian notions of disciplinarity that depend upon "normalization, routines, convention and . . . regularity" for deployment as a technique of power and suggests that in its place we must seek different forms that delink the processes of history making.[25] The neo-Ridiculous artists studied in *Charles Ludlam Lives!* connect to several other legacies as well, both ubiquitous and discrete, with the largest, of course, being the gigantic web that attempts to illustrate a global history of theatrical performance. All are committed to retaining the conventions of Ludlam and moreover the grand historical praxis of theater as tradition, though this tradition is queered through deconstruction and reconfiguration as corroborated by interviews with the artists themselves.

Becoming part of a cultural legacy (whether theatrical or of queer culture) is a conscious effort, honoring the vision of the originator in order to develop new work that is created from the perfect balance of ingenuity, influence, and innovation. As a distinct subculture within the larger gay liberation movement, the queer legacy of the Ridiculous theater tradition is delinked from more traditional forms of genealogical trace by its nature, hovering between a self-motivated exclusivity and socially imposed abjection (another gap created in the mode of Sedgwick). At its origin the Ridiculous manifested a safe space that allowed for freedom of expression without the fear of homophobic discrimination, but as a theatrical form, it also broke down the walls of concealment through the act of public performance. Ludlam achieved this, in part, by securing a permanent space for his repertory company that could securely shut its doors as easily as open them. Moreover, a normative legacy is dependent on the continual success of its succession, whereas a queer legacy ebbs and flows in a state of constant flux and experimentation and does not necessarily move in an unbroken line, existing in the "in-between spaces" of visible cultural consumption.[26] This instability allows for queer legacy to circumvent the normative formula of "trying and trying again," for unmitigated success and instead allows for a layered state of discursive success and failure. As Halberstam suggests, such "queer failure" helps to form the alternative identities that create a surrogate standard of progression if not progress.[27] The equilibrium of success/failure in the Ridiculous theatrical tradition is directly dependent on the time and place in which it is revived. As chapter 4 corroborates, Mac pointedly and explicitly refers to his early failures in the underground East Village scene as the catalyst for the creation of better, more meaningful work.

The Ridiculous legacy is not broadly accessible because it is disseminated and transformed through internal channels of self-formulated kinship. Although kinship, as introduced by Claude Lévi-Strauss has been a highly criticized topic by queer theorists like Judith Butler (and admittedly Butler's criticism of Lévi-Strauss is not without bias), there is, if you look closer, a loophole. Lévi-Strauss defined the kinship system as the key to the structural analysis of generational lineage through male/female alliances (both legal and sexual). He also suggests, however, that beyond the heteronormative model provided by the natural world, "other" models may exist, like homosexuality, "which brings about an integration of [a] group on a new plane."[28] It is on this new plane that queer legacy persists and exclusively normative representations of kinship are made arbitrary. Thus, according to queer scholar David L. Eng, this new construct of kinship can be held together steadfastly through a system of affective feeling (and I would add desire and belonging) as much as biology.[29] Literature scholar Elizabeth Freeman sees this alternative legacy of the nonreproductive as a construct of kinship that is dependent on the formation of distinct community and what anthropologist Kath Weston names in the title of her groundbreaking study of queer kinship: *Families We Choose* (as is demonstrated by Ludlam's aforementioned selection to use the father/son construct to embody his desire for a continuing legacy).[30] Sex and gender theorist Gayle Rubin extends the argument by suggesting that kinship is in the process of losing its "obligatory status,"[31] and queer ethnographer Esther Newton calls for an applicable extraction that dismisses normative and traditional connotations based on biological lineage and consanguinity.[32] Muñoz supports this emerging concept of queer kinship as a building block for the construction of queer legacies by identifying it as "an alternative chain of belonging, of knowing the other and being in the world."[33] I suggest that said construct also introduces distinct modes of internal communication, both linguistic and cultural, as evidenced by Ludlam's layered texts, while also serving to delink from normative traditions of biological continuance. Cultural anthropologist Corinne P. Hayden defines this as "kinetic kinship" rather than "genetic kinship."[34] Ludlam's collagist theater follows this mode of queer kinesis not only through reventionistism, but also by being blatantly exploitative of previous works and even of itself, thus consistently introducing new concepts and genres within the Ridiculous framework—a genre that evolved by constantly falling back on itself. This falling back is illustrated by the fact that many of Ludlam's dramatic texts self-referentially reemployed dialogue and from earlier works. Elizabeth Grosz defines this concept as "a folding [of] the past into the future, beyond the control or limit of the present."[35] In a queer context I argue that this allows for a kind of queer growth that stands apart from biological modes of reproduction. This is further illustrated by embedded references to Ludlam in neo-Ridiculous plays, whether through Busch's historification, Louryk's channeling via lip sync, or Mac's postmodern clown/fool character. My envisioning of queer kinesis as mode of movement within abstract genealogical structures of queer legacy is closely in line with the Aristotelian rendering of kinesis as anything with potential or possibility. A shared trait of Busch, Louryk, Mac, and Ludlam is the desire to create timely work inspired by queer experience, both personal and shared. I cling to the optimistic notion of queer possibility as a productive force that moves through time and hopefully acts as a harbinger for queer continuance (both culturally and theoretically) if not growth.[36] This ties into theater scholar Joseph Roach's suggestion that culture is derived from kinetic/frantic "surrogate" processes. He argues that as culture begins to take shape from a perpetual void of motion it begins to propel itself toward a predetermined direction (what he defines as "kinesthetic imagination"), forging a connection that surpasses traditional notions of time and space.[37] My concept of queer kinesis is also clarified by performance scholar Ramón H. Rivera-Servera's concept of queer subjects as "traveling subjects," first as he uses it to trace the urban migration of rural homosexuals seeking solace and community, and second as I extend it to suggest a traveling through alternative modes on nonlinear temporality and subsequent legacy.[38] This dualistic notion is demonstrated more literally by the continued immigration and convergence of queer artists in places like New York City. In this mode, the success of queer kinesis is reliant on its ability to weave between, under, behind, over, around, through, and even beyond these normative networks of social transmission forged by the kinesthetic imagination, leaving traces of influence behind without necessarily revealing their presence or purpose. My interpretation of trace is a self-professed naive interpretation French deconstructionist Jacques Derrida's use of the same term—where that which is "always-already hidden" inadvertently leaves an impression that can be reconstructed into an archive that represents both a self-directed fiction, and its own truth.[39] Taylor Mac, for example, excavates the tangled lines of his own queer personal narrative (much of which was previously hidden by means of trauma or grief), weaving them together with Ridiculous precedents, creating a new, interconnected, and arguably even stronger version of the genre for a contemporary audience.

As an interpreter of queer legacy, I take it as my responsibility to bring into conversation such contrasting, lateral, and ambivalent perspectives of history, and in this case reveal the Ridiculous theater as a practical example of this applied theory. This methodological approach takes inspiration from feminist scholar Sarah Ahmed's significant work on movement as product of human emotion, wherein "what moves us, what makes us feel, is also that which holds us in place, or gives us a dwelling place," a place for the past to live.[40] Ludlam lives on in the recollections and interpretations of his heirs as driven by their emotions, regardless if these feelings are exaggerated, misunderstood, or even fictional.

A queer legacy is made manifest less by its framework than by its exclusivity of participation and reception, reprojecting arch images back onto a world where they were originally created. Using the lens of affect or emotion to produce such a new history is a daunting task, and the rosy hues of nostalgia and romanticism may quickly be dissipated by feelings of jealousy, resentment, and bitterness. I have tried to retain the role of such contentiousness within the Ridiculous as a "counterpublic" (for example, John Kelly's dismissal of Busch in chapter 2, or Louryk's wry lack of interest in Mac in chapter 3) to demonstrate how such emotional reactions can serve to shift, bend, or even break certain legs of a specific history.[41]

The notion of legacy is still largely undertheorized, and the model of queer legacy is nascent in form. Several scholars have inadvertently begun to foster the idea of a queer legacy in studies focusing on queer temporality and space. Román contributes largely to the conversation through the introduction of "archival drag," which refers to "that nature of contemporary performances that draw on historical embodiment and expertise."[42] When brought into conversation with Freeman's "temporal drag," which she defines as "a kind of historicist *jouissance*, a friction of dead bodies upon live ones, [and] obsolete constructions upon emergent ones,"[43] drag is extended beyond early utopian notions introduced by seminal queer theorist Judith Butler in *Gender Trouble* and favors particular acts of drag drawn from social history.[44] If the Ludlamesque legacy is presented as what contemporary performers figuratively drag behind them as a connection to the past, then I suggest that it is the acknowledgment of this trailing history that allows performers like Busch, Louryk, and Mac to then cut the ties, creating a momentum that propels them forward into new performative manifestations of the Ridiculous; an example of queer kinesis in action. This kind of lineage belies "positivist notions of historical progress" through cross-temporal connections that social and cultural analysis scholar Carolyn Dinshaw calls "touch."[45] This idea of touch, or perhaps more accurately "contact," makes for a performative link between the past and the present that perpetually moves in all directions and across various planes—following the kinetic model and Roach's surrogate. Echoing the Derridean reading of Heraclitus on fire, where the identity of flame is "preserved in its changes," the past stays in habitual contact with the present and vice versa, combining to form a dualistic ontological and affective construct of Western queer identity.[46] Again, drawing insight from Derrida's retro-futurist theory and specifically his neologism *hauntology*—or the "paradoxical state of the spectre," I say that contemporary Ridiculous performers are consciously haunted by the ghost of the original Ridiculous, but rather than as men possessed, they act as a medium to the spirit, which, in the words of Roach, allows them to "bring forth, make manifest and transmit."[47] In simpler terms, this is an act of being and continuance. The works of Busch, Louryk, and Mac all channel Ludlam's ghost, though I'd like to think their success is propagated by the ability to tame that specter by entertaining him through new, innovative works. Derrida, after all, suggests that hauntology may be best employed as "an interpretation that transforms the very thing that it interprets."[48] Literary critic Fredric Jameson reminds us that the hauntological is less about the spirit of the past directing the present than it is a reminder that the living present is scarcely as self-sufficient as it claims to be."[49] In contemporary Ridiculous performance the past and present continue to "haunt" the other, but only as an extension of the gay history that paved its way. I suggest that this transitive and cross-temporal connection may act as the modus operandi by which to create an alternative account of social history constituting a queer legacy that, as David Savran suggests, is "located on the threshold between two worlds and two temporalities."[50] This follows Muñoz's suggestion that "queer art from the past [may be] evoked for the purpose of better understanding work made today . . . [and how] contemporary work lines up with the historical archive."[51] Because Ludlam's unspoken mission was to constantly evolve, his heirs must continue to develop work that honors the Ludlamesque tradition while also "exploiting" his work. Thus, the inertia of this queer legacy is managed through a sort of resuscitative transformation and what historians James Harding and Cindy Rosenthal title a "creative response." Such a response "is a product of the terms of its transference," and in this case the transference is grounded within an exclusively queer network that seeks to "excavate, propagate, and reconstruct."[52] The creative responses of Busch, Louryk, and Mac are highly individualized and personal and also very likely to continue transforming, but all are rooted firmly in the histrionic mythology of the Ludlamesque.

In fact, as the case studies will demonstrate, each of the artist thinks about Ludlam quite differently.

Pansexual artist Nayland Blake suggests that "the legacy of prophetic artists is not to give us specific ways of doing something but, by their example, the permission to be fearless in our own search for a way to do something."[53] The very notion of theoretically unpacking any concept of legacy is a complex one, with transformation, revision, and patchiness as potential factors of transmission. A queer legacy differs in its generative source: transcendent momentum is activated through mimicry and ridicule and propelled by its very indeterminacy and inability to be understood.

Lateral Historiography

My original concept of *lateral historiography* is a method with which to construct alternative queer genealogical (nonbiological) narratives. Lateral historiography extends and provides alternate perspectives that intersect with primary first-person historical accounts ("truths" in the patriarchal/ normative tradition of legacy), offering alternative and even contradictory opinions driven by human emotion and subsequent effects shaped by affect. This formula follows Ahmed's reinterpretation of Karl Marx's notion that temporal periods are shaped by accumulating emotional response and what queer scholar Sara Warner terms "a nuanced avenue of feelings" (jealousy, trauma, joy, gaiety, shame, or any other form of human emotional response).[54] The concept of lateralizing historiography also finds inspiration in Kathryn Bond Stockton's notions of horizontalized history, latitudinal fictions, or "growing sideways."[55] The theory at the core of this study maintains Stockton's embrace of malleable queer history-making that allows for affective fictions as the ground on which to forge alternate nonnormative identities and legacies. In lateralizing the methodological process, I allow for the analysis of queer intersections with the normative world, particularly when the market becomes involved in the shaping and dissemination of products consumed beyond the queer community. Although my carefully selected subjects ground the framework of my study (Ludlam and thereafter Busch, Louryk, and Mac), I unapologetically allow for tangential explorations of contemporary performers who laterally intersect the constellation of the Ridiculous legacy at particular points in time: lateral historiography in practice.

The Post-Ludlam/Neo-Ridiculous

CHAPTER TWO

Charles Busch

More Excitement! More Glamour! More Wigs!

"Life isn't an old movie." Oh yeah? Maybe not a feature, but this
adventure was most definitely made for TV. It seemed only natural
that I should view life as a celluloid fantasy.
—Charles Busch

Prologue

This first case study focuses on Ludlam's continuing influence during the
East Village Renaissance in the 1980s and the impact of the HIV/AIDS
epidemic on the gay community. It unpacks the phenomena of queer legacies that are passed interpersonally and through direct contact, whether
vocational, amicable, or sexual. Tied to Ludlam in time and place, Charles
Busch's approach to the neo-Ridiculous closely embodies Dinshaw's idea
of touch.[1] Touch is a framework with which to create a constellation of
individuals that collectively fall under the category of Halberstam's queer
subjects, linking the notion of physical/affective touch with a kind of
queer subjectivity that informs both the performance of Busch and its reception.[2] Thus, in this formula of touch, or queer contact, Busch becomes
a physical marker of the past verging with the present. This embodiment
is magnified by Busch's tendency to play his roles through the character
of an aging grande dame modeled on nineteenth-century divas, a poor
man's Sarah Bernhardt. Busch performs as his own unique manifestation
of Bernhardt as a particular character in each of his plays.

Referring to Ernst Bloch's theory of escapism, this chapter deconstructs the period's reinterpretation of the Ridiculous genre as a source for
communality and solace by examining the work and texts of John Kelly

and the interloper status of Busch. Busch achieved his own notoriety in the Off-Broadway theater scene by unapologetically appropriating, revising, and mainstreaming the conventions of the Ridiculous genre. He achieved success by snatching the genre from the affluent West Village ruled by Ludlam and his Ridiculous Theatrical Company (RTC) and moving it across the island, dropping it in a condemned antiestablishment club called the Limbo Lounge in the midst of the decaying East Village. The transplanting of a new form of the Ridiculous in the East Village resulted in a kind of "multiplicity" as introduced by Dolan, setting up a queer geography that refracted and shifted what the RTC had started at Sheridan Square, though admittedly much to Ludlam's chagrin.[3] Whereas Ludlam had risen to fame and achieved popular and critical success with the RTC in reaction to the Stonewall/post-Stonewall era of gay liberation and sexual freedom, Busch was propelled by the desire to create a nineteenth-century touring "stock" company; a nostalgic construct intended to whisk the often chronically ill audience to a simpler time. It also demonstrates how Busch successfully extended his theater beyond its early association with the AIDS crisis—taking his own legacy proverbially by the horns.

Busch's neo-Ridiculous originated in a particular time and moment and in what Halberstam deems the legacy-building "in between space," taking shape in the abandoned refuse of the culturally liminal East Village, particularly in his early plays, such as *Vampire Lesbians of Sodom* and *Sleeping Beauty or Coma*.[4] Regardless of its physical location, however, Busch unknowingly helped to create an example of Muñoz's "alternative chain of belonging" that was soldered through disease, fear, and empathy as much as sexual desire and identity.[5] The development of muscle culture (sthenolagnia) and the infected body in Ridiculous performance is also unpacked by considering the cultural semiotics of AIDS in context to the vampire as an apocalyptic figure, as suggested by conservative fundamentalist Christian groups. It also calls upon Román's deconstruction of the "false binary between art and politics," in order to shed light on Busch's sociopolitical relevance in light of his apolitical intent.[6] The notion of the apolitical is ironically magnified through Busch's descent into a Ridiculous historification of the past in his *Red Scare on Sunset*, a play that hilariously critiques the communist witch hunts in McCarthy-era Hollywood, the apolitical driven by the irreverent deconstruction of the distinctly political. Moreover, the apolitical becomes politically charged through the appearance of HIV-positive bodies presented on the stage.

The chapter continues to examine Busch's later, more sophisticated

Figure 4: Charles Busch as Judith of Bethulia in the play of the same name (2012). Photographer: David Rodgers.

plays and films, including *Die Mommie, Die!* and *The Tale of the Allergist's Wife*, representative of the playwright's tendency to switch between plays loosely inspired either by old Hollywood glamor or by urban Jewish-American nostalgia.

Interpersonal Origins

In 1984, the same year that Charles Ludlam's play *The Mystery of Irma Vep* opened to critical acclaim (arguably marking the zenith of his artistic career), a failing, starry-eyed solo performer and Ridiculous acolyte named Charles Busch abandoned his one-man show to form his own troupe: Theatre-in-Limbo. Busch achieved his own notoriety in the Off-Broadway theater scene by unapologetically appropriating and revising the conventions of the Ridiculous theater. In structuring this chapter as a narrative that weaves together different perspectives of the same period (with much of the information drawn from original interviews), it takes on an affective lens, what Ann Cvetkovich terms "an archive of feelings" taking into consideration often less than objective responses to Busch's work.[7] Busch's queer legacy begins interpersonally: he knew and worked with Charles Ludlam. Busch achieved success, however, by carrying the genre, from the affluent West Village ruled by Ludlam and his Ridiculous Theatrical Company (RTC), to a condemned antiestablishment club called the Limbo Lounge in the midst of the decaying East Village. Whereas Ludlam had risen to fame and achieved popular and critical success with the RTC in reaction to the Stonewall/post-Stonewall era of gay liberation and sexual freedom in the 1970s, Busch would extend the Ridiculous tradition into a new era by providing a temporary escape from Manhattan's changing culture of poverty and HIV/AIDS after 1981.

This chapter reconsiders Busch's earlier drag work from the mid-1970s in Chicago and his post-Ludlam work after Theatre-in-Limbo had dissolved in 1991 due to creative differences and the AIDS-related deaths of original company members Robert Carey and Meghan Robinson. Finally, it analyzes the acceptance of Busch's work into mainstream American theater and film culture. Of all the artists analyzed in this book, Busch best represents the transition that bridges Ludlam's performances with the RTC to the post-Ludlam Ridiculous that thrives in the downtown art scene of New York today. Although Busch's playwriting and performance styles intentionally stray from the social commentary that Ludlam and his contemporaries had introduced, he is the linchpin that held together the remnants of the Ridiculous in a time of crisis, allowing the genre to reform as a queer theater of activism and elitism in the late 1990s. Unlike the current generation of Ridiculous artists who were exposed to the Ridiculous genre through academic study or the trickle-down effect of post-1987 performers, Busch became versed in Ludlam's unique style and purpose because he knew him personally.

Neo-Marxist philosopher Ernst Bloch defined escapism as a catalyst for social change. In providing a temporary diversion from a reality created by a rational and technologically advancing society, Bloch saw escapism as "an immature, but honest substitute for revolution."[8] In Busch's era escapism became a self-protective mode for collective agency from the outside in, because the group (in this case gay men at the advent of the HIV/AIDS crisis) were stigmatized by AIDS phobia and paralyzed by a sense of fear-propagated vulnerability. The concept of escapism has been associated with the Ridiculous genre since Jack Smith and Ronald Tavel first invented the genre in the early 1960s. Of this, Tavel wrote, "The escapism [of the Ridiculous Theatre] is of a timeless, universal sort, which is why it was so readily encased in timeless fairy tales."[9] The role of escapism differs between the early Ridiculous and that of Busch because of the shifts in the sociological context of gay life in the United States. The decade between 1980 and 1990 marked a dark time for the gay community as AIDS took its toll, claiming the lives of thousands. The *New York Times* first reported on the disease in 1981and just three years later the metropolis reported the highest population of individuals with AIDS, marking it the failing heart of the epidemic.[10]

AIDS came on insidiously and swiftly, simultaneously occurring with the East Village Renaissance and hitting the theater community especially hard, spreading fear and uncertainty across the urban gay population. The promiscuous sex that had marked the previous decade came to a halt as bathhouses and sexual emporiums across the city were boarded up, and individuals (particularly gay men) sought to fill their time with emotional support, solace, and a renewed cohesive and unifying spirit. Busch's theater became a safe haven for the gay community and beyond, where the Blochian "revolution" became the practical act of giving a survivalist visibility to the disease, both in the audience and on the stage. Original troupe member and Busch scholar Kenneth Elliott corroborates this: "Theatre-in-Limbo began performing in 1984 as the AIDS crisis was escalating. Our 'primarily gay' audience craved 'simple entertainment' as an escape from this relentless tragedy. Busch seized the moment by providing it."[11] As Román notes, almost an entire generation of the American theater succumbed to AIDS in the 1980s (including Charles Ludlam), lending Busch the important status of a firsthand observer and oral archivist of a contextual history that otherwise might be lost, forgotten, or misunderstood.[12] Although Busch's take on the Ridiculous theater was not interventionist, it did become a site of performative resistance. In this sense, Busch's theater is rendered queerer through its ambivalence—its refusal to be categorized. It becomes politicized through reparative analysis, though its original mission is far from grassroots. In both text and performance Busch's early work provides an important contemporary reflection of 1980s and can be read as a performance-based cultural time line that inadvertently traces changes in gay American life over the past two decades.

In Limbo

From whence does Busch's legacy originate? The escapist quality and sim-plistic construction of Busch's early plays is pre-Ludlam and reminiscent of Ronald Tavel, playwright and founder of the Playhouse of the Ridic-ulous. Tavel worked as a filmmaker with Andy Warhol and the Factory before turning his creative energy to theater in 1966. His early plays *The Life of Juanita Castro* and *Shower* were written as screenplays, but Tavel transformed then into short plays for the stage when Warhol rejected him for newer, younger, and more easily controlled artists. In forming the PHR troupe with John Vaccaro, Tavel began composing camp follies or pastiched plays such as *The Life of Lady Godiva* and *Gorilla Queen*.[13] Of his work Bonnie Marranca notes, "Tavel revels in sexual wordplay (most often generating sexual imagery)."[14] It was these early plays that set in mo-tion the Ridiculous spirit and sensibility that Ludlam would perfect and Busch would appropriate.

Whereas the production of Tavel's plays provided a meeting space that foreshadowed the explosion of the gay sexual revolution, Busch's inhabit a safe space that marks the end of a visible gay brotherhood that had been expressed through promiscuous sexual activity. In the late 1960s the Play-house of the Ridiculous became a covert fraternity where the lines be-tween audience and actors were blurred. Within this space gay men and their friends openly celebrated with free love and mind-enhancing drugs while also inadvertently sowing the seeds (and I fully embrace the double entendre) of a united front that would become the watershed of the Stone-wall Riots. Thus, Tavel and Busch are Ridiculous bookends to the period of New York's gay history between the foundation of the gay rights move-ment and the AIDS epidemic. Tavel's escapism was built on a foundation of hope, whereas Busch's attempt was claimed by the attendant audience to combat a widespread stigmatization of the gay community and subse-quent feeling of scapegoating and isolationism.

It is essential to note that the initial development of Busch's theatri-cal vision grew out of a personal curiosity and was neither a reaction to the AIDS crisis nor an act of performative intervention. Theatre-in-Limbo came about within a certain time when it was supported and claimed by a gay community that was suffering from the rapid spread of HIV/AIDS, consumed by inexplicable and seemingly unpreventable premature death. First and foremost the theater genre was gay in its legacy, thematic choices, and aesthetic. It was even more so because Busch and the majority of the actors in the company were living openly gay lives. Because a large portion of the audience identified themselves as gay or bisexual and had been building a community by living in the midst of the city that had promulgated Stonewall fifteen years earlier, their affinity for Busch bonded them and their concerns as a disenfranchised whole. The support and companionship derived from the attendance of social gatherings such as Theatre-in-Limbo's late-night soirees tangibly constructed what anthropologist Benedict Anderson refers to as an "imagined community."[15] Busch created this escapist space by continuing the Ridiculous tradition of creating a community through a theater encoded with exclusive language and symbols intended for a gay reception—Camp—and in this instance an audience impacted by the horrors of the AIDS epidemic. Busch's created space hovers ambivalently between what Mary Bernstein refers to as distinctive modes of "celebration," and "suppression" in a period when the gay community was forced to take a backwards step in the dour Lenten period that followed the queer carnival of the 1970s.[16] The support and companionship derived from the attendance at social gatherings such as Theatre-in-Limbo's late night formed a *geist* that Verta Taylor and Nancy Whittier title "we-ness," in other words a twofold exchange that essentially erased the stage's fourth wall and allowed for human contact, both physical and emotional.[17] Gregg Bordowitz (whose memoir, *The AIDS Crisis is Ridiculous,* was inspired directly by Ludlam) notes that the early years of AIDS manifested as a lens that the gay community focused to create new timely art that balanced "youthful exuberance [with a] palpable sense of fear."[18] This mode of creativity, linked to survival, stood in counterpoint to the incomprehensible weight of the AIDS crisis as a shroud draped over gay identity at large. Although Ludlam largely avoided discussing HIV/AIDS in his essays, and never announced his status publicly, in his final essay, entitled "Politics," he warns of the effect of the disease on the arts, writing, "Unfortunately, American society, and maybe all societies, can't cope with real problems like [AIDS] . . . it's sad that we've had to go back to the nineteenth century, when syphilis was a deadly disease and people couldn't be as free as they once had been."[19] Busch's theater (as well as other gay companies working during the period) was made a part of this larger subcultural body politic through association, using Camp to create "a world in which the real becomes unreal, the threatening, unthreatening."[20] Andrew Holleran refers to the act as a shift in consciousness where "two identities which are most often separated in time and place, merg[ed]: homosexual and American."[21]

Busch's Theatre-in-Limbo troupe was formed not to criticize the social injustices of Regan-era America (particularly around HIV/AIDS), but
rather to provide a few hours of fun and entertainment for an audience
whose lives revolved around a melancholic uncertainty. Busch recollects
of his first production:

> For a long time I was embarrassed by what I considered to be the flim-
> siness of Vampire Lesbians of Sodom. Rereading it recently, I was struck
> by how entertaining a little sketch it is. Never meant to be considered a
> play at all, this little decadent dream achieved its goals quite well. It was
> created merely to entertain a late night crowd on a hot summer night
> in the East Village. The crazy miracle is that the play has had such an
> incredibly long life.[22]

Busch's plays served as an influential step in "the assimilation of Ridiculous Theatre into mainstream culture."[23] Whereas Ludlam's revolutionary
plays were infamous for an intricately pastiched recipe that mixed (low)
pop culture and an (high) academic ethos, Busch's original plays operate
on a shallower level, satirizing familiar stories and cinematic situations
on a fantastical plane with no concern for high-brow humor based on
obscure intellectual references. Laurence Senelick refers to Busch's performances as "a high-spirited game of Trivia," suggesting that the plays serve
to act as diversion from reality in the same way that leisurely parlor games
provide escape from boredom in the guise of lively entertainment.[24] Elliott recalls that Busch's early productions were "like festive parties for the
audience and actors alike."[25] While this comparison is acute in its explanation of how Busch's Ridiculous functions, it is essential to point out that its
social relevance at the time of creation supersedes any literary merit. Furthermore, the larger whole of Busch's pre-Limbo and post-Limbo plays is
far more complex and sophisticated than tongue-in-cheek works such as
Vampire Lesbians of Sodom (1984) (inspired in part by Anne Rice's popular
novel Interview with the Vampire [1976]) and Theodora, She-Bitch of Byz-
antium (1985) (liberally drawn from Victorien Sardou's Theodora [1884]).

Low-Rent/High(ish) Art

Busch's commercial success was supported by the fetishism of East Village
culture as Manhattan's uptown elite flocked to Alphabet City and subse-

quently approved it. Simply stated, Theatre-in-Limbo conveniently developed in the right place at the right time. In Cynthia Carr's 1984 essay "The Hot Bottom: Art and Artifice in the East Village," the author dissects the phenomenon of this period, where the energy that was inherent in the radical creativity of East Village artists (like Busch) was essentially commodified by the wealthy uptown Manhattan gentry through the act of purchasing art and the patronage of avant-garde theater and performance art (which, as in the case of Busch, was often performed in gallery spaces that reopened as clubs at night).[26] Carr suggests, "The highly publicized 'energy' of the scene feels something like gold rush fever."[27] Formerly a place to be avoided if not completely ignored, the East Village became a cultural fad as the new avant-garde quarter of New York. Elliott recalls, "It was not unusual to see limousines parked in front of storefront clubs and galleries on otherwise burned-out blocks."[28] The low rents that initially attracted the artists to the once crime-ridden area soon skyrocketed as real estate followed the booming trend that the art community had unconsciously created. Though Busch's success was assisted by Theatre-in-Limbo's original East Village location, unlike other performers who had lived bohemian lifestyles in the condemned lofts of Alphabet City and created the radical, irreverent, and often drug-induced impulse that defined the neighborhood aesthetic from within, Busch infiltrated an already vibrant area with a different aesthetic that was more West Village with a pinch of Broadway showmanship. Busch describes himself as an "outsider" in the East Village scene and recalls that he and his troupe would quickly retreat back to their favorite haunt, a theater bar called McBell's on Washington and Sixth in their home turf of the West Village.[29] Busch remarks, "I was attracted to the decadence of the thing, but didn't really pursue it."[30] Busch's position in between the East and West Villages is demonstrative (both geographically and artistically) of his ambivalent position and refusal to choose a singular identity for his post-Ludlam Ridiculous and example of the complex nature of queer performance and its resultant legacies.

Kelly Green with Envy

Busch's interloper status is reflected in the opinions of the more hardcore East Village artists such as Busch's contemporary John Kelly, another revisionist Ridiculous performer and celebrated occasional drag artist. Kelly suggests:

The more edgy [East Village] people, unless they did something kind of mainstream, kind of remained underground. Charles Busch did not come from the East Village aesthetic, he came from the Broadway aesthetic in via the West Village. When he came over to Limbo he was really an outsider and he was using the East Village in a perfectly fine way but he was not spawned from the East Village scene, he was spawned from the commercial theatre. He did it incredibly, he had incredible production values and it was great work, but it wasn't really indigenous to the East Village DNA.[31]

Kelly, a classically trained ballet dancer, visual artist, choreographer, and countertenor, is best known for his drag performances as Dagmar Onassis (the mythical lost child of Aristotle Onassis and Maria Callas). Kelly has been unfairly labeled (like Ludlam) merely a solo drag act when in fact his original and complex male personas outnumber his female characters. Although Kelly's work has a strong tie to Ludlam's in its irreverent impulses, dedication to craft, and inspiration drawn from classical disciplines, Kelly considers his primary juvenile inspiration to be the Cockettes, a notorious San Francisco–based drag troupe. Kelly's acknowledgment of the Cockettes as an inspiration is compelling, particularly because he also performed with the Trockadero Gloxinia Ballet, a direct offshoot of Ludlam's troupe and founded by RTC members Larry Ree, Richard Goldberger, and Lohr Wilson in 1972.

Kelly first saw the Cockettes in a production of *Pearls over Shanghai* while still in high school when they played New York's Anderson Theatre during a 1972 tour. Kelly was inspired by the raucous company's fluid genderfuck aesthetic that negated the myopically traditional "man masquerading as woman" form of drag. Kelly remarks,

In a way the drag impulse is a great impulse, it's the impulse to basically be irreverent and to transcend and be extravagant with gesture, but it's not necessarily about male becoming female or female becoming male. The Cockettes were totally genderfuck, and it changed my life. It wasn't the female thing at all, believe me, they had beards, they didn't have tits, some were painted gold—it was total genderfuck. It was basically taking cultural information and amplifying it and fucking with it. And basically shoving up your finger to the culture and saying "No! Let's do this instead." That version of drag I'm alternately all for. But when drag went mainstream it diminished it and made it kind of stupid.[32]

It should be noted that Kelly's enthusiastic response to the Cockettes' New York performances stands in opposition to the general reception of the visiting troupe. Though the Cockettes had gained a cult celebrity status across the country after their spoof film of Trisha Nixon's wedding was released in 1971, the Manhattan audience, who had become accustomed to Ludlam's sophisticated and multilayered pastiched texts and rehearsed performances found the troupe's disorganized spontaneity infantile and pedestrian in comparison. What played well to the post–Summer of Love audiences in the City by the Bay had no footing at the advent of New York's disco age.[33] In counterpoint, though the failure of the Cockettes' Manhattan run is often attributed to their amateurish style, it more than likely was a case of regional taste and loyalty. By 1972 Ludlam had gained a cult following and growing celebrity within Manhattan, perhaps making the Cockettes widely publicized tour destined to fail.

In addition to his classical training at the American Ballet School, Harkness House, the Fashion Institute of Technology, and Parsons throughout the 1970s, Kelly developed a skill set in working with various professional artists. Kelly's performance career originated at the height of the post-Stonewall sexual revolution, and he became a regular at the East Village's slew of hardcore (yet inclusive) gay bars and clubs. It was at the S & M leather bar The Anvil in 1979 that Kelly first performed as his "alter ego" Dagmar to popular success after finding inspiration in resident drag queen Tanya Ransom, who regularly lip-synched to Nina Hagen. Over the next ten years Kelly would become a headliner as Dagmar at the popular Pyramid Club[34] and develop a legitimate biography[35] for the character, adding authenticity to the fantasy by "being photographed for the *Style* section of the *New York Times* [and] entering or leaving fashionable clubs in 'full dress' on the arms of handsome escorts."[36] Kelly continued to develop the queer fiction of Dagmar creatively with drag-on-drag metatheatrical layering, appearing as Dagmar masquerading as other characters: Dagmar as Joni Mitchell, Dagmar as Mr. Butch from Teaneck, New Jersey, or even Dagmar as Callas herself. This act practically represented Judith Butler's theory of drag as a self-conscious expression of desire-induced fluid gender in the decade before she concretely set her theories down in print in the watershed *Gender Trouble* (1990). Kelly's metamorphic drag maintains the Ridiculous affinity for the cult of the diva, as discussed in the introduction, but it is also a highly academic approach that seeks to complicate and erase gender binaries rather than validating them. Senelick orients Kelly's anarchic drag with queer activism, noting that he and his East Village peers "have read all the feminist and queer theory, boned up on hagiography, and perform in a postmodern manner with quotation marks around their drag."[37] Kelly's fractured filtering of celebrity through his stage-worthy self as Dagmar as whomever (Mitchell, Callas, etc.) illuminates the commodification of gendering as a form of cultural capital by embodying genderfuck through performative layering. Rather than using a hodgepodge of gender specific signifiers, as favored by Ludlam and the Cockettes, Kelly preserves a state of transparency in his drag that allows the viewer to see the characters lurking just beneath the surface: Dagmar beneath Mitchell and Kelly beneath Dagmar. This effectively destabilizes the symbolic order of gendering, embodying what Stephen Whittle called "a full frontal . . . practical attack on the dimorphism of gender and sex roles."[38]

Having gained a cult following with his Dagmar act, Kelly began to experiment with a series of diverse yet iconic gay male personae such as Orpheus, Narcissus, Leonardo da Vinci, and Saint Sebastian, using the neoclassical Wilhelm von Gloeden–inspired tableau vivant as medium to draw upon a masculine beauty that was frequently celebrated and cloyingly discussed by critics. Kelly sees himself as a "chameleon" that loves to "inhabit technique without being shackled by it [as well as] existing in shapes that are decided on and reliable [before] transcending them."[39] This approach has led to a remarkably diverse gallery of characters over his lengthy career.

From his initial solo performances Kelly began to develop larger and more intricate multimedia shows just as Busch and his troupe began to gain prominence. These highly cerebral shows included *Go West Junger Man* (1985), a dance narrative about Waldemar Dix, a young East German graffiti artist; *Diary of a Somnambulist* (1986), inspired by early twentieth-century German Expressionist films; and *Pass the Blutwurst, Bitte* (1986–87), the visual diary of neo-Expressionist artist Egon Schiele, for which Kelly was awarded his first Obie. Wishing to return to his roots as a classical dancer, Kelly also joined the all-male Trockadero Gloxinia Ballet (founded by former RTC troupe member Larry Ree [Ekathrina Sobechanskaya] in 1972) and was able to perform some of the most iconic women's roles in tutu and en pointe. Throughout the 1990s he also continued to develop a broad range of solo and group work. Kelly developed a working relationship with Harvard University and the American Repertory Theatre, where he played Cupid in Neil Bartlett's production of Marlowe's

Dido Queen of Carthage (2005) and appeared in dual roles as John/Persephone in the world premiere of Rinde Eckert, Denise Marika, and Robert Woodruff's collaborative retelling of the Orpheus and Eurydice myth *Orpheus X* (2006) prior to its run in Edinburgh (2007). Kelly is also committed to recording his performance inspired by Caravaggio in video and still images with *Carav(i)aggio* (2007) as a fellow at the American Academy in Rome. With this process he attempted to technologically preserve his work for posterity in order to combat its ephemeral nature and what he terms "rampant cultural amnesia."[40] In an effort to "galvanize" his work in order to leave "some kind of tangible object to the world"[41] that on some level may be considered if not comprehended by the average person, Kelly has been tirelessly creating an online video library of his complete works on YouTube and following the trend of creating a personal web page.[42] Thus Kelly's queer legacy veers into the posthuman, a record of oral histories made digital and accessible beyond the ephemeral nature of live performance.

Kelly's most recent works include *Paved-Paradise Redux,* an updated homage to Joni Mitchell (2007–10), *Cohesion,* a movement-based performance, *Muse Ascending a Staircase,* a multimedia exhibition (2011), *Beauty Kills Me*, a recording (2014), and *Escape Artist Redux*, a performance and video installation based on a graphic novel (2011–14). Kelly has also resurrected productions of *Diary of a Somnambulist* and *Love of a Poet* (both 2015). A regular feature at Bard College's Live Arts, curated by Gideon Lester, Kelly is also developing *Memoir*, a performance of legacy and his personal journey drawn from his journals, no doubt an important contribution to both queer history-making and a performative record of his own distinct queer legacy.

Unlike Busch, whose brief stint at the Limbo Lounge in the East Village lasted less than a year before he was catapulted to a producer-based Off-Broadway format, Kelly continued to produce work in the same grant-dependent bohemian style, long after the downtown renaissance had been snuffed out by rampant gentrification. Furthermore, performance artists like Kelly were struck a hard blow in 1990 when the National Endowment for the Arts (NEA) chairman, John Frohnmayer, was pressured by the conservative administration of George H. W. Bush and vetoed the grants of four artists because of the sexual themes in their work, even though they had been previously selected and approved after a peer review. The four artists, Karen Finley, Holly Hughes, Tim Miller, and John Fleck, were labeled the "NEA Four." Although the artists appealed the case to the U.S.

Supreme Court in *National Endowment for the Arts v. Finley* (1993), in turn winning a settlement in the same amount as the revoked grants, the NEA buckled under pressure from Congress, ceasing all grants awarded to individuals thereafter. Sixteen years after this landmark change Kelly is discouraged by the state of the arts in the United States. Kelly says, "Culturally it's more about finances and practicality at this point, although there are certain cultural issues that I would dwell on in my work, and really I'm working on reconfiguring my process, not so much to adjust to the world, but to adjust to the realities of being in this country and this moment in time."[43]

Because Busch built his career on a midtown professional model that only borrowed from the East Village aesthetic and hype, he has continued to achieve a financial and popular success in theater and cinema that Kelly has not. Like Kelly, Busch continues to perform in new original theatrical and cinematic works as writer and actor over thirty years after his premiere of *Vampire Lesbians*. This achievement surpasses Ludlam's incredible run of twenty years with his own ever-changing troupe prior to his AIDS-related death in 1987.

Kelly's independently developed performance genre is a unique addition to the Ridiculous because it is primarily nonnarrative, relying upon singing (both live and lip-synched), movement, and dance. In this way, his performance must be considered in a different context than either Ludlam's or Busch's work because it does not make reference to literature or cinema via dialogue-centered pastiche. Kelly's work should be analyzed in terms of both dance and performance history. Though the affective connections to New York, Ludlam, and Busch are rife, Kelly also chooses to trace his queer legacy from the Cockettes rather than his Gotham-based contemporaries, opening the possibility of another scholarly project in queer legacy and performance.

All about Eve

In an introductory essay that appears in his published collection of plays (2001) Busch remarks, "I was never in a school play, and for good reason: I couldn't remember a line of dialogue. I nearly hyperventilated the moment I hit the stage. It was because I loved it too much. To be 'up there' was almost too magical to imagine."[44] This expression of youthful reticence is the antithesis of Ludlam's childhood approach to the theater, which was reliant on a constant struggle to be the center of attention. Busch's off-stage persona as a nice Jewish boy from uptown was contradictory to the larger-than-life grandes dames that he presents onstage. Since the early days of the Ridiculous movement its creators have always been dependent upon the establishment and capitalization of commanding and often bizarre personae that blurred the lines between their everyday and performative identities. Ludlam's command of the stage while in role was in part a reflection of his often difficult and demanding behavior as director and playwright. In counterpoint, Busch's offstage persona is more wealthy urban gay man than it is contrived eccentric. Though grand and effeminate gestures occasionally color his conversation when off the stage, Busch uses them ironically; he could easily slip into a crowd unnoticed. This desire for anonymity often accompanies commercial success, whereas many contemporary Ridiculous performers such as Justin Vivian Bond and occasionally Taylor Mac blend their stage personae into their everyday life as avant-garde self-promotion. Busch chooses not to appear in drag for public appearances because he desires to be identified as an actor capable of self-transformation rather than a radical drag queen. His freedom to do this is supported by the fact that he has already developed a name for himself that is immediately associated with his successful work in the cultural coteries of New York.

Busch first became aware of Ludlam's RTC in the early 1970s when he was still a high school student in Manhattan. Afterward he attended productions of *Eunuchs of the Forbidden City* (1971) and *Camille* (1973).[45] Busch's perception of theater changed completely in watching the reckless abandon that Ludlam encouraged onstage in stark contrast to the Broadway shows that he had regularly attended with his wealthy aunt Lillian. He recalls of these early RTC productions: "It was so decadent, and dangerous, and funny . . . and the whole operatic nineteenth-century feeling of it, yet crossed with the primitive . . . I just was hooked."[46] In the spring of 1976, Ludlam took his company on a tour of the American Midwest, culminating with a performance and a symposium on the Ridiculous held at the University of Chicago. Busch, who three years before had relocated to the Windy City and was a senior at Northwestern University, attended the symposium followed by a question-and-answer session with Ludlam. There he became acquainted with RTC troupe members George Osterman and John Brockmeyer because, as Busch recollects, he and his best friend Ed Taussig, who accompanied him, were "cute."[47] Osterman and Brockmeyer invited Busch and Taussig to attend a closing-night party after the performance of *Stage Blood* that they would be attending that evening. At the play, an undervalued masterpiece based on a meta-metatheatrical retelling of Shakespeare's *Hamlet* and Chekhov's *The Seagull*, Busch immediately noticed that a poster for his upcoming play *Sister Act* (about a pair of showgirl Siamese twins trying to separate) that he had presented to Osterman and Ludlam had been posted on the wall of the dressing room set. Encouraged by this generous display and hoping to gain favor with Ludlam before the party, Busch went backstage to help strike the set after the performance. He recollects:

> I had this one, very weird, "All About Eve" moment. When we were packing up the costumes, somebody tossed Camille's ball gown to me; and as I was holding it up, I noticed Charles watching me with this odd look: I put it down *very* quickly.[48]

Busch's reference to the Bette Davis star vehicle *All About Eve* (1950) reflects the continuous Ridiculous convention of employing references drawn from an obsession with old Hollywood film stars, and a pastiche of these icons as metaphors for their own lives. This began when Ridiculous forefathers Jack Smith and Ronald Tavel initiated a cult around B movie "Queen of Technicolor" Maria Montez. Of his "patron saint," Jack Smith said, "[Maria Montez] believed and thereby made the people who went to see her movies believe. Those who could believe did. Those who saw the world's worst actress couldn't and they missed the magic."[49] In much the same way that Busch's plays would come to represent an escape for the disenfranchised in the mid-1980s, Maria Montez films provided "the escapism of a timeless universal sort" for individuals with a Ridiculous mentality before the Ridiculous movement began.[50] Although he was a generation younger than Smith, Tavel, and Ludlam, Busch also found his inspiration in the films of a bygone era.

In *The Lady in Question Is Charles Busch: A Drag to Riches Story*, John Catania and Charles Ignacio's 2006 biographical documentary that covers Busch's life from childhood through the premiere of his film *Die Mommie, Die!* (2003), Busch appears to graduate from college to go on to a solo career before he haphazardly falls into his drag career at the Limbo Lounge in 1984.[51] In reality, Busch had already developed his skills as a drag star with his first acting troupe, the forgotten Imitation of Life Theatre (ILT) in Chicago (1976–78). Encouraged by his introduction to the aesthetic of the RTC and its members, Busch began writing more short plays in the style of Ludlam. The first, entitled *Old Coozies*, was a parody of the classic film and high-camp gem *Old Acquaintance* (1943), starring Bette Davis and Miriam Hopkins. Billing themselves under the drag pseudonyms, the sisters Elsa and Shatze Van Allen, Busch and Taussig opened at Chicago gay punk bar, La Mère Vipère. Retrospectively Busch realized that *Old Coozies* was in fact "an embryonic version of what would become years later *Vampire Lesbians of Sodom*."[52] While in a Chicago-based homoerotic production of Sartre's *The Flies*, Busch met several other young actors who had recently graduated from Northern Illinois University. It was with this group that Busch formed the ILT as a Chicago-based emulation of the RTC, opening with his self-penned production of *Myrtle Pope: The Story of a Woman Possessed* (1977). A pastiche of a "slew of women's pictures," *Myrtle Pope* became a cult favorite among audiences, playing in diverse venues including straight and gay bars, bathhouse, and late-night movie theaters across Chicago.[53] While this experience resulted in the honing of Busch's drag skills, for which he was lauded by Chicago's gay and counter-cultural journalists, the troupe dissolved amid feelings of resentment and jealousy as other company members faded before the attention bestowed on their rising star.[54] This is reminiscent of Ludlam's deliberate choice to surround himself with novice actors to highlight his own acting talent. The frustrating behavior that ended ILT was the catalyst for Busch to work as a solo performer playing multiple characters and genders and informed his decision to return to New York.

The acquaintance of Busch and Ludlam was revived two years later when Busch began performing his solo show *Hollywood Confidential* (1979) in New York. Busch was struck by the difficulty of finding space to perform within the city and was relegated to scrounging for a night at Scene Once, a cabaret space on Hudson Street that "would book just about anybody."[55] As he was paying his dues as a solo performer trying to make his way in the challenging world of professional theater in Manhattan, Busch became determined to reconnect with an aloof and seemingly unapproachable Ludlam. Since Busch made his acquaintance in Chicago, Ludlam's star continued to rise: he found a permanent home for the RTC at One Sheridan Square in the West Village and continued to be the toast of the downtown theater scene, balancing now classic and new productions in repertory. In an attempt to gain Ludlam's attention (and hopefully his audience) Busch plastered the RTC theater with flyers after running into RTC company member Black-Eyed Susan (Susan Carlson) on the street. Carlson was a longtime RTC member who initially met Ludlam while they were undergrads at Hofstra and would remain a member of the company until Ludlam's death. Fortuitously, Ludlam saw a flyer and attended an evening of Busch's show, but much to Busch's chagrin Ludlam and his partner and fellow RTC member Everett Quinton left without going backstage to offer congratulations or criticism. Disappointed, but not willing to give up, Busch found what seemed to be an ideal opportunity to corner Ludlam when he saw an advertisement for a comedy awards presentation called "The Charlie Awards" for which the RTC head had been nominated. Taking his sister Meg, Busch bravely approached Ludlam and Quinton's table and introduced himself, mentioning that he had seen his comic idol in his audience the week before. Ludlam was warm and supportive, explaining that he was too shy to come backstage and laud Busch for a performance that he thought "marvelous."[56]

Inquiring where Busch was to play next, Ludlam invited the young actor to perform midnight shows at his One Sheridan Square Theatre in the upcoming months. Thrilled by the opportunity, Busch immediately began mailing flyers to advertise his upcoming show at this impressive venue. The week before Busch was scheduled to begin his run of *Hollywood Confidential* at the RTC, he approached Ludlam backstage to inquire about scheduling a technical rehearsal. Ludlam, clearly having forgotten his promise to the young actor, seemed flustered and sent him off to speak to Catherine Smith, the business manager of the playhouse and company. Smith was puzzled and annoyed by Busch's request, explaining that she had no prior knowledge of the show and thus had not reserved funds to produce it out of dwindling grant money. Busch pleaded and begged, agreeing to provide a technical staff on his own, and eventually Smith caved in and agreed to list his show in the weekly prerecorded telephone advertisement of the RTC. Busch played every Friday and Saturday midnight for the next two months at Ludlam's theater, and though the performances were poorly attended, the appointment resulted in Busch's first major reviews in the New York gay press, including the *Village Voice* and the *Advocate*.

With the professional relationship that Busch had always desired with Ludlam now blooming, another opportunity took place when Ludlam invited him to take the role of Hecate, Goddess of Hell, in the RTC's production of *Bluebeard*, which had become a signature piece of the troupe since its premiere in 1970. Busch jumped at the opportunity, offering to provide his own costume since the clownish garments and makeup that the previous actor had worn in the role put him off. Piecing together a red dance skirt, black bustier, platform shoes, and a ratted-out red wig, Busch glamorized the character's appearance, foreshadowing his signature style of drag that was yet to come. With only fifteen minutes of rehearsal sans Ludlam, Busch prepared to take the stage at the climax of the play when Ludlam as Bluebeard summons Hecate from the bowels of hell. Though Busch received the highest of compliments from several cast members for his uniquely subtle performance, Ludlam was displeased, encouraging Busch to "ham it up more."[57] Afraid that he would come across as an amateur and convinced that Ludlam was jealous that he had stolen the moment, Busch decided to change very little for the next performance, infuriating Ludlam. Busch recalls Ludlam saying, "Who the fuck do you think you are?" before storming off.[58] On the following night Busch attempted to bend his performance to meet Ludlam's demands, and Ludlam as Bluebeard reacted by pulling down Busch's bustier in the midst of the scene. When Busch questioned Ludlam about the incident after the performance, Ludlam responded with a resounding, "I'll stick my finger up your ass if I feel like it!" and Busch came to the realization that he had no interest in becoming a member of the RTC troupe.[59] Christopher Scott stated, "Charles was quite in control of how he manipulated people. But I don't think that he was in control of that desperate quality of needing to be at the center of things."[60] The rift between Ludlam and Busch may have in fact on some level stemmed from the physical differences that molded their different approaches to drag. According to biographer David Kaufman, Ludlam lacked confidence in his thick features, receding hairline, and compact physique, though he fully embraced these physical traits in developing the genderfuck aesthetic that would color his characters such as the hirsute Marguerite Gautier in *Camille*. Busch, on the other hand, had a slight frame and delicate features and thus could "actually look like a girl."[61] Thus Busch possessed a physical beauty that Ludlam did not, and Ludlam possessed the public adoration that Busch had yet to achieve.

For the next four years Busch gained continued success with his touring solo performances in San Francisco and Washington, DC, though he struggled to find performance space and a consistent audience in New York. During this period Busch developed a handful of other solo performances, including *Vagabond Vignettes* (1979), *A Theatrical Party* (1980), and *After You've Gone* (1982). Busch recollects of this uncertain period that was marked by either performative feast or famine,

The eight years I worked as a solo performer were essential to my development as an actor/writer but filled with loneliness and frustration. It was hard showing up alone in a strange city and forced to rely on the good graces of the mostly impoverished nonprofit theaters that had engaged me. I longed for the sense of camaraderie that can be such a magical part of theater. I also had reached a certain level of professionalism where I received great reviews and could even sell out on a rainy Sunday in Santa Cruz, but just couldn't earn a living.[62]

Although the same monetary stresses that plague many young artists made Busch's vocational choice a challenge, his perseverance and resolve would soon pay off.

East Meets West

In order to support himself while in New York, Busch began working as a temp and moonlighting on summer weekends as a quick-sketch artist at the local Renaissance Fair. It was here that Busch first met Bina Sharif, an eccentric Pakistani performance artist who lived and often performed in the still decrepit East Village. Sharif invited Busch and Elliott (then a struggling theater director and Busch's roommate) to attend one of her bizarre performances at the storefront gallery / performance space/ bar called the Limbo Lounge on Avenue C in the spring of 1984. The same night that Busch saw Sharif's performance (which was primarily composed of the dramatic recitation of designer perfume brands) he was intoxicated by the exotic freedom and Weimaresque decadence of the space and audience. He immediately approached the manager of Limbo Lounge, a young punk East Villager going by the moniker Michael Limbo, and inquired about performing in the space. The carefree Limbo immediately scheduled Busch to open three weeks from that night. Busch remembers,

> I'd always had these longings for this decadent avant-garde kind of world, to be a part of it, but I never was. I was just enraptured. I was doing my act in non-profit theatres. Even if I was playing in a gay bar, it wasn't particularly exotic. So I knew that I didn't want to do my act, I wanted to do something decadent . . . like Lindsay Kemp![63]

Kemp became known for his unconventional blend of drag, mime, burlesque, and the intricate and often grotesque Japanese dance form of butoh. After first performing at the Edinburgh festival in 1968, Kemp continued to perform in original works on the stage, film, and television. He collaborated across many art forms and genres with such artists as David Bowie and Derek Jarman. With his self-proclaimed dance troupe, Kemp created graphic productions drawn from any number of sources, featuring himself as a perverse clown playing roles as diverse as Wilde's Salomé to a nineteenth-century Bavarian Cinderella. Senelick suggests that "through Kemp's mixture of high camp and martyrology British art of the 1960s became imbued with overt images of homosexual taboo."[64] Although Kemp's aesthetic drew from the crude, often verging on the sensational, the core of his vision is the British equivalent to the radical social changes that spawned the uniquely American Ridiculous theater across the Atlantic. Busch traces one alternative leg of his queer legacy back to Kemp.

Within three weeks Busch had cobbled together a company of actors from friends and acquaintances. Conceptually, Busch formed the troupe around the metatheatrical Pirandellian theme of contemporary actors as a nineteenth-century touring company, composed of stock characters, who in turn played various roles. Busch figureheaded this effort as the aging starlet who plays the lead regardless of her age, in the footsteps of Sarah Bernhardt, who had stubbornly played the role of the teenaged Joan of Arc at fifty-four. The stock company consisted of Arnie Kolodner, the leading man, Kenneth Elliott, the villain, Theresa Marlowe, the ingénue, Andy Halliday, the character actor, Julie Halston, the comedienne, Meghan Robinson, the villainess, and Robert (aka Bobby) Carey, the juvenile. Richard Niles theorizes that this approach of tailoring roles produced celebrity acting: "In essence, a double role was being performed. The Limbo actor presented himself first in the role of an actor in the company, then as the character defined by the given circumstances of the play."[65] This sense of layered performance can be traced back to the origins of the Ridiculous when Ronald Tavel explained in a reinterpretation of Brecht's *verfremdungseffekt* that the illusion created by the Ridiculous theater "was that we were presenting the real actor, not some character. The true mentality of the actor."[66]

Before Halston joined the company former RTC alumna Lola Pashalinski originally performed the role of La Condesa at the premiere the troupe's first play, *Vampire Lesbians of Sodom*.[67] The troupe decided to call itself Theatre-in-Limbo in honor of the space that would host its premiere and become its first permanent home. Busch selected the outlandish title prior to writing the script because he thought he could "costume ancient Sodom easily with just G-strings, tulle, and netting."[68] After writing a brief innuendo-ridden scene about a vampire succubus and a virgin sacrifice, Busch decided to compose a second scene that would place the immortal characters as rivals in the future. He chose 1920s Hollywood, because again, it would be simple to costume with "slips and sashes" and make filmic reference to the Hollywood fetishism that was at the core of the early Ridiculous movement and drawn from Busch's early obsession with the sirens of silent film.[69] Although the script of *Vampire Lesbians* is frothy when compared to Ludlam's *chefs d'oeuvre* or Busch's later works, it is must be analyzed for its rich pastiche of cinematic references and how they reflect the gay culture of the period. Additional analysis of how his first play helped to shape what would become Busch's unique reinterpretation of the Ridiculous genre is also revelatory.

Setting Ridiculous plays in exotic settings of the past had been commonplace since at least Jack Smith's *Rehearsal for the Destruction of Atlantis: A Dream Weapon Ritual* (1965).[70] Aside from the ease that the setting of ancient Sodom provided for design elements, the reference of the ancient city was also a tongue-in-cheek snub of the right-wing Christian fundamentalist movement that had been likening the ill-fated Old Testament city with the United States and the visibility of gay rights and HIV/AIDS. The comparison of Sodom to cities such as New York and San Francisco became a frequently used metaphor for the conservative campaign against gay rights. Evangelist and television personality Jerry Falwell used AIDS as sign of apocalyptic doom, advancing his earlier argument that homosexuality was a contagious disease. In the mid-1970s David Wilkerson, a Pentecostal reformed gang member referred to Sodom in his book *The Vision*. His sensationalizing rhetoric states:

> The sin of Sodom will again be repeated in our generation. Of all the sins Sodom was guilty of, the most grievous of all were the homosexual attacks by angry Sodomite mobs attempting to molest innocent people. . . . I have seen things in my vision which makes [sic] me fear for the future of our children. I speak of wild, roving mobs of homosexual men publicly assaulting innocent people in parks, on the streets, and in secret places. . . . Believe me when I tell you the time is not far off

that you will pick up your local newspaper and read sordid accounts of children being attacked by wild homosexual mobs.[71]

The theory behind this alarmist and fear-mongering statement became instant fodder for the Ridiculous tradition filtered through Busch. In the spirit of Ludlam, who built his theater by ridiculing heteronormative conservatism rather than radically protesting against it, Busch takes the vitriolic bigotry of the antigay movement (with Senator Jesse Helms and Anita Bryant as figureheads) and magnifies its absurdity through parody and satire. When read critically in the context of the component culture of the AIDS crisis at its genesis, the vampire may be read as a figure that represents both sexual seduction and death. Marty Fink notes that "since their popularization in the nineteenth century, vampires have evolved as literary signifiers of sexual deviance [and] embodying illnesses."[72] The allegorical association of the vampire with those suffering from AIDS positions the mythical figure as a sexual predator, whose immortality can only be snuffed through an act of righteous fundamentalism. In this formula the religious Right becomes emblematic of the vampire killer, and this metaphor forms a series of binary oppositions: evil against the righteous, dark against the light, the weak against the strong. In his book *AIDS and American Apocalypticism*, Thomas L. Long notes that Americans have a frequent history of "redefine[ing] our commitments to social actions by declaring metaphorical war," and in the case of AIDS a moral war with apocalyptic undertones.[73] Long's suggestion that a revealing fluidity between the past and the present can be made through other narratives of disease, trauma, and scapegoating also inadvertently supports queer legacy-making through a lateral process.

Although Busch wasn't motivated by the political agenda surrounding the vampire figure while writing *VLOS*, the act of deflecting the political through satire inadvertently falls in line with Ludlam's formula of packaging irreverence in the form of Camp. This approach is queerer still for its ambivalent position, implementing Camp to eschew labels and stigma that comment wryly on the social construct rather than participating in dualistic rhetoric of the (minority vs. the majority) binary. This sort of Camp aesthetic is the very backbone of *VLOS*. The first act is centered on a virgin maiden who is sacrificed to a Lesbian succubus vampire by two muscular, handsome guards in loincloths. This premise playfully draws upon every stereotype presented in the Wilkerson extract. The virgin sacrifice as portrayed by Busch in a long wig, a bit of tulle tied around his narrow waist, and spike heels was intended to suggest a "a stripper performing a burlesque sketch about Vestal virgins."[74] The scene climaxes as the girl awaits the arrival of the Succubus, and Ali the guard inquires what he can do to calm her:

> ALI: Is there nothing I can do to ease your pain?
> GIRL: Yes, there is something you could do. Break my hymen. Rape me and I'll no longer be a virgin fit for sacrifice.
> ALI: But, I . . .

The girl rips off Ali's loincloth and chases him around screaming "break my hymen, break my hymen!" Hujar pushes her to the ground.[75]

The comic irony of this scene comes in the contradictory promiscuity of the supposedly innocent virgin girl, and then the sight gag as she rips the loincloth from Ali, exposing his nude muscular body. The display of over-developed musculature as the ideal gay body type is linked directly to the gym culture of the early 1980s. Replacing the flannel-clad mustachioed clone of the 1970s, the muscular physique became central to gay body culture and the development of the "himbo" aesthetic.[76] When read in context to vampirism, the display of taut male flesh goes beyond constructs of desire to symbolize youth culture as embodied by corporeal perfection. This alternative reading is relevant because it presents the vampire as a figure that eternally preserves the facade of youth and beauty sans the magic waters of conquistadorial fantasy. Taylor's recent work on queer subcultures that cling to youthful characteristics defines communities of aging queers as "hotbeds of post-adolescen[ce] . . . that exist largely outside of traditional kinship notions" and helps to clarify the vampire as another model of queer legacy and a metaphoric embodiment of eternal youth(fullness).[77] In other words, in a queer construct the consumption of youth, whether in the form of flesh or cultural capital, is key to avoiding the pitfalls of aging.[78] In this vein the vampire may be read as an underground symbol of youth and sexual virility rather than infection and death. Carey, the actor who originated the role of Ali, was known far more for his statuesque physique than his acting talent, and in every show that followed his body would be revealed as a Camp-infused signature of his performance in a carnal display that was highly anticipated by the audience in each Theatre-in-Limbo production.

The muscle culture of the 1980s also grew in part because anabolic steroids became a common prescription for those suffering from AIDS. Incongruously, the muscular body that appeared to be at the apex of physical health was often the infected body, reliant on steroids to treat chronic weight loss and other forms of physical wasting. In fact, Carey would pass away from AIDS-related complications in Los Angeles in 1991. As the muscular physique became an iconic type in gay culture, the Ridiculous theater embraced it as another stock figure in its cast of postmodern American commedia dell'arte characters. After Busch had introduced Carey to the stage the year before, Ludlam recruited the hunky plumber and occasional stripper Philip Campanaro into his company in 1985 to play the loincloth-clad lead Matho in his *Salammbo*, not to mention the chorus of bodybuilders that were snatched up from various gyms and escort advertisements and hired to play barbarians. Kaufman posits:

> Just when the gay world suddenly had compelling reason to become more monogamous or even celibate, Ludlam was going to celebrate the lascivious promiscuity it had reveled in before—primarily by putting a lot of raw muscle onstage.[79]

More recently, contemporary Ridiculous performer Taylor Mac continued the tradition of the half-nude muscle boy stock character with actor Todd D'Amour as the evangelical weatherman Colin Clement in his production of *Red Tide Blooming* (2006) at Manhattan's PS122. Prior to Busch's introduction of Carey as the first muscle boy in his Ridiculous fold, nudity had been primarily used as an irreverent and comic convention in the genre, thumbing its theatrical nose at the antiporn movement. Ludlam said,

> Pornography is the highest development of naturalism. It was the seriousness of pornography that the [RTC] was never into. It is not in depicting the sexual act that one becomes a pornographer; it is in demanding to be taken seriously. Depicting sexual things—nudity and all that—we were taking a satirical view, rather than trying to arouse the audience sexually.[80]

Ludlam regularly employed nudity and heightened sexual situations in his productions, though most often in the form of the grotesque. The hilarious climax (both figurative and literal) of his infamous production of *Bluebeard* came in the nude sex scene between Ludlam as the hirsute

Bluebeard and the obese, malapropism-spewing Pashalinski as Miss Cubbidge. Rather than this shocking and provocative approach, Busch was far
more interested in exploring the ironies of beauty and glamour. Ludlam's
camp was "motivated by [a] rage"[81] that was spawned by gay oppression,
whereas Busch was using his theater as a celebration of life that was too
often cut short.

Although the gay culture of the 1980s embraced and then exploded the
culture of superfluous muscle, Busch had created Carey's stock image as a
hyperbolized type, not something to emulate in the performance of daily
life. This late twentieth-century reincarnation of the cult of the body developed because American popular culture was overrun with images of the
nude body. This overt use of nudity became a soft-core pornographic exhi-
bitionism rather than the thinly veiled declaration of freedom developed
by the flower children two decades before. In his article "The World Made
Flesh: Staging Pornography in Eighteenth-Century Paris," Senelick states
that pornography is "meant to arouse a sexual response" and "is expected
to culminate in orgasm," before concluding that the public consumption
of such material makes the desired orgasm impossible.[82] Although Busch
delightedly takes full advantage of exposing the male body beautiful, he
consistently juxtaposes the moment of revealing with a sharp anachronistic
irony that dissolves the physical fantasy. As Ali and Hujar appear onstage in
all of their masculine glory, they exchange the following dialogue:

> HUJAR: So what brings you to Sodom?
> ALI: Don't scoff but I've come to seek my fortune.
> HUJAR: My friend, you've made a wise move. This city has everything.
>   Have you been to the bars?
> ALI: Last night I was taken to a place called "The Galley Slave." The
>   whole place was supposed to look like a slave ship. There was this
>   fellow who they tied up in a sling and . . . and . . . and they shoved
>   a golden pestle up his you know what.
> HUJAR: (*lewdly*) You don't say. Last night my lover and I went to the
>   baths in Gomorrah. Talk about trolls. It was like open house at a
>   leper colony.
> ALI: I don't want to offend you but I'm really not into bars and baths.
>   I'm looking for a relationship.[83]

Herein the ancient guards become typical Manhattan gay twenty-
something's, with Ali "seeking his fortune" in the materialistic New York

of Reaganomics. The "Galley Slave" could easily be any of the backrooms in hardcore gay bars that grew out of the sexually free atmosphere in the late 1970s and dotted lower Manhattan. In Busch's fictionalized account of his East Village beginnings, the novel *Whore of Lost Atlantis*, he even renames the Limbo Lounge "Gomorrah." It can be argued that "leprosy" may be read as a metaphor for AIDS, as Ludlam would also use leprosy in the same context in his aforementioned AIDS play *Salammbo.* Additionally, Ali's search for a relationship supports the desire for commitment and companionship that grew in part out of the AIDS crisis, as well as smashing the stereotype or fantasy that the beautiful Sodomite guard would be sexually promiscuous and accessible.

After the virgin succumbs to advances of the vampire Succubus in the first scene, the second opens with the Succubus reincarnated as La Condesa, a silent screen vamp and the virgin as Madeleiné Astarté, a stage actress. The women, both immortal vampires, have been passing through the centuries as rivals and enemies. The old-Hollywood location of the second scene refers to the eccentric and flamboyant silent film star Alla Nazimova, whose hotel complex "The Garden of Allah" on Sunset Boulevard in the early 1920s was often the location of exclusive lesbian parties. Resplendent with lush foliage, a Black Sea–shaped swimming pool, and twenty-five bungalows, the Garden of Allah became the hot spot for Hollywood's elite to live and play with carnal abandon. Nazimova's role as a gay cult figure had been solidified after her eccentric version of Wilde's *Salomé* was released in 1923. Purported to have an all-gay cast in homage to Wilde (though this has been proven to be myth), Nazimova's film was excessively rich in Camp aesthetics and theatrics, assuring it a place in the repository of the Ridiculous impulse and conscience.

La Condesa and Astarté are pursued by the vampire hunter Gregory Salazar (an homage to Stoker's Van Helsing), who is disguised in drag as the gossip columnist Oatsie Carewe before the second scene blends into the final installment, which takes place in contemporary Las Vegas. When *Vampire Lesbians* first premiered at the Limbo Lounge in 1984, only the first two scenes were presented; the play then concluded with the suspenseful question "Will they escape, or will they perish?" before the melodramatic tag of "to be continued . . ."[84] The third and final Las Vegas scene was not added until *Vampire Lesbians* moved from the Limbo Lounge to its second home, another East Village club called 8 BC, before going back to a new and larger Limbo Lounge and finally settling at the historic Off-Broadway Provincetown Playhouse.

The Las Vegas scene opens with three chorus boys exchanging a flamboyant patois that re-creates the affected dialect that arose in the gay ghettos of New York and San Francisco. Madeleiné is now Madeleine Andrews, a middle-aged Vegas headliner. The characters are introduced by the following exchange:

ZACK: . . . Take this tip, buddy, stay away from the queens in this
company.
DANNY: I heard that, Miss Zack. Stay away from the queens, indeed.
Sweetie, has Miss Thing invited you to her dungeon room? Or did
I arrive too soon?
P.J.: Hey guys, come on. Miss Andrews will be here any minute.
DANNY: I hope she is. It's about time she discovered this one's true
colors.
ZACK: Jealousy, jealousy, jealousy.
DANNY: If you're referring to the one night we slept together. I'd talk
about your cock but I've got respect for the dead.
ZACK: You goddamm . . .

Zack tries to attack Danny but P.J. stops them.

P.J.: Hey guys, come on, can't you discuss this calmly?
DANNY: I'll tell you what's going on. I've been dancing in Madeleine
Andrew's Vegas act for five years. Before that I was a dancer on
her TV Variety Show. I've paid my dues with that broad. My lover
David has been with her just as long. Then Mata Hari here joins
the company and tries to turn her against us.
ZACK: First we have vampires on the strip, now I've got an hysterical
faggot to deal with.
DANNY: I wouldn't be worried about vampires, Whorina. Your ass is
hardly virgin territory.[85]

This conversation operates on a variety of levels. The hyperbolized masculinity of the muscled actors is humorously inflated when they open their mouths and a slew of purses torrentially fall out. This contradictory effeminacy works to deconstruct the erotic desirability of the actors on the stage, separating the pornographic myth from reality. Performed before an audience that was primarily composed of gay men and their supporters, the language that might otherwise be considered as irresponsible, offensive, or blatantly homophobic is reclaimed and celebrated. Elliott points out that this can be linked to Muñoz's theory of "disidentification" wherein "damaged stereotypes" are recycled "as powerful and seductive sites of self-creation."[86] This is reminiscent of Ludlam's reliance on the encoded inferences or passwords that litter his own work, and which he broadly defined as Camp. For Busch, the Campy use of the patois, paired with gay-specific references, becomes a common ground, which becomes the catalyst for conversation and cathartic bonding in the midst of crisis. Moreover, the inclusion of encoded language heightened a feeling of belonging in the ephemeral escapist world that only existed as the show was performed. Cleto traces the development of gay "argot" from Harold Beaver's groundbreaking 1981 essay "Homosexual Signs," built upon the Barthesian principle of "persona" to frame Camp as a homosexual language, to Phillip Core, who expanded this idea to define Camp as a "[gay] Masonic gesture" that utilized secret signs to share occultic and "secret knowledge."[87] Linguist William Leap surmised that gay slang, which he terms the "lavender lexicon," developed through the modern era as a sort of protective armor in an otherwise hostile world where homosexuality was directly associated with deviance and perversion.[88] Don Kulick extends Leap's notion by making reference to D. Sonenschein's Stonewall-era theory that gay slang was not merely isolationist, but also served to "reflect common interests, problems, and needs of the population."[89] Although the nightclub scene is satirical bordering on absurd, it does provide a reflection of gay culture that speaks beyond the specificity of the period when it was written.

Carey and Kolodner, the same actors who portrayed the guards of ancient Sodom in scene 1, also play the roles of the gay dancers. This conscious doubling implies that just as fictional vampires have existed since ancient times, so have gay men been a vital part of culture and society. This is a reaction to Falwell's and Bryant's accusation of gay recruitment, the latter's explanation of a seemingly instant gay visibility that had previously been hidden in the dangerous climate of the pre-civil rights era. Busch bookends the play with another snub of the religious Right when the character of Tracy (played by Marlowe), who has "been on tour with the Young Republican First College Christian Review," pulls a Sally Bowles, abandoning her morals to become Madeleine's "latest protégée."[90]

It was also during the initial run of *Vampire Lesbians* that Busch developed his signature curtain speech at the end of every performance. Always opening with the statement "Bless you, darlings," Busch channeled a nineteenth-century diva exhausted from her hour sacrificed on the stage and lending a Camp-infused authenticity to the shtick of a touring stock company. Company designer Brian Whitehall added to this illusion with a series of interchangeable painted drops and by adding footlights to the edge of the stage.

The longevity of *Vampire Lesbians* Off-Broadway arose from a combination of cult status (some evenings audience members would recite dialogue à la *The Rocky Horror Picture Show*) and a glowing review by D. J. R. Bruckner in the *New York Times*. He wrote of the production,

> One can imagine a cult forming. Costumes flashier than pinball machines, outrageous lines, awful puns, sinister innocence, harmless depravity—it's all here. And it's contagious; this kind of campy show that transforms everything it touches attracts audiences that could take over and finish the performance if the cast walked out in the middle.[91]

The reference to the potential for the cast to walk out hearkens back to the early days of Ludlam's company when in the epic productions of *Big Hotel* and *Turds from Hell* the cast followed a revolving door policy and changed like the wind on any given night. Busch's rapid rise to success using the Ridiculous genre did not sit well with his old mentor. In the midst of the *Vampire Lesbians* fad, Ludlam and Quinton went to see the production unbeknownst to Busch and the company. Kaufman suggests that "Ludlam returned from the performance enraged, griping that superficial elements of his work had indeed been stolen, but without any of their substance."[92] Busch relates that he had no knowledge of this and only learned of Ludlam's anger and disappointment upon reading Kaufman's account long after Ludlam's death. As reported by several original RTC members, Ludlam's jealousy was a vice that often plagued him, stewed up from a combination of self-doubt and the need to be in control. If Ludlam was indeed angry with Busch, his disappointment was contradictory since all of his work had also been influenced and collaged from preexisting genres and works. Because Ludlam's life was cut prematurely short in the midst of a prolific and expanding career, perhaps he was not yet prepared to pass off the Ridiculous torch to his heirs, and particularly not to those outside the grasp of his controlling fist and the RTC. While Ludlam saw himself and his work in the present, the next generation was already looking to his work as a theater that represented a watershed moment in the recent gay past.

From 1984 until 1991 Theatre-in-Limbo produced eight cultish and popular plays at the Limbo Lounge, the Provincetown Playhouse, and the WPA
Theatre. Aside from *Vampire Lesbians* and *Theodora* the plays consisted of
Sleeping Beauty or Coma (1984), a postmodern fairy tale set in 1960s swing-
ing London, *Times Square Angel* (1984), the annual Theatre-in-Limbo holiday show, *Pardon My Inquisition* (1986), Busch's satire of fifteenth-century
Spain as metaphor for Reagan-era Manhattan, *Psycho Beach Party* (1986), a
dark comedy drawn from bubblegum Frankie and Annette beach blanket
films of the 1960s, *The Lady in Question* (1988), a riff on Nazi-era suspense
thrillers, and finally *Red Scare on Sunset* (1991), a farce about witch hunts in
McCarthy-era Hollywood. Theatre-in-Limbo went on several highly successful tours to Los Angeles and Japan, producing more quality work with
every season. Before dissolving Theatre-in-Limbo due to internal conflicts
and external circumstances (such as the severe illness and resultant AIDS-
related deaths of Carey and Robinson) Busch began to explore the possibility that his drag identity was limiting his potential. This promulgated his
decision to return to independent work.

As Busch's company gained critical respect and popular success, major changes occurred regarding the treatment of and public visibility of
AIDS. The gay and theater communities responded immediately to the
epidemic in the form of vigils, fund-raisers, and new plays that tackled the
still disconcertingly difficult theme of the disease. While Busch was still
in the early phase of Theatre-in-Limbo, ACT UP founder Larry Kramer's
AIDS play *The Normal Heart* (1985) was produced to critical acclaim at
Manhattan's Joseph Papp Public Theater and Robert Chesley's *Night Sweat*
was featured at San Francisco's Theatre Rhinoceros the same year. As
the 1980s bled into the following decade, the identity of AIDS shifted as
the disease moved beyond the stigma of *only* a gay epidemic. With the
death of blood-transfusion victim Ryan White in 1990 and heterosexual
basketball superstar Magic Johnson's public admission to suffering from
the disease in 1991, the face of HIV/AIDS drastically changed. Additionally, advancement in medicines such as antiviral and protease-inhibiting
"cocktail" therapy helped AIDS to become a chronic disease rather than
an immediate death sentence.

This cultural shift allowed for a return to normality within the gay
community, and as safe-sex campaigns became a sign of the times, the
fear that hovered over New York in the early days of the AIDS epidemic
lessened. Busch's Ridiculous plays became assimilated into popular theater culture in the 1980s. Though his theater continued to attract a gay

audience with its use of Camp and innuendo, its role as an escapist commune was no longer as relevant or appropriate. *VLOS* became a staple of
the New York theater tourist trade (Busch and the company were even
featured in the widely read tabloid magazine *People*, on August 20, 1984),
making it one of the longest-running Off-Broadway shows in New York's
history. Busch's drag was no longer a decadent and eccentric manifestation of the East Village avant-garde, but rather something wild to bring
Mom and Dad to when they were seeking urban adventure while visiting
from small-town America.

La Grande Dame

When asked what he considered to be the seminal works of his career,
Busch responded with the predictable *Vampire Lesbians*, but also with two
works from the post-Limbo period: the Tony-nominated *Tale of the Allergist's Wife,* for which Busch stepped away from the makeup table and
served as playwright, and the stage production and major motion picture
Die Mommie, Die!

After the members of Theatre-in-Limbo had gone their separate ways,
Busch penned his first play in which he would forgo drag to play a gay
man. He had always been impressed by the fact that Ludlam dynamically
played all of his characters with equal charisma and power regardless of
gender. In fact, Ludlam's male roles were more than triple the number of
his dragged-up leading ladies. In the play *You Should Be So Lucky*, Busch
portrayed Christopher, a young New York electrologist who is swept up
into a Cinderella tale of an enchanted ball and a wealthy benefactor in the
midst of pop-cultural references that run the gamut from old Hollywood
films to contemporary New York. In his first major post-Limbo project,
Busch brought along troupe members Elliott to direct and Halston to play
the role of Lenore, the brassy Jewish daughter of Christopher's benefactor,
Mr. Rosenberg. After an initial reading at the Bay Street Theatre in Sag
Harbor, the production played for a limited run at Primary Stages beginning in November 1994, and received affectionate reviews ("a hymn to
the sanctuary of escapism") from critics who were already supporters of
Busch's work.[93] It was Halston, however, who received the major acclaim
for a vivid characterization that far outshone Busch's "suppressed flamboyance" and "shrinking-violet persona."[94] Furthermore Busch recollects,

At best I was this very withdrawn and shy kind of person who blossoms, and it wasn't much of a fun part to do. I'm so female-centric in my writing that it turned out that women's roles were the best ones. I just didn't like playing that nerdy kind of guy. I liked playing the glamorous lady who's desired—and everybody wants to make love to her! I also resented when in reviews people said that this was me playing myself.... Honey, I am *much* more like Irish O'Flannagan [from *Times Square Angel*], and Gertrude Garnet [from *The Lady in Question*] than I am that boy.[95]

This experience confirmed to Busch that he was best suited for drag, and Halston's rave reviews resulted in a bitter feud that ended their friendship until it was reinstated several years later. During this period Busch also wrote his novel *Whores of Lost Atlantis* (1996) and continued to develop several new productions, including a World War II USO show satire called *Swingtime Canteen* (1995); a new musical, *The Green Heart* (1997), based on Jack Ritchie's short story of the same name; *Queen Amarantha* (1997), an homage to a nineteenth-century historical melodrama; and *Shanghai Moon* (1999), a Theatre-in-Limbo-style production set in exotic 1930s China.

Working off the popularity of Halston's character type in *You Should Be So Lucky*, Busch developed an extended monologue as a "raging Jewish lady" named Miriam Passman for his new solo cabaret act *Flipping My Wig*.[96] In addition to the Passman role Busch created a range of other characters in the performance, including a Prohibition Era tough-as-nails nightclub chanteuse and a suburban housewife who lives her fantasy of transforming into Edith Piaf for one night. The show was originally performed in Philadelphia and directed by Elliott before transferring to the Manhattan Theatre Club. It was through exploring this Upper West Side, pseudointelligentsia, Jewish character initially in *You Should Be So Lucky* and then in *Flipping My Wig* that Busch came to create what he considers to be one of his most important works, *Tale of the Allergist's Wife*, which opened at the Manhattan Theatre Club in November 2000. The production was directed by Lynne Meadow and was nominated for a Tony Award for best play the following spring along with Busch for best playwright. Busch was not featured in this production, but instead gave over the leading lady reins to Linda Lavin as the neurotic Marjorie. Drawing upon his own experience growing up culturally Jewish in New York along with verbatim fragments of borrowed conversations between his aunt and sister, Busch composed a succinct and uproarious boulevard comedy that had the Broadway community suddenly proclaiming him "the next Neil Simon."[97] Just as Ludlam's Catholic upbringing played heavily into the themes of his plays, this was an opportunity for Busch to express a satire of his own urban Jewish-American experience. In order for the work to reach its full potential, he knew that he had to find the perfect lead to carry off the challenging but familiar role of Marjorie. Busch professes to have convinced Lavin to take a role in the production by "pursuing her like I had Ludlam . . . [and] writing her an outrageous letter comparing her to Bernhardt and Duse."[98]

The intersection of urban Jewish and gay identities that plays heavily into Busch's work had been a traceable part of New York City's culture since the early days of the gay liberation movement. Scholars including Judith Butler, Eve Sedgwick, and Jay Geller have laid solid groundwork on the relationship between gayness and Jewishness.[99] Although Jews have been strong supporters and producers of the New York theater scene since the origins of Broadway, it was not until the early 1980s that playwrights who were Jewish, gay, and dedicated to writing about gay/Jewish themes (such as Harvey Fierstein, Tony Kushner, and Martin Sherman) began to have a regular presence. The conflation of Jewish and gay ideologies is successful because themes of Jewish identity in such dramas echo those found in gay-themed works. For example, questions may address assimilation (whether cultural or religious), alienation and persecution (paralleling anti-Semitism with homophobia), or the source of social definition (cultural or individual). Furthermore, Reform and Reconstructionist movements as well as secular cultural approaches to Judaism have been largely accepting of homosexuality throughout the twentieth century (which is not to ignore the rampant homophobia that has been reported in some Orthodox communities).

A 2007 *Washington Post* article entitled "Gay Jews Connect Their Experience to Story of Purim" goes as far as declaring the holiday as a "National Jewish Coming-Out Day."[100] Purim celebrates the ancient triumph of the Jews over Haman (an evil royal vizier who ordered the Jews exterminated) with Esther's revelation (or "coming out") to the love-struck Persian king Ahasuerus that she was indeed Jewish. Sometimes called the "Jewish Halloween," Purim celebrations "embrace cross-dressing and debauchery, [and] serve as unofficial gay pride events."[101] The carnival atmosphere, subversive gender practices, and allegorical implications of these celebrations provide a safe and comfortable environment for experimentation and have in turn been appropriated by the gay Jewish community. Abe Rybeck, artistic director of Boston's resident queer company The Theatre Offensive, drew upon this phenomenon in his Purim-themed drag musical *Pure PolyEsther* (2007). Rybeck connects his own life experience back to the story, relating, "Me coming out as queer, as gay, as part of the power of being able to do that comes from the book of Esther. It really helps people to understand oppression and what it looks like to fight for liberation . . . from the threat of death or slavery or the closet."[102] Busch's drag practices and performances are propelled by this amalgam of gay and Jewish identities, as is their reception by an audience fluent in the cultural symbols and innuendos. The mainstreaming of these characters was partially due to convenient timing.

The popular inclusive reception of Busch's Jewish matron was partially set in motion by the widespread cultural exposure of comedian Mike Myers's drag character of Linda Richman on the weekly sketch comedy program *Saturday Night Live* from 1991 to 1994. Based in part on his mother-in-law, Myers-as-Richman hosted a fictional local cable talk show entitled *Coffee Talk*. Myers hyperbolized and conflated Jewish stereotypes including a heavy New York accent, a sprinkling of Yiddish idioms (with the trademark catchphrases "It's like buttah," and "I'm a little *verklempt*"), and veneration for Barbra Streisand.[103] Myers-as-Richman furthered the Jewish stereotype by wearing tacky sweaters, huge glasses, and garishly painted acrylic fingernails with which she constantly adjusted her bouffant hair. Because Myers's image as a comedian on *Saturday Night Live* was initially based on his reputation as a hockey-loving Canadian "guy's guy" (cemented by his other characters like "Wayne" from the "Wayne's World" sketch), his performance in drag helped to shift the perception of drag solely from a gay bar pastime to a (still) viable comic convention. Furthermore, the presentation of urban "Jewishness" exposed a cultural stock-character (already recognizable in the city) to a suburban or even rural audience distanced from the cultural practices that were being magnified. Thus, an audience was already prepared to accommodate the spirited fun of the *Allergist's Wife*, which tells the story of Marjorie, a depressed and wealthy Jewish wife of a retired allergist, Ira, living a comfortable life taking care of her aging, vulgar mother in the social bastion of the Upper West Side. Though Myers's widely received television performances are not part of Busch's direct queer legacy, I argue that his presence does help to better clarify the cultural relevance of *Allergist's Wife* and the accessibility of the legacy I have traced herein.

When Marjorie's adventurous childhood friend Lee suddenly reappears, all of the characters are hilariously left questioning their sanity. In his *New York Times* review, critic Ben Brantley declared that with *Allergist's Wife* Busch had "swum into the mainstream."[104] Although he was thrilled by the critical acclaim that the play received, Busch was resentful of this limiting statement. He responds,

> I guess that I didn't realize that I was so out of the loop, which I guess was because in my way of thinking each of the plays that we had done post–Limbo Lounge had been at reputable nonprofit theatres and had transferred commercially. I guess if you're in drag and your work is mostly movie pastiche, then you're not in the mainstream.[105]

Busch's sentiment reflects the precarious situation that he found himself in the New York theater scene: ambivalently hovering between the disenfranchised avant-garde and the commercial popular stage, but belonging to neither. *Allergist's Wife* pinpoints Busch's desire to be taken seriously as part of the uptown theater community, though it has also disenchanted many of the lower Manhattan performers, like Kelly, whom he originally struggled alongside.

In creating *Allergist's Wife* Busch turned to Ludlam's recipe of mixing literary and academic references with vulgar humor and pop-cultural inferences. Scene 1 opens with the following exchange as Mohammed the doorman struggles to assist Marjorie in installing a new light fixture:

> MOHAMMED: Mrs. Taub, describe to me your vision once more.
> MARJORIE: It should be a feverish dream out of Baudelaire. Exotic, mesmerizing. This doesn't say "Extravagant decadence." This says "Lighting fixture."
> MOHAMMED: No, it says "Romantic opulence."
> MARJORIE: (*Losing her patience*) It says, "Repro bought at cost."[106]

This dialogue exemplifies the Ludlamesque formula of pairing the intellectually elite, "Baudelaire," with the crass juxtaposition of daily life. The metaphor of a counterfeit antique bought at a discount works particularly well as analogous to Busch's style of work: it relishes the paradox of a cheap foundation masquerading with an obviously fake but still luxurious facade (while also providing a wry to connection to Sontag's connection of Tiffany lamps to the Camp aesthetic). This is particularly reminiscent of Ludlam's later plays such as *Le Bourgeois Avant-Garde* (1983) and *The Artificial Jungle* (1986), which explored the contradictory schisms of the American Dream versus the realities of a contemporary American existence.

The references in *Allergist's Wife* are diverse and complex, including Kafka, Rimbaud, Beauvoir, Hesse, Helen Keller, Plato, Böll, Grass, Mann, Tolstoy, Turgenev, Flaubert, Nietzsche, Kierkegaard, Spinoza, *Dracula*, Goethe, *The Vagina Monologues*, Blanche DuBois, *Waiting for Godot*, Weimar Berlin, Judaic ritual, *Siddhartha*, Cocteau, *La Bohème*, and Shakespeare. Typically, Marjorie makes these references with the intention of pretentious name-dropping (another stereotype of New York City's Jewish upper class). This connects back to the Myers-as-Richman character that encouraged viewers to talk about esoteric and ridiculous topics such as "The Romanesque Church design was based on the Roman Basilica, discuss," or "The Thighmaster is neither a thigh nor a master, discuss," as she collected herself from her *verklempt* state (usually brought on by a reference to Streisand).[107] The success of *Allergist's Wife* on Broadway confirmed Busch's reputation as a theatrical force to be reckoned with, though his downtown fans had known this for years.

While *Allergist's Wife* was still in final rewrites and rehearsals, Busch had migrated to the West Coast, where he starred in a new play, *Die Mommie, Die!* (1999). Again directed by Elliott, the play evoked a Grand Guignol film of the 1950s while also drawing upon the ancient Greek (and Ridiculous favorite) Electra myth to convey the dramatic downfall of a family smothered in the kitsch of late-1960s Hollywood. The basic plot is as follows:

Angela Arden, an aging pop star, has a torrid affair with a young, macho, out-of-work actor and tennis pro named Tony Parker to escape from her unhappy marriage to Sol Sussman, a film producer. Angela retaliates against her husband's emotional abuse and viciously murders him with a poisoned suppository. Angela's bitter daughter Edith (in the Electra role) convinces her gay, black-sheep brother Lance that they must get to the bottom of the suspicious situation and avenge their father's death. In the meantime Parker, who is really a secret agent, seduces everyone in the house. Finally, by slipping LSD into their mother's coffee, the children take Angela on a wild acid trip in which she reveals that she is actually their Aunt Barbara, having killed her sister and stolen her identity years before. The play satirically critiques the notion of celebrity in America, highlighting first the ecstatic rise and then the bitterness that follows as a product of the fleeting nature of fame. Additionally, the play sends up the potentially dire fate of actresses in a culture obsessed with youth and beauty. The erratic aging star-let has been a common movie trope since at least Gloria Swanson's dynamic portrayal of Norma Desmond in *Sunset Boulevard* (1950) and continued to be represented throughout the 1960s in films such as *Whatever Happened to Baby Jane?* (1962), *Hush . . . Hush, Sweet Charlotte* (1964) and *Berserk* (1967). While Busch is unabashedly satirizing these films with neo-Ridiculous aplomb, his portrayal of Angela also embodies a kind of empathy for his predecessors, with Busch years older than when he convincingly portrayed pretty, youthful ingenues at the Limbo Lounge.

The structure of *Die Mommie, Die!* is reminiscent of Ludlam's "well-made play" period (1973–80), in which he created scripts based around the format codified by Eugène Scribe and Victorien Sardou and the farces of Georges Feydeau. Arguably Busch's most sophisticated script to date, *Die Mommie, Die!* achieves success because Busch retained his trademark glamorous aesthetic while also embracing the multiple plots and complex literary references that made Ludlam famous in his own work. Busch's maturation as a playwright is a product of both experience and experimentation. For example, the notorious suppository murder scene at the end of act 1 plays as follows:

(SOL takes the huge wrapped suppository out of his robe.)

SOL: How are you supposed to open this damn thing?
ANGELA: Let me do it.

(She takes the suppository from him and begins taking the wrapper off. SOL walks away from her.)

SOL: Angela, Angela, what time has wrought. I remember when I first laid eyes on you. You were in a sound booth in that forcockta recording studio on Fiftieth and Third Street. So lovely and fresh. I said to myself "Someday that delicate songbird's gonna be mine and I'm gonna boff her brains out."

(While he's talking and not looking, she dips the suppository into her quite lethal glass of warm milk. She hands him the suppository.)[108]

In this scene Busch as Angela plays out to the audience members, letting them in on her sly secret unbeknownst to her ill-fated husband. As she dips the suppository into the poisoned milk, Busch as Angela stares

ominously at the audience with a suggestive wink. Sol's chauvinistic demeanor blatantly convinces the audience to take the seemingly victimized
Angela's side (who is already the center of attention—Busch in a signature
role). The self-conscious acting style employed by Busch obliterates the
fourth wall and was the essence that made Ludlam's early Ridiculous plays
feel more like parties than traditional theatrical performances. Ludlam
and Busch invite the audience to partake in the intrigue of the plays. The
scene continues in a carnal ballet that could have been extracted from one
of Ludlam's plays: the aforementioned raucous sex scene in *Bluebeard*, the
climaxing Empress dildo scene in *Eunuchs of the Forbidden City*, or the
consumptive blow job that concludes *Camille*. Busch takes on the insertion of Sol's suppository for the theme of his own clownishly macabre pas
de deux.

ANGELA: Here you go. Ready for insertion . . .
SOL: It's the size of a Nathan's hotdog, I can't do this.

(She takes it from him)

ANGELA: Here. I'll help you.
SOL: Are you kidding?
ANGELA: I'm tired of hearing you complain about the bloat. Bend
over. Come on, Sol, bend over.
SOL: What the hell? Just be careful. I can't believe this.

*(She lifts up his robe. Away from the audience's view, she pulls down his
underpants. She looks around for a brief moment wondering where
she can find a lubricant. Giving up, she tries to insert the suppository.)*

SOL: Be careful. I've got a hemorrhoid! Ow!! You're killing me.
ANGELA: Now you know how I felt every night you forced yourself on
me.
SOL: *(She sticks it in him once more.)* Ow! Motherfucker!
ANGELA: Darling, just trying to get the whole thing in. You're very
tight. You must do your utmost to relax.

*(With a violent shove, she pushes the suppository into him. SOL cries
out in agony.)*

SOL: Oy!!!
ANGELA: All done. Operation complete.

(Sol sits down on the sofa.)

SOL: I wonder how long it takes before I feel anything.
ANGELA: Almost immediately from what I understand.
SOL: You've got a queer expression on your face. What are you think-
    ing about?
ANGELA: Perhaps how nothing turns out exactly as one plans.[109]

The scene concludes with Sol's violent death from the poisoned suppository. Busch owns the scene by mugging for the audience with both
pleasure and disgust as he inserts the suppository onstage, blocked by a
large sofa. The grotesque situation mixed with gay innuendo is pure Ludlamesque ridiculosity with a clear influence from the farce of Molière. As
Angela inserts the suppository into Sol's anus, both dialogue and actions
suggest a gay first-time sexual encounter, as Angela in the guise of the
"dominant" eases Sol, the hesitant "submissive," to relax. This double entendre is heightened by the fact that Busch is a man in drag, in much the
same way that Ludlam used drag in *Camille* to showcase a gay kiss with
Bill Vehr as Armand. The joke climaxes when after Angela completes her
dirty task Sol inquires about the "queer expression" on her face. Though
the innuendo is obvious in its delivery, it uses an exaggerated version of a
straight perspective that is then filtered through Camp to speak uniquely
to the contagion of the gay audience that potentially finds humor in similar life experiences.

Another scene of note is when Angela is drugged by Edith and Lance
to force a confession. Relying on manic gestures, sporadic sound cues,
and bizarre lighting, the scene is transformed into a hazy manifestation
straight out of 1960s drug culture. This acts as another unintentional homage to the early Ridiculous theater that was more often than not watched
through a drug haze by its audience, as were the early days of the East
Village renaissance.

While Busch was in Hollywood performing in *Die Mommie, Die!* he received a telephone call from a young up-and-coming director named Robert Lee King, who was interested in turning *Psycho Beach Party* into a major
motion picture through the gay-owned production company Strand. Busch
jumped at the chance of reformatting the short play into a longer screenplay.
Rather than play the revised Gidget-like character of Chicklet (as he origi-

nally had at Theatre-in-Limbo), Busch created the role of a no-nonsense police investigator, Monica Stark, for himself. King ambitiously shot the film in only twenty-one days. Although Busch expresses disappointment in the casting of "model types" rather than actors and the lack of transitional shots in the film, he was pleased in the way that he was presented.[110] The task of presenting himself as the iconic "leading lady" Charles Busch was a challenge since he was no longer appropriate to play the role of sixteen-year-old Chicklet. In the original Theatre-in-Limbo production the Ridiculous sensibility was pushed to its limit when Busch as Chicklet removed his bikini top and exposed his thin male torso and remarked, "I'm hopeless. I'm built just like a boy. I wonder if I'll ever fill out."[111] This clever sight gag defines the Ridiculous device to reach beyond the stage and invite the audience to be part of theatrical clique that is an active player in the game. In the film, Busch's shining moment comes in a car sex scene with Gibson as surf king Kanaka. The scene showcases Busch and Gibson kissing passionately in close-up before pulling away to a wide shot revealing the side view of a female body double's naked breast. Working on the same principle as the original gag, this sequence serves to remind the audience of the ludicrous fakery that the characters are completely oblivious to.

The release of the film *Psycho Beach Party* in 2000 coincided with Busch's annus mirabilis. The year was hallmarked by the opening and eager reception of *Allergist's Wife* that November. In 2001, after feeling out of sorts, Busch was rushed to Manhattan's Presbyterian Hospital, where he underwent open heart surgery for a genetic defect that had ripped his aorta. Busch's mother had suddenly passed away from heart failure when he was a young boy, and he unknowingly suffered from the same condition. Busch recovered fully from the operation and says that the experience "gave [him] clarification that [he] doesn't want to spend time working on projects that make [him] miserable."[112] Several television production companies had pursued Busch to take a position as a writer, but he abandoned this unsatisfactory work and returned to his childhood obsession—the movies.

In 2003 Busch was approached to make *Die Mommie, Die!* into a motion picture by producers Dante De Loreto and Anthony Edwards. Displeased with the final editing of *Psycho Beach Party*, Busch was excited by the opportunity to take part in a film that better showcased his personal aesthetic and approach to the Ridiculous. In adapting the screenplay, Busch closely followed the theatrical plot, creating a tight production that was marked with a filmic theatricality. With an all-star cast including 1990s television heartthrob Jason Priestley in the role of Tony, and directed by Mark Rucker, the film caused a minor sensation, with Busch winning a Special Jury Prize for outstanding performance at the 2003 Sundance Film Festival. Busch fondly recollects:

> We shot the movie in nineteen days and shot more footage than was planned. There were scenes that were designed to be shot in just one master shot, and we did it early and got close-ups, so it was just a dream! Maybe the most exciting nineteen days of my life. I mean most of the time in our lives we aren't aware that something great is going on until after the fact, but I was aware of every moment. I thought, "I can't believe this is happening to me."[113]

Following the success of the film, Busch revived the theatrical production of *Die Mommie, Die!* Off-Broadway in November 2007. Consistently developing new projects that retain his unique revision of the Ridiculous aesthetic, Busch occasionally presents summer productions in Sag Harbor, Long Island.

As epidemiological advances have been made in the fight against HIV/AIDS since the 1990s Busch has shifted his authorial perspective, producing new works that maintain his original Camp sensibility but that are intended to speak to a larger and more mainstream audience, such as his Tony Award–nominated *Tale of the Allergist's Wife* (2000). *Vampire Lesbians of Sodom* continues to be produced throughout amateur and regional theater across the globe. Though contemporary performances of *Vampire Lesbians* may no longer resonate with the play's original impact as a site of respite from the threat of HIV/AIDS, such productions maintain a seminal importance as a preservative of a specific time and place in LGBTQ history. This step toward the formulation of a queer narrative is achieved through the collective reading of performance and oral history as an alternative archive, revealing an intersection between dramaturgy, performance ethnography, and social history.

Epilogue

Charles Busch has continued to work consistently both as a playwright and as a drag performer. Since 2007 Busch has primarily moved back and forth between sentimental Jewish plays that draw from his youth and Hollywood homage plays that continue the silver screen diva-worship initiated by the original Ridiculous.

For his play *Our Leading Lady* (2007), Busch returned to his Ridiculous roots, where he had envisioned himself as an ingénue in a nineteenth-century touring theater company. From this he drew the inspiration to write the story of Laura Keene, the actress who was performing at Ford's Theatre the night of Abraham Lincoln's assassination. The play was produced by the Manhattan Theatre Club, directed by Lynne Meadow, and starred noted television actress Kate Mulgrew (now famous for her role of Red in the Netflix series *Orange is the New Black*) in the title role. Don Shewey noted the connection between Busch and Ludlam, writing, "Just as Ludlam's *The Mystery of Irma Vep* continues to be a regional theater staple, I can imagine Our Leading Lady being snapped up by every rep company in the country."[114] Shewey also used this forum to ponder, "What kind of work would Ludlam doing if he hadn't died of AIDS?"[115] While romancing the "what if" of any situation is certainly fun after-dinner conversation, in the case of a queer legacy like this, it seems to negate Busch's distinct contribution by comparing him to a mentor who he has become distanced from both temporally and culturally. As evidenced, Ludlam's Ridiculous inspired Busch, but Busch's neo-Ridiculous is not Ludlam's.

After the success of *Our Leading Lady* Busch was driven to return to the stage, first in his self-penned send-up of vintage Hollywood in *The Third Story* (2008) at the Lucille Lortel Theatre in 2009 and the following year in *The Divine Sister*, first at Theatre for a New City before moving to the Soho Playhouse. Busch continued a tradition of Camping-up Catholic rituals that had been a staple of his Ridiculous forebears by writing a pastiche of classic films that featured stories about nuns, including *The Song of Bernadette*, *The Bells of Saint Mary's*, *The Singing Nun*, *The Sound of Music*, and *Agnes of God*. Starring as the Mother Superior, Busch also invited early Theatre-in-Limbo actress Julie Halston to play one of the convent sisters.

In 2011 Busch was awarded the title of "Off-Broadway Legend" by the Off-Broadway Alliance, and his play *Olive and the Bitter Herbs*, essentially a seder gone awry, premiered at Manhattan's Primary Stages, setting up a sort of formula where he continues to write while acting in only every other play. A successful production of *Judith of Bethulia* premiered at Theater for a New City in 2012, a Ridiculous pastiche of D. W. Griffith's 1914 silent film of the same name, with other biblical epics including *The Ten Commandments* (1956) and *Samson and Delilah* (1949). This marked the first time in the history of Theater for a New City that a show was completely sold out for its entire run before its opening performance. Busch portrayed the title character as an aesthetic homage to his own theatrical heroine, Sarah Bernhardt, by wearing a headdress inspired by a photo of Bernhardt as Mélissinde in Rostand's *La Princesse lointaine* (1895). Busch's channeling of Bernhardt through the character of Bethulia (which also makes a subtle and exclusive reference to his role of the Virgin Sacrifice in *Vampire Lesbians of Sodom*) through the histrionic version of himself as a touring actress magnifies Ludlam's traditional method of palimpsest as performance. The fetishizing of Bernhardt harkens back to the diva worship that was a staple of the Ridiculous in its nascence.

After a series of incredibly popular shows, Busch wrote and starred in *The Tribute Artist* (2014), also at Primary Stages. Relying on his traditional formula of using references from the divas of the silver screen, a dragged-up Busch as Jimmy as female impersonator of those famous dames added Julie Halston to the mix, as Rita, the aide-de-camp who explains all of the esoteric references for a contemporary audience. This became a sort of performative footnoting in performance. This new approach is successful in attempting to bring gay cultural references to a new generation, and it received a rave review from Ben Brantley in the *New York Times*. Although I first read this approach as a kind of betrayal to the Ridiculous spirit, after further consideration I read his craft as wise dramaturgy. More than any other artist in this particular book, Busch is the most adept at hovering between a Ridiculous past and present, carefully introducing a new audience to the old-Hollywood references that both he and Ludlam loved, while still charging forward with new work that is both sentimental and contemporary without the nostalgia that weighs down the work of other Ludlam contemporaries like Everett Quinton. In this vein, Busch is a master at writing different plays for different audiences. While plays like *Judith of Bethulia* maintain the formulaic Camp crassness of the 1980s East Village for a downtown audience, other plays like *The Tribute Artist* are shaped for an uptown audience and the potential for a more commercial and subsequently lucrative run. Busch's productions have been a regular feature at Theatre for a New City (downtown) for over twenty years while he has also been a regular at Manhattan Theatre Club and Primary Stages (uptown). Perhaps this is all part of Busch's ruse as a gender illusionist, playing ironically with the Ridiculous genre across communities, sometimes weird and boundary pushing and sometimes couched in a more digestible way that is no less queer in intent. Busch has also moved beyond Manhattan, bravely taking his solo drag cabaret act to the most conservative spots in America, like megachurch-filled Colorado Springs, Colorado. Busch's recent works invite an entirely new dialogue (and likely an entire book) on what it means to mainstream queer identity and queer performance.

CHAPTER THREE

Bradford Louryk

"Not Just Any Woman"

I must say that clothes are simply a side issue—one isn't born to
wear clothes, actually. Ah, clothes are a habit that one accumulates.
—Christine Jorgensen

Prologue

This case study introduces and defines the concepts of *visceral existentialism* and *mimetic ventriloquism* in relation to the more intellectual and
intertextual approaches and legacy of post-Ludlam Ridiculous theater
practitioner Bradford Louryk. In contrast to his predecessors, Louryk
developed his approach to the Ludlamesque from within the academy
while a student at Vassar College, and his queer legacy hangs on more
of a distanced intellectual frame, in contrast to Charles Busch's direct interpersonal connections. Louryk's position of privilege inspires a theoretically based repositioning of the Ridiculous whereby he incongruously
deconstructs the genre through a formulaic restructuring of preexisting
text. This methodology is inclusive of classical texts, as well as the original writings of Ludlam; forming a genre of *hyperpastiche*. Moreover, this
technique embodies Grosz's legacy-building notion of "folding the past
into the future," a future that lies both in the present as a binary term in
relation to the past as a construct and in the possibility of queer evolution within live performance.[1] This is particularly evident in Louryk's *Klytaemnestra's Unmentionables*. Herein the exclusivity of Ludlam's theater
is replaced with an elitism composed of esoteric cultural references and
abstruse language, which is heightened by Louryk's trademark lip-synch.
The use of lip-synch, pulls heavily from the techniques of performer Lyp-

Figure 5: Bradford Louryk on stage as Christine Jorgensen in *Christine Jorgensen Reveals* (2005). Photo: Aaron Epstein.

sinka (John Epperson), while converging the past with the present. This borrowing serves to shift Bhabha's notion of mimicry from the postcolonial and toward the encoded and queer. Louryk's careful selection of his queer legacy embodies Román's provisional collectiveness[2] while still continuing to pull laterally, both backward and forward through time as suggested by Jagose—particularly through the revival of extinguished voices through lip-synch as a kind of queer channeling.[3] This stands apart from the other legacies in the book that form either violently and organically.

Additionally, this chapter examines the current cultural fascination with the conservatism of the American Cold War era regarding the appositeness of iconic postoperative transsexual Christine Jorgensen and how it translates in Louryk's Drama Desk Award–winning drag performance *Christine Jorgensen Reveals* (2005). I divulge the social and economic influence of the paradigmatic stacking of Jorgensen-as-Louryk-as-Jorgensen by elaborating on Judith Butler's theories of gender fluidity as well as Kate Davy's reading of Camp as a magical enchantment that "bewitches" the audience with its performative juxtaposition of discordant symbols.[4] The queer play within the sensual past of *CJR* inhabits a space that resembles

Savran's "threshold between two worlds," a performative space that materializes between the fiction of the narrative and the delicate truth that Louryk relies on to bring his characters to life.[5]

Extending Nostalgia

Bradford Louryk, actor and self-professed "creator," extends the legacy of the Ridiculous theater by reinventing the genre for the twenty-first century.[6] Reared in the academy, Louryk's intellectual approach to the Ridiculous sensibility reflects the gentrification and accompanying rarefication of audiences in Manhattan at the close of the twentieth century and commencement of the twenty-first. Louryk's plays are intended for elite theatergoers rather than the blend of freethinking artists and drugged-out hippies that frequented Ludlam's early plays. Additionally, Louryk interrogates a cultural nostalgia for Cold War conservatism as an apposite critique of the search for a postmillennial American identity. For Louryk the practice of reevaluating the selective past by contrasting it with the performative version of the present allows him to introduce a critical manifestation of nostalgia that, in the words of Ray Cashman, "extends [nostalgia] beyond the realm of imagination into the realm of action or practice."[7] By engaging in this reevaluation of nostalgia, the developing model of queer legacy is expanded through Louryk's examination of "tradition, identity, authenticity and heritage."[8] This exploration is steered by the magnification of his characterizations (women both real and fictional) through the lens of midcentury American conservatism (e.g., Klytaemnestra transformed into a 1950s suburban housewife). Through this conceptual repositioning of temporal frames, Louryk delivers a radical queer critique by fluidly embodying Judith Butler's notion of gender fluidity onstage, "the mundane way in which genders are appropriated, theatricalized, worn and done."[9] Louryk achieves this through the histrionic presentation of metagender, inscribing his body with the nostalgic past through the blending and contrasting of his masculine corporeality with hyperbolized feminine deportment and layered transsexual characterizations. As an act of high-Camp ritual, Louryk's approach to drag is most closely aligned with Kate Davy's notion of "bewitching," crossing the boundaries of the performer and audience.[10] This style of neo-Ridiculous performance is supported by Louryk's onstage transformation through the practices of lip-synching to his own prerecorded voice ("mimetic ventriloquism") and sadomasochistic drag, employing garments (such as a bespoke corset) that constrict and control his body as an expression of public sexual freedom against dominant social accusations of perversion and shame.

Though Ludlam became known for playfully engaging in the convention of theater for theater's sake, he was also responding to the current events of his time, and inevitably drew from and ridiculed the world around him. Of his Ridiculous theater, Ludlam insisted, "I am of my time, of the perfect moment."[11] In the much the same way, Louryk draws from a contemporary culture that is often nostalgic for the past. He fulfills Ludlam's Ridiculous objective by consciously reacting against key points of his predecessor's manifesto in an effort to maintain a genre that reflects and comments on shifts in contemporary social mores. This is instead of favoring a museum re-creation of the work originated by Ludlam, who commented,

> My work is very much for people who might not approve of the gayness. I take them over bumps, make them draw certain conclusions about sexism through parody, hold sexism up to ridicule. The same techniques that other playwrights use to maneuver their audience into a sexist position can also be used to make them accept something they wouldn't ordinarily accept. In a sense, I think it has a big influence on there being such a thing as gay theatre.[12]

In a 2006 interview Louryk referred to Ludlam's mission, asking, "How do you honor someone who is so subversive?" and answering, "You subvert!"[13] Ludlam's Camp-infused text and performance style was intended to speak primarily to a gay audience, advancing social acceptance and community building through coded language, double entendre, and a prepossession of glamour/genderfuck drag.[14] In contrast, Louryk simplifies and deglamorizes drag in an effort to deliver a "visceral existentialist" experience to a broader theatergoing audience, commenting on his disenchantment with the current state of the American theater and too often conservative political climate.

I define the concept of visceral existentialism in theater as a ruggedly individual didactic style that draws from and subverts preexisting Ludlamesque Ridiculous conventions and addresses the audience directly.[15] This is in an effort to reassign historical text and context without attempting to invoke radical activism or enlightenment; instead, it attempts to incite an inner dialogue and intellectual narrative with the autonomous self, promoting communities where individuals coexist while maintaining their individuality and uniqueness. Louryk achieves this objective in performance using a combination of sound play, manipulation and enhancement, precision of gesture, aural formalism, and meticulous timing, to create what I deem *moments of beauty*. These moments of beauty are developed through Louryk's dedication to precision and authenticity in the use of prerecorded sound and the embrace of imperfections on original recordings. This is in an effort to utilize environmental sounds by drawing attention and reassigning imperfections rather than masking them or rendering them inaudible. Of this convention Louryk remarks, "That moment of a sound and the perfection of the moment is in the gesture and the timing and every facet of the execution . . . it represents every ideal that I have."[16]

Ludlam stressed that his Ridiculous "[was] the only avant-garde movement that is not academic."[17] Other avant-garde artistic/theatrical movements such as Tzara's Dada or Artaud's theater of cruelty were preceded and formulated by manifestos that proclaimed the mission behind the movement as well as providing a set of guidelines that the resultant art was supposed to adhere to. Although Ludlam drew inspiration from the early avant-garde, his Ridiculous theater did not grow out of their manifestos; instead, he composed his own manifesto a decade *after* the performances of the RTC. This document was based on pragmatic performance experience rather than precursory theoretical intentions.

Because Louryk is descended from the original Ridiculous movement and to some degree informed by Ludlam's midcareer manifesto, his work has become more academic as scholars have embraced the Ridiculous theater and its theories. However, Louryk's work has metamorphosed in order not to be neutralized as the academy has subsumed it. Therefore, Louryk's Ridiculous is not Ludlam's. Because the relationship between gay culture and mainstream society has changed rapidly in the past forty-plus years, Louryk's theater is responding to new advancements in civil rights as well as previously unconsidered obstacles that challenge marginalized Americans. Within such a culture of change that appropriates and even celebrates gay taste and style in popular culture, the contagion of the contemporary Ridiculous audience has shifted. Nuances and subtextual references that would have been accessible largely to a gay urban audience in Ludlam's lifetime are more universal and poignant to spectators whose political and personal views embrace the concept of a normative homosexuality. With their unique theatrical work Louryk and his occasional writing partner Rob Grace seek to create new and innovative theater drawn from Søren Kierkegaard's ideal that "the thing is to find a truth which is true for me, to find the idea for which I can live and die."[18] Therefore this Ridiculous is more about exploring individual experience and identity than attempting to speak to gay culture as an insular collective. Louryk's approach is almost Nietzschean, embracing the obstacles associated with individualized homosexual identity in the twentieth century and funneling the associative pain and shame through live performance in order to resolve the tension between memory and nostalgia. This moment of discovery (moment of beauty), is closely aligned with Sara Warner's notion of a performative queerness that is expressed in acts of "gaiety," though for Louryk the gaiety is the resultant feeling produced after a self-awareness reached through trauma and subsequent analysis.[19] In fact, it isn't difficult to imagine any of Louryk's filtered female characters lying on a psychoanalytic couch, with the audience sitting opposite and working toward a breakthrough midperformance. This sort of performance continues my concept of queer ambivalence, refusing to be solely pinned to an antirelational affect that is singularly negative (as suggested by Lee Edelman and Leo Bersani) or even Warner's rosier take.

Though the academy has circumspectly neutralized the radical origins of queer art by embracing and dissecting it, Louryk attempts to produce groundbreaking work by refuting such minoritarianism. Norman Bryson introduces the concept of "minoritarian" thinking in a 1999 essay in the electronic journal *Invisible Culture*.[20] He seeks to rectify the historical record by reexamining and reconsidering "relatively familiar events, objects, images or texts" from previous works that were "so constructed, arranged and published that materials of direct interest to lesbian and gay studies have often literally dropped out of immediate view or have completely disappeared."[21] Bryson goes on to define the paradigm that he sees inherent in the minoritarian viewpoint: "that once the visual expression of gay and lesbian desire can be as freely explored as their heterosexual equivalents— end of story."[22] This idea is further dissected in Michael Warner's *Fear of a Queer Planet* wherein he states, "There are many people, gay and straight who think that discrimination should be eliminated, but [once this is accomplished] gay people have no further political interest as a group."[23] This desire for social inclusion is apparent not only in the movement that seeks to reexamine and reassign canonical art and artists within a gay/lesbian context.

Going against this trend, Louryk's projects such as *Klytaemnestra's Un-*

mentionables (2000) and *Christine Jorgensen Reveals* (2005) concentrate on individuality and the acceptance of identity rather than rehashing the social status of women in an effort to reclaim agency in a feminist context. By selecting and shedding light on true-to-life characters like Jorgensen, Louryk creates a theater that is queerly ambivalent in its vision and practice, and subversive in its landmark standpoint of favoring personal narrative(s) (and whatever that may inspire in his audience) over a blatant political agenda. Although Louryk's theater retains the ability to communicate to a gay audience on one level, it also extends beyond a coterie audience defined by sexual preference. Whereas Ludlam's early audience was disproportionately composed of the disenfranchised men and women who literally took to the streets for the Stonewall rebellion, Louryk's subscribers are more likely to be academic and mainstream. Because Louryk's theater is one that demands the comprehension of elitist language and obscure intellectual and historical references, it is geared toward a highly educated audience, and is groundbreaking for its unapologetic reinvention of female impersonation and drag, introducing the form to audience members far from the drag bars of Chelsea and (most recently) Hell's Kitchen and Brooklyn.

Louryk's elitist approach was influenced primarily by an urban influx of wealthier and better-educated people who instigated the revitalization of once poverty-stricken neighborhoods in New York City. This urban gentrification began in the lower neighborhoods in the 1980s and has consistently moved north, most recently taking over the once economically destitute areas of Harlem, Hell's Kitchen, and even Washington Heights. Because Louryk's plays often depend upon costly production elements, either technological or aesthetic, his neo-Ridiculous is far from the do-it-yourself variety propagated by Ludlam and his contemporaries. Thus, Louryk's plays, as a true reflection of his time, are more midtown than lower Manhattan, suggesting that he can shift with the changing economic infrastructure of the city and find a new home within the world of commercial theater without forgetting his roots.

It's All Greek to Me

Louryk first became acquainted with the work of Ludlam in high school when his drama director gave him a copy of *The Complete Plays of Charles*

Ludlam, which he professes to have devoured from cover to cover. It was in reading the collection that Louryk garnered "an appreciation for more traditional theater," motivated by Ludlam's tendency to unapologetically make a collage of great literature and high culture through pop-cultural pastiche.[24] After high school Louryk entered the Experimental Theatre program at Vassar College in Poughkeepsie, New York. Inspired by the work of former Vassar professor Hallie Flanagan (who headed the Federal Theatre Project during the Great Depression), the mission of the program is to use the stage as a laboratory, where new ideas can be tested and theories examined through performative experimentation. Gabrielle Cody, Vassar professor of drama and Louryk's undergraduate advisor, describes the pedagogical purpose of the program as to "produce [theater] primarily in order to experiment with a text or genre."[25] She continues, "We are not interested in putting together a season of dutifully canonical plays. We also encourage our students to create their own work beyond simply participating in productions as actor, designer, director, or dramaturge. And some of the most exciting theatre has come out of student-generated works."[26] It was the exploratory and vanguard nature of this environment that allowed Louryk to flourish and develop a post-Ludlam Ridiculous style that would come to define his work and eventually become what I define as "visceral existentialism." In his freshman year, Louryk directed and acted in an abridged version of Ludlam's epic classic *The Grand Tarot* (1969). Through this initial flirtation with the Ridiculous genre in performance Louryk forged a professional friendship with fellow Vassar student and budding playwright Rob Grace. Louryk was immediately drawn to Grace's "oddball perspective and wicked sense of humor,"[27] promulgating an artistic relationship where Louryk "is the devisor of projects," and Grace serves as "playwright—a 'helmsman' of creative projects."[28] The working dynamic behind this partnership brings to mind Ludlam's self-assessment: "I think of myself as an inventor of plays. The wright as in playwright is worker, maker: one who works in wood such as a shipwright. My plays are wrought as much as written. I work in the theatre as well as the study."[29] This approach, which merges the collection of data (in this case a collection of preexisting literature and cultural references) to forge experimentation with the precision and trained skill of craftsmanship is derivative of the same approach that Louryk and Grace used for collaboration a decade after Ludlam's death. The process began when the two undergraduates began composing "violent and humorous and smart" plays, and then formed a performance group to give readings.[30] These early works prompted Louryk to introduce Grace to Ludlam's epic style. Louryk recollects,

> I knew that Rob had a great deal of talent and I knew that sometimes his scope was limited. My perspective was always maximal and epic— like Ludlam's plays. I'm not sure which came first. I've always had a tendency in me to like things that are epic, or if that was informed by Ludlam, I'd have to project backward. I remember having a conversation with somebody on a train coming back from New York and talking about how Rob needs to stop thinking so small. Trying to get him to create character and situations that are much larger . . . I always find that he is most successful, interesting, and truest to himself when his plays are enormous and oddball.[31]

Louryk's influence via Ludlam within his collaborative partnership with Grace resulted in their first Ridiculous play, *The Tragedy of Hamlet, Prince of Denmark*, at Vassar in 1999. The text episodically intersects thirty bizarre characters who are searching for contentment in circumstances that range from priestly molestation and alien invasion to the Judeo-Christian God's secret desire to become a funk singer. The overarching story line involves a family of siblings named after characters from Shakespeare's Hamlet; Laertes (played by Louryk in the original production) seeks to lure unsuspecting audience members into his pornographic theater by titling the unrelated plays after great works of the Western canon, hence the title of the play: *The Tragedy of Hamlet, Prince of Denmark*. Louryk's Laertes as theater producer-cum-pornographer epitomizes a Ridiculous sensibility drawn from Ludlam's chosen conventions as driven by Louryk's skill and personal taste. For example, in scene 4 of the play, Laertes's monologue reveals his opinion on the current state of the theater:

LAERTES: About ten years ago I was at this production of *Ivanov*. It was very decadent. Very naturalistic and—Well, I was a starving artist at the time, before I really made it, and seeing this play was a very big deal for me. Imagine the most colorful, imaginative, brilliantly crafted version of *Ivanov* you can possibly imagine. That was what I was watching that night. Chekhov himself rose from the grave to see this production. That's how good it was. The acting was phenomenal. Lebedev, especially—Brilliant. Best performance of that character I've seen to this date. The costumes and set had this emerald green motif—They had these curtains—It was beyond words. And I'm sitting there, completely taken in by the performance and the perfection of it all, and I'm intensely bored. Understand, you couldn't ask for a more talented group of actors and designers. And I'm sitting there completely bored. . . . What do people want? When they wake up in the morning . . . when they're doing their dishes . . . when they're paying their taxes, what do they really want? Sex. Sex! Let's face it, theater can't compete with television and film anymore. The intimacy of the close-ups, the special effects, the music. At this point in time, the only thing theater can provide that no other medium can is live sex. And that's what people want. They want to see live sex, happening right in front of them, and they want to see it in a socially accept-able fashion. As I was staring at this man, in complete awe, my duty as a writer, a director became clear: To create pornographic theater. I ran home after the show and that very evening I penned my first work, *Rozencranz* [sic] *and Guildenstern Give Head*. At first, of course, nobody understood. People incessantly asked me, how can live sex have dramatic merit. Sex is drama. Drama is sex. They are one and the same. What about that moment when the male reaches orgasm, the woman has not, but the man is too tired and falls asleep? Finally, a medium that can explore moments like these. How the little things get in the way. One of the themes of my play *Clítoris, Clitóris*. Jenkinson here starred in *Pleasure for Pleasure*, my first iambic pentameter work. Since then, he's worked with me on almost every single one of my projects.[32]

This section of text is an example of Louryk and Grace's first original work that is informed by a Ridiculous sensibility, and the closest to Ludlam's, prior to Louryk and Grace's defection from the Ludlamesque toward their own aesthetic. Nods to Ludlam include the use of high-cultural forms (references to Chekhovian plays and characters),[33] sexual plays on words (*Rozencranz and Guildenstern Give Head*), and the discussion of pornography on the stage, which the conservative press had often accused the RTC of exhibiting due to the use of nudity and erotic situations in their plays. Ludlam was tolerant toward pornography as a performative medium because, like his work, it was "held in low esteem," but he also firmly denied that his theater was pornographic in form or intent[34] He explicated this opinion in *Confessions of a Farceur*: "Pornography is the highest development of naturalism. It was the seriousness of pornography that [the RTC actors] were never into. It is not in depicting the sexual act that one becomes a pornographer; it is in demanding to be taken seriously."[35] Louryk and Grace also borrowed from this concept—the first scene of *Hamlet* has a priest being fellated onstage by a prepubescent boy named Timothy. This situation is presented as tongue-in-check satire (Timothy is bound by a chain that he drags around the stage with him throughout the play, only to discover that the other end is attached to a young girl who faces the same sticky situation with her own rabbi at the play's conclusion) that is intended to incite laughter and stimulate commentary, not to arouse the audience sexually. This is also a prime example of the "ridiculing" of social matters and their resultant discourse (such as the sex scandals that have recently plagued the Roman Catholic Church) within a world that promotes heteronormative morality, and arguably from whence the Ridiculous derived its name.

It was the collaborative process and success of *Hamlet* that led Louryk and Grace to continue their relationship, creating Louryk's senior thesis project, which would become the initial version of *Klytaemnestra's Unmentionables* in 2000. This was the first self-devised piece textually constructed with Grace in which Louryk would play all of the characters in an evening of solo performance. This project originated with Ethyl Eichelberger, who stated in *Extreme Exposure: An Anthology of Solo Performance Texts from the Twentieth Century*, "I wanted to play the great roles but who would cast me as Medea?"[36] Louryk responds, "I identified with Ethyl Eichelberger. . . . I knew that my thesis would be in drag, but I didn't feel that at that point I could sustain a single character for any lengthy piece."[37] Eichelberger, a classically trained actor like Ludlam, developed her unique and personal Ridiculous sensibility when she migrated from the RTC in the West Village to the bohemian world of the Lower East Side in the early 1980s. In turn she became a seminal figure in the post-Stonewall queer theater movement before committing suicide in 1990, unable to tolerate the harsh side effects of the prescribed AIDS medication. Most scholars have referred to the Eichelberger as *he*, perhaps because she was biologically male. I have selected to resurrect *she* in honor of her work and as a reflection of the shift that has taken place with the post-queer theory introduction of preferred gender pronouns as a talking point. Colloquial play with female pronouns in the gay community is hardly revolutionary and a common form of both familiarity and Camp, used to express affection or to throw shade. In selecting the female pronoun, however, I honor Eichelberger as a predecessor of gender-bending pathbreakers like Justin Vivian Bond (who uses the gender pronoun *v* and prefix *Mx.*) and Taylor Mac (who prefers the gender pronoun *judy*) both winners of Performance Space 122's coveted Ethyl Eichelberger commissioning award.

Thus, in the Ludlam-Eichelberger tradition, Louryk set out to take on, if not extend, Eichelberger's challenge, by portraying several iconic women derived from Greek tragedy in an evening of gender-bending performance. The concept of transforming mythic characters and epic themes was derived from Vassar's 1999–2000 theatrical season, which was dedicated to presenting ancient Greek plays, adaptations of Greek plays, and original works inspired by ancient Greek themes. Though the project's theme was conceived by the Drama Department, the concept was inspired by Louryk's intensive study of and passion for art history. The image of Jacques-Louis David's famous painting *Marat Assassinated* (1793) inspired the central element of the set design as well as the climax of the play. The painting depicts the stabbed, pallid corpse of the Jacobin revolutionary Jean-Paul Marat submerged in a slipper bath. Drawing upon this, Louryk conceived that all action of the play would take place around a Victorian claw-foot bathtub elevated on a central dais that was filled manually by Louryk during scene transitions, which were layered with recorded text. The tub would become a central metaphor and the "site of Klytaemnestra's killing of Agamemnon, Electra's enforced washing of the family's dirty laundry, Medea's infanticide," culminating when Louryk as Phaedra drowns herself in the now overflowing tub.[38] Furthermore, this convention mirrors Eichelberger's 1990 suicide, where she slit her wrists in a bathtub, theatrically mimicking the David Marat while literally expelling the HIV from her body through the release of her infected blood. Joe E. Jeffreys suggests that Eichelberger's AIDS-related suicide may be read as "a call to arms and icon for a revolution," just as David's painting served as a propagandistic device where "the blood of the martyr is the seed of revolution."[39]

With these images serving as the inspirational framework, Louryk approached Grace with his ideas for a script. First, Louryk selected the women that he would portray; a diverse group reflecting various ages, types, and personas as filtered through contemporary archetypes of femininity. Helene Foley thoroughly yet succinctly lists the antecedent performances that informed Louryk's selections:

Louryk's portrait of a Klytaemnestra paralyzed by fear of retribution was influenced by Greek tragedy, Charles Mee's 1994 *Agamemnon*, and Jean-Paul Sartre's *Les Mouches* [1943] (as Louryk put it in interview, Klytaemnestra's "dead-white look" is borrowed from Sartre's guilt-ridden heroine with her deathly white make-up); his Electra by Aeschylus, Sophocles, and Euripides, *Les Mouches*, and Eichelberger; his Medea by Ludlam, Heiner Müller, Cherubini's Opera *Medea* [1797] as performed by Maria Callas [1953], and the story of Andrea Yates, the troubled Houston housewife who drowned her five children in 2001; his Phaedra by Euripides, Racine, Eichelberger, and Sarah Kane's *Phaedra's Love*.[40]

Additionally, Louryk created the original character of the Fury in order to present a performance drawn specifically from his own set of skills. Foley's research corroborates Louryk's use of Ludlam's original Ridiculous formula in playmaking: combining a variety of literary and cultural references as well as current events in a collage that both embraces and rejects influences in order to create new characters who relate to contemporary contexts and issues (i.e., presenting Yates in the guise of a modern-day Medea).

While the text (divided into sections each dedicated to a character) draws from these influences, it proved problematic, for it was a series of disconnected monologues, lacking a trajectory that brought together the characters and themes. This was remedied through a direct homage to Ludlam and Eichelberger, drawing from their preexisting texts and in turn inserting them as transitions between the episodes of the performance—a concrete and tangible connection to the writers as forebears in Louryk's queer legacy. These transitions took the form of voice-over film footage of Louryk that played as he changed into the costume and makeup of each character at a dressing table before circling the stage to pour water into the bathtub. The transitional text, which presented Louryk discussing his cross-dressing performance, was divided into six sections. In the initial projected section Louryk mimicking Eichelberger and, after defining his purpose (drawn from Ludlam/Eichelberger), sought to answer the question:

> LOURYK: The characters I play tend to be women who are misunderstood. And given enough distance in time, I can distort who they were for my own "nefarious" ends.
>
> It's all a matter of whom you want to emulate. Whom you play affects your life, so I decided to play the most beautiful, eminent women I could find.

I wanted to play the great roles, but who would cast me as Medea? Who would cast me as Phaedra?[41]

In setting up the performance with his prerecorded naturally masculine voice and deportment, and in reinterpreting celebrated Ludlam/Eichelberger quotations, Louryk makes clear his pursuit of the Ridiculous tradition and sensibility in a performance that, as Ludlam stated of his Camille, "Is simultaneously both terribly funny and terribly moving, both ethereally beautiful and grotesque, both real and artificial, both a man and a woman in a dress."[42] Here Louryk completes the introductory monologue:

LOURYK: To Frantz [*sic*] Salieri, transvestitism was a spectacular act with no sexual or erotic meaning. To one interviewer, he explained that he found boys were the most prodigious actors, and when they played women, there was "a double phenomenon of distance between the character and his interpretation."

I have to convince myself that I am beautiful before I go on. If I believe it . . . Belief is the secret to reality.

I know it's acting. I never think I'm a woman. I am not trying to kid anyone into thinking I am a woman. I am trying to wrench something artistic from the experience.[43]

With Louryk's mission as an actor and artist firmly defined, the play continues with Klytaemnestra's monologue before the second transition that defines the marginal social position of the drag artist-as-performer in American society:

LOURYK: When his dream of the part calls for playing the opposite sex, the actor must reconcile his sense of truth with his sense of the theatrical. Drag embodies the paradox of acting. People are disturbed by female impersonation. They don't realize or understand its inner motive. They see something that is humorous. They don't understand what it means to play a woman. To defiantly do that and say women are worthwhile creatures, and to put my whole soul and being into creating this woman and to give her everything I have, including my emotions (remembering that the greatest taboo is to experience feminine emotions), and to take myself seriously in the face of ridicule was the highest statement. It allows audiences to experience the universality of emotion, rather to believe that women are one species and men another, and that what one feels, the other never does.[44]

Here, Louryk comments on the origin of the Ridiculous sensibility. In taking himself seriously "in the face of ridicule" he stresses the function of the Ridiculous theater to reflect and mimic heteronormative and moralistic social judgments, while also subtly invoking the bigotry and intolerance that Ludlam and Eichelberger faced and in turn challenged in their own time for being openly gay. The other transitions that separate the monologues borrowed directly from Ludlam's and Eichelberger's essays and performance texts, including Ludlam's essay "Costume Fetishism or Clothes Make the Man," which defines costume tenets essential to presenting oneself as "butch" or "drag." Louryk's interpretation of Ludlam's list declares:

> LOURYK: Be artificial. Wear as much underwear as possible. Foundation garments, garters and shoes should be tight enough that you are always conscious of them. Suggest a captive in some aspect of your dress. If you are wearing them, see to it that your heels are too high to walk or run comfortably. Take on yourself the burdens of your womanhood, the seven dolors of the Blessed Virgin Mary. The transvestite "berdache" of the Apache Indians cut themselves on the inside of the thigh and let the blood run down their legs once a month . . .

Finally, after the Fury, Medea, and Phaedra's monologues (interspersed with more Ludlam-/Eichelberger-generated wisdom in the transitions), the play closes with a direct homage to Eichelberger's performance, as a lingerie-clad Louryk (just drowned by suicide as Phaedra) rises from the bathtub to lip-synch Eichelberger's trademark song *Women Who Survive*, which concludes with the chorus:

> LOURYK: We are women who survive; our world is hard.
> We are women who survive; our world is mean.
> We are women who survive; scratch us, we bleed.
> We are women who survive; but we will live to fight
> another day.[45]

The lyrics of the song, which were initially sung by a concertina-wielding Eichelberger at the conclusion of her solo performances of grandes dames, such as *Jocasta, Medea, Nefertiti, Clytemnestra*, and the Obie Award–winning *Lucrezia Borgia*, deliver a survivalist message that speaks beyond gender in order to address any audience member who has fallen victim to discrimination or marginalization within the construct of American society. This final scene, which relies on his self-styled impersonation of Eichelberger, is unique to *Klytaemnestra*. Louryk avoids such direct impersonations in his more recent work, because he reflects that it held "too much hubris."[46] Nonetheless, this conclusion becomes the "moment of beauty" in the production. By fusing Eichelberger's song with his own prerecorded voice, for the first time in the performance, Louryk is dedragged and revealed in person, as he has to this point appeared as himself only in the media-generated transitions. With the layered makeup of the six characters streaking his face, he emerges in a Botticelliesque fashion, rising from the water in the claw-foot tub as an actor stripped to a bare minimum: without his voice and only remnants of a now transparent costume, he appears as both himself and the personification of the "Other" in one, blending gender lines and aesthetics in an almost shamanistic fashion. Additionally, he serves to represent a Venus-like rebirth of the Ridiculous spirit, embodying Ludlam's and Eichelberger's texts to cheat death emblematically and return to the living in ritualistic honor of his prematurely deceased Ridiculous forefathers. Louryk's split body is sacrificial, reoriented as a living archive, layering his experience and queer Ridiculous legacy at the intersection of Greek tragic women read through the lens of his contemporaries. This intertextual approach to performance extends Marvin Carlson's notion of the haunted stage to the haunted body (the performer's body, the body politic, and the collective body of work), manifesting onstage the impression that "we are seeing what we saw before."[47]

To achieve this symbolic and histrionic reincarnation, instead of applying Camp as his primary modus operandi, as Ludlam did, Louryk favors declamatory acting, lip-synch, and mimetic ventriloquism to deliver his message and Ridiculous sensibility. This mimetic ventriloquism, which demands a precision of every bodily function down to the last breath, is the ideal example of Louryk's subversion of one of Ludlam's Ridiculous performance theories. Although Ludlam was self-trained as a master ventriloquist, skills he exhibited in his production of *The Ventriloquist's Wife* (1978), he was averse to more traditional drag performance that was dependent on lip-synching, where "performers were their own dummies."[48] Ludlam insisted that his live, liberated approach to drag, sans lip-synch, was an effort to give an "honest, bona fide account of [the actors] as characters in a play," not the mimesis of a singer whose recorded voice controlled the live drag artist, who gave a projected (and often campy) interpretation informed by the original performance. Louryk combats this idea by reincorporating the conventions of lip-synch/ventriloquism as a post-Ludlam Ridiculous convention. Louryk's lip-synch performances take on different forms depending on the intention of the project. Of his lip-synching in *Klytaemnestra's Unmentionables*, Foley remarks:

> Louryk adopts the lip-syncing of drag performance but performs to his own voice, thus opening the possibility for tensions between voice and body movement and creating the effect of a ventriloquism in which the performer becomes his own dummy and as well the victim of the larger narrative in which s/he is embedded.[49]

When lip-synching Louryk performs in a medium-like fashion, disembodying his voice and reclaiming it in order to speak through himself to portray the "Other" as himself and finally being transformed into what Senelick refers to as "a heightened self or total identification with what lies opposite."[50] Cody compares Louryk's work to that of the Kabuki *onnegata*, delivering a heightened, performative womanliness that is channeled beyond his masculine, physical self-embodiment. Louryk is not attempting to fool his audience, but rather to engage viewers to a point of committed belief that what they are watching unfold before them is genuine. From a Western feminist perspective, critiquing the role of the *onnegata* is complex: a biologically male actor embodying feminine perfection through masculine eyes. I believe that Louryk's Western version of this cross-gendered portrayal may be read productively as a kind of inverse ambiguity, where his performance layers generations and generations of male actors who have played the roles of women since the City Dionysia of ancient Greece.

This technique is drawn in part from Ludlam and his drag performances of other canonical characters such as Marguerite Gautier. Ludlam explained how he reinvented the tragic story by using his acting talent and charisma paired with cross-dressing and references to earlier performances of the courtesan in order to "lure [the audience] gradually into forgetting, to make it more amazing later on."[51] The movement used in *Klytaemnestra's Unmentionables* strays from naturalism, instead relying on a magnitude of presence that is closer to the declamatory style of the eighteenth and nineteenth centuries. Thus each of the five characters presented in the play (Klytaemnestra, Electra, Fury, Medea, Phaedra) takes on a unique voice and movement style, all bound by the fact that Louryk has recorded and crafted them to create conflicting presentations of both harmony and chaos; for example, the Fury's violent physicality seems disconnected and out of keeping with her calm and soothing voice. This juxtaposition serves to inspire the audience to raise questions about surface appearances, first impressions, and presuppositions.

Louryk's drag aesthetic strays from the sequins and feather boa formula that defined the female impersonation for most of the twentieth century. Ludlam became famous for a genderfuck aesthetic that manipulated the sartorially feminine by exposing masculine characteristics rather than trying to minimize them (as in *Camille* or *Galas*). In *Klytaemnestra's Unmentionables* Louryk borrows this convention, exposing his sideburns that reveal a male persona beneath a corset and panties, making a visible link between the history of oppression for women and gay men. These feminine undergarments act as the base on which all of the female costumes and in turn characterizations are built, character by character. Louryk's insistence on wearing a corset is driven by his chosen technique of psychologically transforming into the female characters that he portrays rather than mimicking or shallowly presenting them. Of this he states, "The corset supports the psychological function that enforces my physical change."[52] Furthermore, the corset may be read as a powerful symbol that in the past has regulated a woman's behavior by controlling her physical deportment as well as a signifier of a woman's subordinate cultural status prior to advancement in feminism and women's rights. For Louryk, the corset is the semiotic modus operandi that pragmatically allows for a transformation of gender and can be read in a variety of ways by the viewer in the context of characters that Louryk is creating and presenting. In *Klytaemnestra* the corset (the first version was actually designed and worn in ancient Crete, made of metal, and worn by both men and women)[53] may read as the representation and cross-representation of a variety of different symbols: male-enforced oppression and bondage (both cultural and literal), (Klytaemnestra, Electra, Phaedra, and Medea), the passage from adolescence to womanhood (Electra), sexual dominance (the Fury and Medea), masochism (Klytaemnestra and Phaedra), and so on. Additionally, it is the base garment that Louryk constantly wears, literally binding all of the women together into one larger narrative. The corset also mediates Louryk's physical deportment as a form of what David Kunzle deems "body sculpture," which, he argues, is "designed to enhance and sexualize the movements of everyday life as much as it is designed to enhance and sexualize the shape of the human form itself."[54] Although Louryk's transformations appear magical in performance, it is essential to note that his success is derived from years of acting training, academic study, and exhaustive physical and mental preparation for each role that he crafts as his body is reshaped though the combination of garments, text, and performance.

The original thesis production of *Klytaemnestra* performed at Vassar in 2000 was met with excitement from both the student body and faculty. Cody commented on this performance: "Louryk reconnected [the Experimental Theatre Program at Vassar] to the essence of what of what theatre is: a ghosting of truths. It demonstrated both to students and faculty how much bold virtuoso theatricality can accomplish, how much it can help deepen our understanding of theatre as an art form, and to remind us why we need theatre."[55] The eager reception, effectiveness, and popularity of *Klytaemnestra* led to its revival performance at New York City's HERE Arts Center running from December 1 to 17, 2001, centrally if not coincidentally located between the lower Manhattan neighborhoods where Ludlam and Eichelberger had performed twenty years before.

Life's a Drag

Having achieved success with his first off-off-Broadway production of *Klytaemnestra*, Louryk, with the textual assistance of Grace as playwright, set out to tackle the infamous Lucrezia Borgia, who had inspired a solo performance piece that won Eichelberger an Obie Award in 1982. It was during the process of constructing a conceptual framework that would examine the conflicting accounts of the Italian Renaissance noblewoman that Louryk found unique inspiration. While browsing in the East Village's Footlight Records, Louryk stumbled upon a 1958 record of Christine Jorgensen. Jorgensen (né George William Jorgensen) was credited with receiving the first "sex change" operation to become "Christine," as reported by the *New York Daily News* in 1952.[56] Louryk purchased the record because he thought that it might yield some material to be used in the third act of the new *Lucrezia Borgia* script, borrowing from the lip-synch conventions that he had developed for *Klytaemnestra*. Louryk was initially drawn to the cover, featuring a smartly dressed, attractive blond woman surrounded by salacious questions: "Is she a woman? Can she have children? What about her love life?" and finally "The answers to all of these questions with the world's most sensational celebrity!"[57] After taking the record home and listening to it repeatedly, Louryk "fell in love with the text of [the recording] and Christine. What I could hear clearly was some of the most exciting, stunning, articulate perspectives on identity, on personhood, on gender, on sexuality, on many topics that people have a hard time being articulate about today."[58] The potential for theater to be derived from the recording seemed destined, and Louryk began to consider how best to approach the piece in a form that would stay true to Jorgensen's experience while also speaking with a contemporary nonmoralistic intention.

With the script of *Lucrezia Borgia* in its eleventh draft and in need of more attention, Louryk and Grace temporarily abandoned the project (the failure to fully write and produce *Lucrezia Borgia* is a significant representation of the incomplete and obsolete so important to the framing of queer legacy) and separated briefly to work on several independent theater projects not associated with a Ridiculous sensibility. It was then that Louryk realized the unique opportunity that the Jorgensen recording could offer. He was driven to create a piece of theater from the original recording because, as he explained in a 2006 interview,

> As both an audience member and as a person who makes theatre, I often feel that [most plays] are not theatrical enough for me. I always want something to be as grand and as operatic in its scope and its scale as possible. I want to be blown away by whatever it is that I see onstage. I don't want to go to a play and see something that I could sit in my living room and get the same thing out of. This interview and [Jorgensen's] story just felt very theatrical.[59]

The passion behind this sentiment is inspired by Ludlam's maxim, "I hate minimal art. I hate conceptual art. I am for *execution*. I am for *maximal* art."[60]

It was in the winter of 2004–5 that Louryk and Grace reconnected to discuss their next collaborative work. They decided to shelve the *Lucrezia* script and concentrate instead on the recording of Christine's 1958 interview with comedian Nipsey Russell.[61] This would also provide the opportunity for Louryk and Grace to act together for the first time; though the two had known each other since 1996, they had been given little opportunity to appear on the stage jointly, as Grace had primarily served the role of playwright in the artistic partnership.[62] It would also continue their pursuit of lip-synch as a signature post-Ludlam Ridiculous theatrical device. Louryk's decision to use Jorgensen's original voice rather than his own stemmed from the desire to share "this sociological, historical document with other people" and because he was charmed by Jorgensen's voice, "which is just so extraordinary."[63] Louryk would appear in drag to interpret Christine, and Grace would portray the role of the male interviewer, Russell. The approach to this project reflects Henry James's phenomenological and intersectional definition of character and incident, where character determines incident and incident illustrates character.[64]

Because Grace had relocated to Los Angeles to pursue another career path, he would be filmed to appear as Russell on a period television set, lending another layer to the performative detachment and then repossession of voice and sound. The portrayal of Russell on the television also sets Christine in a delineated space that is isolated from the normative world, a padded television studio that becomes an ambivalent limbo, trapping her in a bell jar between reality and fantasy. A specimen kept behind a cultural pane of glass.

Because the performance was dependent on the original recording, the first step was to have the record digitally remastered and enhanced. In the meantime, Grace attempted to edit and rework the recording in an effort to create a more theatrical structure with an engaging arc, but in the end only two words were lost. Because the recording was nearly fifty years old, even in its restored state one section was marked by a series of scratches that could not be erased. It was the decision to embrace this imperfection that led to the most poignant *moment of beauty* in the performance. Louryk originated the idea to reclaim and even highlight the scratching sounds: when Jorgensen loses composure as Russell grills her with the question,

> MR. RUSSELL: Christine—do you think the time will ever come when your complete past, or at least this episode in your life, will disappear? When people will think of you as Christine Jorgensen—photographer, or Christine Jorgensen—actress, or whatever your pursuits might be at that time? And not as Christine Jorgensen, woman-formerly-man?[65]

Clearly straining to stay composed, Christine responds with dignity,

> CHRISTINE: No, Mr. Russell, I don't think the time will ever really come when the past—as you say—Christine Jorgensen, formerly a man, will ever be forgotten, should any event come up in my life

such as my marriage, or, even, my death, the newspapers would have a Roman holiday and rehash the whole past, but the strange part of it is, is that the people who know me—know me a very short time, and they forget about the past.[66]

It is in the midst of this tense exchange the record is marked by the scratches. In an effort to stay true to the emotion and intention in this brief dialogical exchange, Louryk as Jorgensen brushes her taffeta skirt, so that the scratches become a nervous physical manifestation, in reaction to Russell's condescending query. The metacommentary behind the moment of beauty borrows from Brecht's *gestus*. As I understand it, gestus is dependent on the expression of basic human attitudes and emotions in counterpoint to the outside world. Unlike gesture, however, the exterior forces of society control the physicality of gestus. It is this gestic moment of beauty that Louryk says "represents every ideal that I have."[67]

Lip-Synchopation

Louryk stresses that he is not giving a "drag performance"; it is rather an exhibition of both the complexity and subtlety of the female body, the female voice.[68] He uses lip-synch as a subversive medium, because his predecessors (Ludlam and Eichelberger) were so against it. In a 2006 interview in the *Boston Globe*, Louryk referred to this:

Ludlam [compares] drag queens who lip-sync to ventriloquism—that they're both the ventriloquist and the dummy simultaneously. He had a low opinion of them. And I thought: Well, here's this man who is so irreverent in everything he does, it seems that the best way to honor him would be to slap him in the face, to thumb my nose at whatever he thinks and do the opposite—to subvert that paradigm. And hopefully by doing that, you come out with something new at the end. So I started recording myself and then lip-syncing to the recording—basically taking away one of the tools that an actor has, voice and body, so that I only had one left and was at the mercy of the other. I wanted to challenge myself as an actor to overcome this hurdle, so that hopefully the audience will see the story more clearly. Which is kind of how we get to Christine Jorgensen. I'm at the mercy of that recording. I can't stop. I can't breathe at the wrong moment. I can't sneeze. I can't cough.[69]

In *Christine Jorgensen* Louryk reinterprets lip-synching by reviving it in its original form: by acting as ventriloquist dummy to a preexisting recording.[70] This is turned on its head not by technical convention, but rather through Louryk's deportment, body language, complimented by restrained sartorial and performative aesthetics. Whereas male-to-female drag lip-synch traditionally presents the male performer as a larger-than-life fictional character embodying if not hyperbolizing a glamorous woman, Louryk presents a restrained interpretive homage to Jorgensen's character as a pioneer for the repressed 1950s woman. This is the approach of a classically trained actor, not an amateur drag queen. Herein, Louryk reinvents a sociological and historical document with grand theatricality that uses the universality of the past to speak to the present, a performative reconstitution of the archive. Louryk says,

> People think drag is some tacky, fat guy in a bad wig and loud clothes and awful makeup. They don't know about Lypsinka, Charles Ludlam, Charles Busch—people who have elevated drag to an art form. I never think that I am a woman. I'm trying to wrench something artistic from the experience.[71]

As mentioned, Louryk's use of lip-synch in performance is also inspired by Lypsinka, a drag persona first created by John Epperson in 1984. Epperson, who gained fame when working with fellow Ridiculous performer Charles Busch in the mid-1980s bohemian East Village, uses female impersonation in an effort to fight clichéd misogynistic drag humor. Adelina Anthony refers to Lypsinka as "a master of mad elegance, hilarious timing, and perfect physical expression. [Epperson's] gender-bending show is also a refreshing delight in the way he explores the dilemma of being pigeonholed, stereotyped, and feared. His work is very pro-woman, pro-individual, and pro-dignity, without the political preaching."[72] Best known for his solo cabaret act, Epperson crafts performances by meticulously combining recordings of music and spoken word, which are lip-synched and interpreted with choreographed gesture, expression, and emotion. These "sound collages" are similar to the pastiched texts that Ludlam composed in the self-titled "epic" phase of his playwriting career in the mid-1960s, in plays like *Big Hotel* and *Conquest of the Universe / When Queens Collide*.[73] Jeffreys notes that this genre forwarded by Ludlam and now repossessed by Epperson as Lypsinka and by Louryk works to "challenge the audience as half familiar snatches go by and challenge the actor to connect the emotional and logical dots between and among the quotes [and references]."[74]

The concept of lip-synching as a serious theatrical discipline demands a reevaluation of the form as a mode of performative transsexuality. The origins of lip-synching as a drag convention can be traced to the use of canned music when live musical accompaniment (whether individuals or orchestras) became too expensive for failing gay clubs and piano bars. Although Thomas Edison might be considered the father of the front parlor lip-synch with the introduction of his cylinder phonograph in 1877, the practice was an essential component to large-scale production numbers after "talkies" premiered in 1929. It was not until the 1960s that prerecorded music became the standard mode of performance for drag artistes. In *The Changing Room* Senelick considers the initial negative audience reception of the form, largely because it allowed for amateurs to pull the carpet out from under highly skilled drag musicians. This practice also set the stage for drag "impressions" of famous female entertainers (Judy Garland, Marlene Dietrich, Edith Piaf, etc.) who were largely adored by the gay community for both their wit and demonstrations of strength or vulnerability. Senelick also points out that the "parody of celebrated performers, especially prima donnas, had been a staple of the minstrel wench, a showcase for soprano-virtuosity; and most music hall impersonators would spoof a danseuse or *grande horizontale* as a topical gag."[75]

Jeffreys suggests lip-synch has unfairly been labeled as "bastardization," for its controversial roots as a form of low art that was originated to cover up a lack of talent.[76] Louryk's use of lip-synch coincidentally took place amid a sea of controversy in 2004 when several young pop princesses, including Ashlee Simpson, Britney Spears, and Lindsay Lohan, were caught lip-synching (and poorly at that) to their own songs on live television.[77] The common defense of the artists is an inability to maintain pitch and strength while performing physically taxing dance routines. Louryk combats this by taking lip-synch from a place of disreputability and heightening the craft upon which his entire performance is based. For Louryk, the practice of lip-synching is as central to his own transformation as the making-up process of the *onnegata* or the drag king's binding of his breasts. Louryk's act of memorizing, mimicking, and embodying prerecorded sound is a ritual process that prepares the actor for a transformation that is both literal and metaphysical.

Though Louryk's use of lip-synch in his work to date differs from the use of his own voice (*Klytaemnestra*) and the historiographic retention of complete extant recordings (*Christine*), the precision required to lip-synch effectively and believably is inspired by Lypsinka's work. Furthermore, Epperson stresses the Ludlamesque Ridiculous sentiment of individualism and gay social acceptance without assimilation. In an interview he says, "When I see gay people who want to be assimilated into the mainstream, I can only say that if Tennessee Williams had wanted to be assimilated into the mainstream, he would never have written *Streetcar*. Being an outsider made him who he was."[78] Furthermore, Epperson stresses the importance of lip-synching to gay artistic expression: "I felt it had to be rooted in tradition. When I say tradition, lip-synching is a very traditional gay form. The Irish dance jigs, Native Americans do tribal dances and gay men get in drag and lip-sync. It's just something that happens. But I've tried to push it to extremes."[79] Although Louryk's message is intended to be more universal rather than specifically gay, it speaks to the same sentiment. Additionally, Louryk seeks to humanize the often larger-than-life characters in his plays, whereas Lypsinka's aural works fully embrace the mythic status of pop-cultural icons by retaining recontextualized snippets of iconic voices (Judy Garland, Bette Davis, Ethel Merman, Joan Crawford, etc.). In this way, Lypsinka's works rely on a nostalgic escapism that invites the audience to rediscover voices of another era and with this a remembrance of gay life prior to Stonewall, the AIDS crisis, and the other shifts that have forever altered queer American culture. In his essay "It's My Party and I'll Die If I Want To!" Román supports this idea:

> Lypsinka (re)occupies the place in gay culture and (re)provides that once flourishing space for gay men. Lypsinka's camp and drag is more readily familiar as the camp and drag of a lost era. The more recent radical drag of both gays and lesbians is a deliberate departure from earlier "apolitical" entertainments of piano bars and burlesque reviews. This newer drag . . . is much more about the visibility politics of current gay movements.[80]

Louryk succinctly uses his acting training in order to channel the essence of Jorgensen theatrically, not to imitate her as a traditional drag queen might. Ironically, the article where this quotation originally appeared opens with: "Bradford Louryk might be wearing a shiny-form fitting dress, high heels, and a platinum blond Marilyn Monroe–style wig while lip-syncing to the voice of a famous woman from the 1950s, but he wants people to know that *Christine Jorgensen Reveals* is no campy drag act."[81] Christopher Wallen-

berg, the journalist, implies that though Louryk uses traditional drag conventions such as the "Marilyn Monroe–style wig," in his performance he is
striving to present something that subverts the given aesthetic. Wallenberg
errs in his description of Louryk as Jorgensen, relying on clichéd description in an effort to paint him as a cheap drag queen that might appear in
any local gay bar. As the creative visionary of the entire project, Louryk is
extremely selective about his hair, makeup, and wardrobe in an attempt to
make himself appear as genuine as possible. Inspired by the original album
photograph of Jorgensen in a smart green 1950s dress and tasteful period
costume jewelry, Louryk's Jorgensen wears an understated custom-tailored
green taffeta suit over "three layers of panty-hose and a corset."[82] Although
Wallenberg plays up the "shininess" of the dress and the "high heeled
shoes," Louryk's appearance is closer to that of a mid-twentieth-century
society matron than a sequin-bedecked femme fatale. In fact, it is Louryk's
conservative restraint in appearance that marks his subversive intention to
commit fully to the presentation of Jorgensen as a character, not a female
impersonation. The combination of design elements and Louryk's attention to articulation and the precision of every breath with resulting movement (as controlled by the original recording) is an effort by Louryk to
"convince the audience that [he's] not a 5-foot-11 man weighing 155 pounds,
but 5-foot-6 1/2 inches tall, weighing 120 pounds."[83]

In *Christine Jorgensen*, the corset allows Louryk figuratively to transform himself into a "woman," but in this case it also represents a personal
victory for the character being portrayed: the opportunity for Jorgensen
finally to don the garment that symbolizes both her physical transformation into female and the resultant feeling of self-acceptance. The post-
third-wave feminist movement has rejected and stigmatized the corset for
its association with female subordination, inadequacy, objectification, and
heteronormative privilege, but one must not singularly impose these strict
criticisms on Louryk's characterizations and decision to truss himself
with the corset without also considering the various and often contradictory relationships that each character has with her corset and the inherent meanings therein. Louryk intends his resurrection of Jorgensen as a
woman attempting to achieve a 1950s ideal as a form of self-completion,
not a critique of postwar gender codes and misogyny.[84] From this position
Louryk queerly negotiates that past and the present through performance,
blurring the lines of a temporal history in favor of an affectively ambivalent narrative that uses the deconstruction of his own gender (through
genderfuck) to highlight the very construction of Jorgensen's.

The use of genderfuck and solo performance by Louryk also draws inspiration from Eichelberger. Eichelberger became famous for displaying a full back tattoo of herself as a cross-dressed angel ascending to heaven while she performed in drag. In displaying this body art, she offered a radical edge to her transgendered performance, providing a constant visual reminder that biologically he was a man dedicated to using drag in an effort to attack the repression of women, gay men, and drag queens in American society. For example, in her *Medea*, Eichelberger used the character to speak to the issue of identity and marginalization. Medea says, "People will strike at one who glitters; I'm an exotic—we're popular this year."[85] Additionally, Eichelberger's tattoo literally branded her as a bohemian outsider—an East Village pioneer, in an age when tattoos had not yet been appropriated by mainstream youth culture.

With the recording and text prepared, Louryk contacted producers in New York and London, who were immediately interested in staging the new play, which was titled *Christine Jorgensen Reveals*. The original production, directed by Josh Hecht, opened at the Manhattan venue 59E59 on July 12, 2005. Louryk opted to work with Hecht rather than self-direct because he was seeking a more traditional theatrical experience. Additionally, because the complexity of the lip-synching was both mentally and physically taxing, Louryk felt it was necessary to dedicate all of his creative energy to his performance. The play was part of the "East to Edinburgh" series, featuring plays that would travel to be part of the Scottish capital's Fringe Festival the following month. With a run of three weeks and six total performances, by the closing performance the production had been critically praised. The first review to appear read:

> Louryk is so natural in his performance that the result is something completely unexpected. Rather than a camp send-up of unenlightened people dealing with what they considered a "freak," the show quickly settles into a genuine appreciation of Jorgensen as a pioneer. She was a remarkably poised and articulate woman who was able to deal with the world in her own terms . . . looking back at Christine Jorgensen, one can't help but be impressed with her courage and fortitude. The play is a fascinating testament to an amazing human being.[86]

This review is accurate in its recognition that the production and Louryk as Jorgensen subvert the common formula of Camp and drag, in favor of a restrained and *gestic* characterization that results in a visceral existentialist experience.

The last production of *Christine* took place as part of the 2006 Dublin Gay Theatre Festival, May 8–13, 2006. While the critical reception of the play continued to be positive, Louryk received some initial criticism from the contingent of local Irish drag queens, who saw his nontraditional lip-synch performance as poaching a bit too closely on their own creative territory, but once they saw the performance, they too were won over by the spirit of the play and, according to Louryk, became one of his most effective non-media-generated advertisements for the Dublin production.

Nominations for various 2006 awards began to accumulate for *Christine* after the play had been performed for nearly a year. Louryk was nominated for the Media GLAAD award, was a finalist for first annual Ethyl Eichelberger Award sponsored by PS 122, received a nomination for the Dublin Gay Theatre Festival's Micheál MacLiammóir Award for best actor, and finally won the Drama Desk Award for "Unique Theatrical Experience."

The audience appeal of *Christine Jorgensen Reveals* is in part a direct reaction to the schisms that populate the sociopolitical climate. The conservative nature of twenty-first-century America has led to a cultural fascination with the conformity of the 1950s as well as the appositeness of Christine Jorgensen, and furthermore a heightened exposure of transsexuality in mainstream society. Todd Haynes, director of the films *Poison* (1990), *Far From Heaven* (2002), and *Carol* (2015), and one of the major proponents of the "New Queer Cinema," is a prime example of a gay artist whose work has dissected American Eisenhower-era attitudes, and in turn set the stage for work like Louryk's to thrive.[87] Haynes's films, as precursory to Louryk's plays, follow the same formula of the original Ridiculous, when the golden age of Hollywood and the avant-garde films of Jack Smith acted as the catalyst that enabled Ludlam's earliest plays. Furthermore, like Louryk's handling of the Christine Jorgensen saga, Haynes seeks to create an oeuvre that reclaims history, retellings that are not revisionist. Instead Haynes conceives and creates works that are essentialist in an effort to represent stories by liberating identities and vantage points that were previously hidden and closeted. Of this, Haynes states:

There is an attempt to link homosexuality to other forms that society is threatened by—deviance that threatened the status quo or our sense of what normalcy is. I don't believe that there is an essential gay sensibility either. What is so interesting about minorities identifying themselves historically and rewriting their own history is that, in a sense, it is an attempt to create an essential difference that isn't really true. But it's one that *they* are writing, as opposed to the status quo. So it's a way of disarming the conventions of difference that have been imposed on us and rewriting our own differences.[88]

A closer biographical examination of Jorgensen the individual versus Jorgensen the pop-cultural icon reveals how her story contradicts the strictly gay sensibility defined in Haynes, both in its origins and in Louryk's theatrical repossession of it. Jorgensen sought sexual reassignment surgery in an effort physically to claim the self-professed "sissified" ways of her preoperative male adolescence.[89] Jorgensen chose to go to Denmark for the surgery because she sought a quiet and escapist location for her sexual reassignment. Jorgensen's private affair soon turned into a national obsession, when, after her third and final surgery her story was leaked to the *Daily News* and broke under the headline "Ex-GI Becomes Blonde Bombshell" on December 5, 1952. When she returned to the United States after her recovery, Jorgensen emerged from the plane at Idlewild Airport on February 12, 1953, to be met by a hoard of photographers and curious onlookers. Although Jorgensen was a photographer, her primary income was derived from a lucrative touring nightclub act in which she told her story through personal anecdotes and capitalized on the public curiosity that it incited. Even until her death in 1989, Jorgensen remained more freak than pioneer in the public eye, as she was the brunt of off-color jokes as often as she was noted for her bravery or beauty. In a 1986 interview she said, "I could never understand why I was receiving so much attention. Now, looking back, I realize it was the beginning of the Sexual Revolution, and I just happened to be one of the trigger mechanisms."[90] Although there has been a revival of interest in Jorgensen as an LGBT icon and the landmark figure for sexual reassignment, before she passed away she stressed that her primary intention was to remain true to herself, rather than advocating change in the conservative climate of midcentury America or creating a legacy for others harboring the same desires. Commenting on her unrivaled fame as a public figure, Jorgensen once said,

> Does it take bravery and courage for a person with polio to want to walk? It's very hard to speculate on, but if I hadn't done what I did, I may not have survived. I may not have wanted to live. Life simply wasn't worth

much. Some people may find it easy to live a lie, I can't. And that what it would have been—telling the world something I'm not.[91]

Louryk's performance as Jorgensen eschews the glamorous persona that was a concocted by the media to sell glossy magazines (a photo spread in *Newsday* was dedicated to her first Easter bonnet in 1953). For the repressed 1950s woman Jorgensen represented a unique and unfamiliar freedom, fusing the rights of her male birth with the pleasures of feminine desire. For some men she held a fetishized fascination as a beautiful statuesque woman, lacking a vagina (Jorgensen never had reconstructive surgery to form a neovagina), a menstrual cycle, and the threat of undesired pregnancy. Although Jorgensen was most certainly the topic of many tabloid headlines and dirty jokes during this period, the curiosity, courage, or desire that she might have incited in the average American was overtly consumed by the scandalous nature of a white man's choice to subordinate his given gender in favor of becoming the fairer sex in the conservative postwar United States. In *Christine Jorgensen Reveals*, Louryk seeks to present Jorgensen as she wanted others to see her. Her calm demeanor, modesty, sharp sense of humor, and nervous self-doubt are all extracted and channeled from the original recording and brought back to life through Louryk's dramatic reenactment. In lip-synching to her original voice Louryk rejects his own vocal skills as an actor, allowing his body to possess the essence of Jorgensen rather than a mimetic posthumous representation of her.

Louryk reflects on the Lucrezia Borgia script, which still remains a work in progress. The delay of its completion is in part due to the challenging nature of the piece. Louryk relates::

Lucrezia Borgia is more difficult to talk about than anything else, because the underpinnings are so diverse. It's ostensibly about, simultaneously about, exploring the ideas of communication and technology—the technology of communication—and exploring this character. Each of the streams informs the other. It's about, for example, Lucrezia had an epistolary romance with a poet and the letters were collected. We use these letters as text for parts of the play. We're also looking at what letter writing does to thought and communication, what the telephone does to thought, the speed of the communication, the philology. It's about premeditation of thought versus speaking extemporaneously on a subject. Writing a letter—the parchment was expensive, the ink was expensive, you had to send it by a messenger on horseback to some destination. You have to be careful of executing the thing so that it can be done in a timely manner, get where it's going to go versus a phone call versus an email. The character is informed by the modes of communication, and the modes of communication inform the way we constructed the character of Lucrezia Borgia. Also, we're looking at how history is made—by people who are on payroll for, or enemies of, the nobility. So you have different interpretations of the same people, depending on who is writing the account. In a way we present many perspectives of Lucrezia Borgia chronically [sic] throughout her life, in an attempt to come away knowing more about Lucrezia Borgia.[92]

In its current draft *Lucrezia* is the next step of Louryk's performative work, merging the use of lip-synch with his own voice as well as a series of unexpected sound bites drawn from a huge variety of sources akin to Ludlam's early epic plays, such as *Big Hotel* (1966). The rapid nature of this section most closely resembles Lypsinka's manic style, which mimics her mental state "as she works her way through the existential crises of her life."[93] In its present form Grace's script draws directly from the films *The Talented Mr. Ripley, Sugar and Spice,* John Waters's *Female Trouble, The Thin Blue Line, Grey Gardens, All About Eve, Waking Life,* Hugo's *Lucrezia Borgia,* and the recordings *Knockers Up, Judy Speaks, The Sensuous Woman, Phyllis Diller Laughs, Christine Jorgensen Reveals,* and *Joan Crawford Live at Town Hall.* In July 2007 *Lucrezia Borgia* was workshopped by Louryk and Grace at the Sundance Theatre Laboratory in Salt Lake City Utah, where Broadway successes and Tony Award winners such as *I Am My Own Wife* (2004) and *Grey Gardens* (2006) were originated.

Louryk's post-Ludlam take on the Ridiculous theater results in a dialogue between the audience and the performer, providing a visceral existentialist experience—that is, an experience both approachable and tactile—while also prompting the individual to ask larger theoretical questions drawn from his ability to relate to and personalize the identities and experiences presented. Just as Ludlam and Eichelberger were responding to the contemporary state of American society, Louryk (with the textual collaboration of Rob Grace) is driven to create new works that speak to a current theatergoing audience; he relates, "There's so much discussion about sexuality and identity now, particularly in the wake of the wave of moral righteousness that swept the country after George W. Bush was elected. Everything in the States is so Right right now."[94] Louryk's self-conscious take on iconic women is unique from his Ridiculous predecessors because of his use of lip-synch to channel femininity and womanhood, while still retaining the masculine essence of his natural voice, creating a performance that blurs gender lines and challenges preconceived social norms for the twenty-first century and ushers in a new relevancy for the Ridiculous tradition.

Epilogue

In contrast to neo-Ridiculous artists Charles Busch and Taylor Mac, who regularly take their performances on tour, Busch to Europe and across the United States, and Mac all over the globe, from Sydney to Edinburgh, Bradford Louryk has chosen to stay primarily in New York City since his own European tour of *Christine Jorgensen Reveals*. After winning his Drama Desk Award, Louryk's career has been directed more toward development and appearing as an actor in plays rather than his own devised performance. He continues to develop the now titled *Lucrezia Borgia Project* around the theme "The despicable poison that is history," deconstructing normative temporality and history-making through a queer lens.[95]

Perhaps most intriguing in a Ridiculous context is the way that Louryk continues to perform himself in the public sphere. Wearing a signature bandana as headband and Jackie O–style sunglasses, Louryk has deemed himself an "icon," creating a presence of invented celebrity that runs closely to Warhol's Factory superstars of Ludlam's era, with a bit of projected diva-worship thrown in. This artistic practice began while Louryk was an undergrad at Vassar when he sent a valentine stating, "Be my icon, I'm yours" to the entire student body and faculty.[96] His online presence is used to support his iconic public persona, and his self-penned Facebook profile refers to him as a "Drama Desk Award Winning Treasure of the American Theatre."[97] Such antics stand in contrast to the public profiles of Busch and Mac, who simply refer to themselves as actor and playwright. In 2013 Louryk attended the Metropolitan Opera in a custom-made sweater reading "Herpès," a tongue-in-cheek take on the luxury French brand Hermès, and a biting jab at commercialism, performance. and the attending audience. Louryk is a consummate satirist, poking fun at how capitalism dictates commercial success from within, and in a Ludlamesque fashion he often gleefully contradicts himself:

I've never been interested in playing the starving artist. . . . I never wanted to do the East Village thing. I'm not interested in playing that role because it's not what I am. I was on a panel . . . with Taylor Mac and Neo-Futurists, great people, and there was this conversation where people were saying, "Oh, I'm doing my work for myself; I don't care if anyone's there. I want to find my stuff in the garbage and do it in the downstairs of a bar." I said, "Bring me a contract for the Helen Hayes and I'll move in tomorrow!" Give me a Broadway house with a cushy dressing room and a couple of dressers and I'm there. If people aren't seeing it, if you're not reaching the greatest audience possible, what's the point of doing it?[98]

Louryk's vision proved falsely prophetic. While he may have pretentiously lusted for mainstream success, it is Taylor Mac who has skyrocketed to mainstream fame by sticking to an avant-garde vision that honors his own humble beginnings. Nonetheless, Louryk is a thoughtfully self-constructed enigma, and part of his queer charm is the inability to pin down the line between individual and artist, both of whom embody and enact his own individual interpretation of Ridiculousness.

Most recently, Louryk has embarked on the pursuit of a new career in film and television while continuing to develop a play on the late British fashion icon Isabella Blow and an opera based on Roald Dahl's children's novel *The Witches* (1983).

CHAPTER FOUR

Taylor Mac

"The Determined Trickster"

Art is one big thrift shop.
—Jack Smith

Prologue

The following and final case study narrates the role of the Ridiculous as an aesthetic spark that instigated Taylor Mac's queer legacy. More specifically, Mac's neo-Ridiculous was transformed into a mouthpiece for the city of New York in the aftermath of September 11, 2001. The early work of Mac, a postmodern clown, was arguably the first politically driven satire performed in New York City after the attack on the World Trade Center. Mac and his contemporaries have declared themselves as carnivalesque "neo-neo-Romantic freaks" who "embrace all pronouns" and reject socialized gender codes.[1] Led by Mac, this fraternity of anarchic pacifists seeks to refute Savran's theory of "no brow"[2] cultural capital while inadvertently supporting Halberstam's postmodern construct of "queer failure," whereby the act of failing can be read as both a "way of being" and a "style."[3] The formation of this group adheres to Weston's concepts of chosen families over the biological, thus propagating a legacy that adheres Eng's affective kinship, a nuanced formula to unhinge the genetic with the self-selective kinetic as a means to a continuing. As demonstrated in *Red Tide Blooming* and several of his plays, Mac builds his legacy through the construction of what Ahmed deems queer "dwelling place(s)," physical and spiritual spaces that give the past a place to live, while nursing the seeds for queer production to mature both culturally and generationally.[4]

I argue that the current manifestation of the Ridiculous genre ushers in a new phase in the avant-garde community that cyclically reflects the original intention behind Ludlam's manifesto. In his retroactive discovery of the Ridiculous legacy via genderfuck aesthetics, Mac considers himself to be a part of a formulaic zeitgeist that extends throughout the history of gay performance, consistently building on its antecedents and altering them. This queer legacy applies Román's temporal drag as a kind of snail trail, a performative residue that links the past and the present in performance.[5] Within the performance space Mac draws out the map of his legacy as one of Rivera-Servera's traveling subjects, traversing the past and the present in attempt to find a queer, community-driven place of belonging.[6]

Mac generates his provocative approach to the Ridiculous theater by (re)employing Camp as a tool for political satire and radical social commentary by transforming Ludlam's clown into the more specific persona of the *fool*. The fool can be seen across all of Mac's plays, but is especially prominent in *The Be(a)st of Taylor Mac* and the commedia dell'arte-driven *Walk Across America for Mother Earth*. The act of politicizing the Ridiculous became particularly relevant when Mac reimagined the genre and became one of the first artists to publicly challenge the Bush administration in a media-generated culture of jingoism and xenophobia following 9/11.

In later autobiographical works such as *The Young Ladies of . . .* Mac proves himself to be the most philosophical of Ludlam's legatees covered herein, playing with queer temporality and history and reveling in a Derridean notion of the past as a specter that both haunts and sustains him.

Political Style

In the two decades since the death of Charles Ludlam, artists have found new ways to reinvent and subvert the legacy of the Ridiculous theater, reflecting shifts in the gay subculture of postmillennial New York City. Taylor Mac (né Taylor Mac Bowyer) is a contemporary actor and playwright who developed a personal Ridiculous sensibility. After solidifying his reputation as a formally trained performing artist, Mac discovered his Ridiculous predecessors and immersed himself in the first-wave Ridiculous canon of Jack Smith, Ronald Tavel, Ludlam, and Ethyl Eichelberger. From this he germinated his own style of genderfuck drag. Mac confesses that his initial affinity for the Ridiculous aesthetic stems from the exposure to images of genderfuck drag performers without understanding their artistic roles, performative objectives, or sociological/historical con-

Figure 6: Taylor Mac in *The Be(a)st of Taylor Mac* (2008). Photo: Lucien Samaha.

texts. It was the unique style of this Ridiculous aesthetic that inspired Mac to learn more about the playwrights and actors who originally introduced the genre. Mac generates his provocative approach to the Ridiculous genre by employing it as a tool for political satire and radical commentary. This chapter traces the queer genealogy between Ludlam and Mac as well as Mac's performative career through his development of a signature character, a "Pierrot figure for the modern age."[7] It attempts to unpack the tension between having one's own style while being part of a legacy, as well as the tension between the Ridiculous "style" and its political claims. Mac was initially drawn singularly to the aesthetic strategies and conventions of the Ludlamesque but extended his approach to the Ridiculous sensibility into a broader context that attempts to address all Americans in the paradigmatic search for national identity in the post-9/11 era.

Although drag is his chosen form of expression, Mac equates himself more with the "fool" trope than with a traditional drag queen:

A Fool is a person who speaks truths that others, who do not have such a phantasmagorical aesthetic, are unable to get away with speaking. . . .

The Fool is a perpetual outsider. A shaman. A queer. And a queer is not exclusively merely a homosexual, but a person who at an early age who was ostracized by society to such a degree that he could never possibly ostracize another human being. The fool brings an understanding of the social context because he was born into it, but has the ability to release people from the social contract because he was rejected from it and can see what's on the outside.[8]

Mac's eloquent description of the fool not only politicizes the queer and the implications inherent in his drag but also connects back to Ludlam's concept of the "clown," which he saw as bringing an approachable veri-similitude to postmodern, avant-garde performance. Ludlam declared, "[There] has always been a special power of the clown, because he can say serious things in a way that he cannot be punished for."[9] Ludlam's decla-ration establishes a long and continuous trope in performance history: the Aristophanic clown, Shakespeare's fool, the Auguste (not to mention Eastern forms with which Ludlam was admittedly less familiar). Ludlam exemplified the clown in his characters Saint Obnoxious (*Turds in Hell*, 1968), The Fool (*The Grand Tarot*, 1969), and Mr. Foufas the farceur (*Le Bourgeois Avant-Garde*, 1983). Ludlam relied on Camp to construct his clown personae, becoming a covert spokesperson for the gay community that was gaining visibility in New York in the 1970s. His distinct sense of Camp as "an outsider's view of things" was employed as a method by which marginalized outsiders could communicate with like-minded individuals through a series of codes—a secret language.[10] For Ludlam, the concept of Camp was thus a combination of the ideas inherent in his plays and the larger-than-life aesthetic choices in his productions. By layering Ludlam's clown (an entertainer combining traditional comic skills with Camp) with the alternative persona of the fool (a figure whose comic identity is a re-flection of his status as a born outsider), Mac provocatively adopts and extends Ludlam's Ridiculous, employing it as a tool for political satire and radical social commentary.

Traceable to the Fifth Dynasty of ancient Egypt, the "fool" as icon and entertainer perfects his buffoonery by drawing upon the color, tone, and infrastructure of the time and place in which he lives. Enid Welsford de-fines the fool as one with "the mouthpiece of a spirit, or power external to himself, and so has access to hidden knowledge—especially knowledge of the future."[11] Herein is the fool's seemingly clairvoyant ability to see beyond the imposed boundaries of a society and then expose injustices through performative jest, making him a gauge of the moral underpinnings of a civilized culture. The fool can take on a variety of forms, from the physically grotesque to the henpecked husband. Mac's exuberance lies closest to what Petit de Julleville referred to in his taxonomy of fools as "la jeunesse abandonée à la nature," which I translate as the young social outsider who is banished from society and abandoned to the wilds, though in his case Mac is the gay youth rejected by a heteronormative culture and given up to the "wilds" of the city.[12] This is where the fool finds the opportunity to found and perfect his own "fool society." The formulation of such a society that exists outside of the cultural mainstream allows members of the LGBTQ community to invent new cultural customs and conventions. Rather than relying on the esoteric subtextual messages of codified symbols and references that Ludlam used to speak to a contemporary self-segregated gay community, Mac's theater represents a new generation of self-proclaimed "neo-neo-Romantic freaks."[13] This group professes to "queer society" through the exposure of political corruption and projecting Ridiculous personae beyond the stage, in the performance of everyday life.[14] Thus Mac's foolery is one of metatheatrics, embracing his socially imposed role and hyperbolizing it into a heightened stage presence.

Describing his stylistic approach as "Hey, let's put on a show!"[15] Mac is continuing the tradition of the "moldy aesthetic" introduced by Jack Smith, founding "fool" of the Ridiculous, one of the common ideas about postmodern performance as a reframing of cultural detritus.[16] The "moldy aesthetic" refers to art recycled from the abandoned refuse of others. In his 1962 essay "The Perfect Film Appositeness of Maria Montez," Smith states that "trash is the material of creators."[17] Over a decade later he further outlined his plan on how this praxis could help to create an improved society:

> In the middle of the city should be a repository of objects that people don't want anymore, which they would take to this giant junkyard. . . . This center of unused objects would become a center of intellectual activity. Things would grow up around it.[18]

The communal freedom and opportunity for improvisatory creation or deconstruction implied in Smith's eccentric vision is communicated directly through his films and plays. In both performative mediums Smith developed his work as ritualistic rehearsals that were the presentation of his daily routine framed by an audience. His approach was to create something divine from nothing. This inadvertently took on a pseudo-Brechtian tone in its debasement of naturalism with the projection of uninformed "actors" playing roles that were directed only by the unpredictable whims of Smith and the trash surrounding them. Smith's work was irrefutably political in its attack on American capitalism, couched in metaphors such as his use of a lobster to represent "the epitome of the avaricious landlord who increasingly held the world in his grip."[19] It was in this carefully mediated vacuum, with Smith as omnipotent yet ambivalent magician, that the early tenets of the Ridiculous were originally engaged. The theme of material and social refuse became emblematic of the era, with works such as John Water's *Mondo Trasho* (1969) or Andy Warhol's *Trash* (1970), and is clarified by Wayne Koestenbaum's suggestion that "collecting [may be read as] a code for homosexual activity and identity."[20] Ludlam continued this adoration of the disposed by rifling through the "trash heaps of culture," in order to compose his plays that Michael Feingold of the *Village Voice* said were "like objects rescued from an antique shop and given new value by restoration."[21] In this tradition, Mac creates new art that is thematically born from the destruction and refuse (both figural and literal) of the 9/11 attacks, in the same way Smith, Warhol, and Ludlam generated work from their own beloved trash heaps.

Mac's work, in the vein of Smith's distinct imagining, is a continuance of the Ridiculous genre as a mouthpiece for political protest through satire and pastiche. Mac professes to be "a strong believer in grass-roots action."[22] This is in counterpoint to Ludlam, who shifted his performative intention from the blatant sociopolitical commentary on which Smith had been reliant. Whereas Smith's performances took the form of esoteric radical protests, Ludlam's Ridiculous was more interested in putting on queer(er) versions of classical texts and theatrical traditions. From his loft space, "The Plaster Foundation," in the Lower East Side in the 1960s and 1970s, Smith introduced films and theatrical performances that juxtaposed political commentary with a slew of Hollywood references.[23] These early versions of performance art occurred amid Smith's handcrafted sets that were precisely constructed from the refuse scrounged from the streets and garbage cans of New York. Thus, with its framework and purpose the closest to the Ridiculous in its nascent form, Mac's interpretation comes full circle in the sixty-year history of the Ridiculous tradition.

In spite of his departure from Smith's theater, Ludlam asserts that his theater is indeed political, but also adds, "What is political is perhaps misunderstood." He continues,

New York is the super-society that is, at the same time, the jungle. They both exist in man. It is not that the outside world doesn't work, it is that we *are* this. . . . The more you accept the rules of society, the freer you are as an individual. The more you are able to conform to the small issues, the unimportant things, the more you are able to be wild or eccentric.[24]

Ludlam communicated to and communed with his audience by creating a persona to "pass" in day-to-day life. Aside from a few known cross-dressing high jinks in his youth, Ludlam reserved his larger-than-life drag (though not necessarily female) personae for the stage. Though Ludlam's plays benefited from a period of freedom and reckless self-discovery that was spurred by the Stonewall Riots, his rise to success came about at a time when homosexuality was still considered to be a mental illness (it was not removed from the list of mental disorders by the American Psychiatric Association until 1975). Thus, Ludlam was using his gay theater not only to speak to a coterie audience of downtown New York, but also to prove that his subversive viewpoint was a worthwhile component of late twentieth-century American culture.

Mac, on the other hand, performs in the era of post-9/11 American conservatism, and thus makes an impact by appearing in his drag personas in public spaces and protests. Mac's approach is designed to combat a different set of cultural circumstances than Ludlam, who was essentially trying to emphasize the sanity of gay men in a time when homosexual desire was still considered a criminal/insane act. This difference is highlighted in Mac's manifesto:

As a theatre artist, it is my responsibility to make a change, to wake up people's unconsciousness, to present ideas and feelings that are unusual to them and confrontational but also surprisingly relevant to their daily lives. Surprise often yields emotion. My goal is to continually surprise the audience with aspects of themselves that they are not aware of. My plays blend tradition with new, comfort with unrest, respect with shock for shock's sake. I am committed to theatre that recognizes and cherishes its power to make a difference.[25]

The result of Mac's singular vision with universal themes has produced a diverse liberal following. Though he initially started performing in gay sex clubs with adjacent bars, Mac's plays have now garnered bookings at festivals, theaters, galleries, museums, and spaces as large as Brooklyn's Prospect Park.

California Dreamin' / New York State of Mind

Although Mac was initially unaware of the Ridiculous antecedents to his performances (as will be traced in this section), he was inadvertently exposed to the subcultural Ridiculous sensibility via mainstream reformations of it. Mac grew up on the West Coast and had no access to downtown New York theater until he was an adult. Because of this distance, in both location and culture, Mac's original approach to performance developed independently before he eventually became a vibrant part of the New York City's queer avant-garde tradition. Mac sees his role as a storyteller and traces his performative lineage to the ancient theater, based on ritual, amateur staging, and the development of plot (in an Aristotelian sense). Like Mac, Ludlam also saw the liberation inherent in theatrical ritual as the inspiration behind his praxis:

> From time immemorial, music from within has inspired slaves to dance. It is in this way that joy and relief make themselves felt. But theatre is more than casting off shackles. We must find harmony with the order of the universe. The celebrations of sacrificial feasts and sacred rights are the means employed by great rulers to unite men. They give expression to the interrelation of the family and its social articulation to the state.[26]

If one critically interprets Ludlam's reference to "slaves" as the socially marginalized, and the "family" as the patriarchal normative, it is implied that Protean ritual is the ideal medium by which to attain freedom as well as independence. Herein, theater is inherently subversive in its purpose to improve on society by inciting positive change, rather than attempting to destroy it with puritanical intention. This quote, however, is considerably more complex; if "great rulers" also manipulate the masses for state-imposed norms, the subversive potential is actually, in some way, leashed to the state. I read this as a radical subversion of the preexisting tradition. Though "gayness" dates only to the turn of the twentieth century (post–Oscar Wilde), its cultural antecedents are tied closely to time and culture immemorial. The same goes for the theater. The Ridiculous was not born in a vacuum; it constantly and consistently excavates and reforms the past. Though Ludlam and Mac both use performance to satirize their personal disenchantment with American culture at different times and to different ends, they both show respect without revering the past. This is achieved by underscoring the necessity of historical knowledge and tradition in order to generate new forms that are both innovative and influential, while also providing performance that entertains. Using the tools of theatrical tradition lends the Ridiculous agency by pointing to the roots of historical oppression and thus clarifying current and contemporary problems. Thus, Mac innovatively creates new theatrical forms and approaches by studying and reinterpreting performance traditions and techniques of the past just as Ludlam sought to reinseminate the tradition of narrative drama using techniques borrowed from the theatrical past. As Ludlam humorously revealed in his list of "Assorted Maxims and Epigrams," "I embrace Aristotle. I kiss his sexy Greek feet."[27]

An admittedly lateral foray into Mac's biography is crucial to better understand the development of his performance-based politics. This information is not readily available and aside from my brief article that appeared in *Theatre Journal* (2012), has never been discussed in a public forum or recorded.

Mac's first memory of theater was during his adolescence in the suburban town of Stockton, California, directly east of the San Francisco Bay Area. Founded during the Dust Bowl of the 1930s, Stockton was incorporated by a group of displaced Oklahomans looking for fertile land to farm. By the time of Mac's childhood in the late 1970s and early 1980s, Stockton had become a homogenous and politically conservative American community of characterless strip malls. In his play *Red Tide Blooming* (2006), Mac as the character Olokun relates:

> OLOKUN: Stockton, California. Not the California of the sea but the land of tract housing—of blending into nothing.[28]

Although the cultural opportunities in the area were severely limited, Mac credits his mother, Joy Aldrich, who ran an after-school creative arts program, as the catalyst for expanding his imaginative possibilities. He notes that his mother "influenced [him] in that way of just looking at things with curiosity rather than judgment."[29] At the age of thirteen, he enrolled in a children's community theater program run by Mark McClellan, who had trained as an actor at the Juilliard School before coming

back to Stockton after a rumored mental breakdown. Mac remembers Mc-
Clellan fondly as "really gay and flamboyant" in the midst an otherwise
bleakly heteronormative community.[30] In selecting atypical productions
to direct as children's theater, McLellan opened Mac's eyes to all of the
bizarre and magical possibilities that theater could be beyond the scope
of Rodgers and Hammerstein musicals (though admittedly R & H would
later prove to be a seminal part of Mac's play *The Young Ladies of . . .*).
Mac specifically recalls McClellan's production of Andrew Lloyd Webber's
Jesus Christ Superstar, in which the juvenile cast sported sadomasochistic
rubber costumes that seemed more related to Robert Mapplethorpe than
middle school.

After graduating from high school in Stockton, Mac decided to move
west to San Francisco because it was the "closest city, and gayest city," and
seemingly the ideal place for Mac to come out and experience life as a
young gay man.[31] San Francisco offered Mac a hodgepodge education that
included professional acting training in the classroom and practical experience as a working actor. It was during his residence in San Francisco that
Mac also began working with the San Francisco Mime Troupe under director Dan Chumley (the SFMT had been founded in 1959 by R. G. Davis
as an experimental offshoot of the Actors' Workshop). As the originator of
"guerilla theater," the SFMT gained notoriety for presenting political satire
in the spoken style of the Greek mimes or the commedia dell'arte rather
than the contemporary mode as silent, pantomimic performers. For the
next four decades the SFMT continued to present radical works that dealt
with contemporary events including the Vietnam War, Reaganomics, the
Israeli-Palestinian conflict, and the 1990 right-wing attack on the NEA.
Regardless of the controversy that they incited, the troupe secured its reputation by winning a Tony Award and three Obie Awards. Mac acknowledges that it was at the SFMT where he learned about politics and how to
incorporate political themes into his own original work.

It was also in San Francisco in 1993 that Mac began performing as an
ensemble chorus member in *Beach Blanket Babylon*, Steve Silver's infamous San Francisco–themed variety show. Currently America's longest
running musical revue, *BBB* first opened in 1974 in San Francisco's North
Beach neighborhood at Club Fugazi. With a plot structure that revolves
around Snow White searching for Prince Charming, the show is constantly updated with references to contemporary pop culture and is well
known for its drag stars in gravity-defying hats, one of which holds an
entire model of San Francisco's best-known landmarks. The show gained

national attention when it was mentioned in Armistead Maupin's *Tales of the City*, a revealing fictional slice of life of San Francisco in the 1970s and 1980s. Mac joined the company in the third decade of its performance in time to participate in *BBB*'s twentieth-anniversary spectacular at the San Francisco Opera House in 1994. Though he deferentially acknowledges his experience as a cast member of *BBB* for providing him the opportunity to perform in a professional theatrical environment with large audiences, Mac admits that at the time he hated the experience.

The desire to perform as "a more serious actor" drove his decision to move to New York City and study at the American Academy of Dramatic Arts.[32] At the AADA Mac studied formal acting training and history. During his tenure as a student Mac learned that the institution had also been the training ground for Ethyl Eichelberger, who would influence his aesthetic and reverence for Ridiculous performance. This relationship represents an important phase in Mac's development as a performer.

Aside from his unique reinterpretation of Eichelberger's genderfuck drag and self-penned solo texts, Mac's greatest homage to Eichelberger is in his use of a ukulele to accompany his singing. Eichelberger, who saw herself as "a storyteller and performer," became known for her signature use of the concertina in her solo concert shows.[33] She took up playing concertina in order to cut out the necessity of hiring an accompanist for her shows. This bare-bones "do-it-yourself" approach to performance was also the motivation for Mac to take up the ukulele. Mac also chose the ukulele as his signature instrument because of its small size and symbolic vulnerability. In contrast to his histrionic and gigantic genderfuck drag, the ukulele appears even more delicate in its appearance and sound. Mac confesses that he chose the ukulele because it is a culturally "un-cool instrument," that is, associated with indigenous Hawaiian music rather than more popular American or classical forms.[34] Mac capitalizes on the unexpectedness of the ukulele as a component of the multifaceted composition of his cut-and-paste performance style, creating visual juxtapositions of vulnerability and confidence.

Upon graduating from the AADA, Mac began performing widely in regional theaters across the country, including the Jean Cocteau Repertory in New York. This traditional experience as an acting apprentice is also reminiscent of Ludlam (who worked as a summer intern at the Red Barn Theatre on Long Island) and Eichelberger (who spent seven years as a character actor at Trinity Repertory Company). The practical exposure to a theatrical repertory tradition also instigated Mac's interest in ac-

quainting himself with classical themes and canonical plays. While touring with various companies throughout small-town America, Mac began
reading broadly and voraciously, from eighteenth-century kabuki to the
French theater of the absurd.

It was in playing supporting roles while touring that Mac began applying his own ideas as a playwright. Seeking an outlet to express his frustration with the state and reception of live theater in the United States, Mac
began writing self-proclaimed thematically "kooky" plays with traditional
structures.[35] Mac's first play, *The Hot Month*, was written in 1997–98 and
premiered in 1999 in Manhattan, produced by Center Stage. In 2003 Boo-
merang Theatre Company produced the play a second time with a new
cast. *The Hot Month* tells the story of a sister, brother, and his male lover
as they seek to find their own identities while struggling to come to grips
with each other in the face of death. Mac uses the beat of a heart monitor to
set the pace and tone of the entire play. It was also during this period that
Mac penned *The Levee*, a kitchen-sink drama about a heterosexual couple
attempting to deal with the pain and pressure of repeated miscarriages.
Premiering at Chasama's Oasis Festival in Los Angeles, the play was soon
published, and it received several more productions, gaining popularity
for its simple production demands and universal themes. With *The Levee*
Mac coined the term "interlocked happenings" to describe his composi-
tional style. Mac defines "interlocked happenings" as the convention of
overlapping and collaged scenes and dialogue that are transformed when
they are heard in the context of unrelated action on the stage.[36] Although
Mac takes pride in the success of this early work, he is also frustrated by
its remaining popularity through community theater productions since it
is no longer reflective of his current theatrical agenda.

In the summer of 2000, while still exploring his newfound vocation
as playwright, Mac ceased his theatrical touring across small American
towns and headed to the gay mecca of Provincetown, Massachusetts. It
was in the colorful village at the end of Cape Cod, where Smith had first
developed his own moldy aesthetic in the late 1950s, that Mac found his
way to solo drag performance. Because in the summer season "P-town"
supplies a constant liberal audience and no-holds-barred climate for experimentation (artistic and otherwise), Mac found it the ideal location
in which to workshop his larger-than-life characterization and aesthetic.
Mac turned to this new style of solo performance because he missed singing, which he not had the opportunity to do while touring as a supporting cast member in spoken dramas. Furthermore, by performing alone,

he was able to control all of the elements of the production, relying on a low-budget "Let's make a play" model. In these early performances, Mac would sing original songs and overlay them over preexisting tracks in a convention that he describes as "singing with an underscore."[37] He adds, "I was interested in appropriation and what appropriation is, and so I started forming the idea of pastiche."[38] The motivation to create new innovative works by employing the collage of diverse extant sources through the schema of pastiche has been the genesis of the Ridiculous theater since the early days of Smith, Tavel, and Ludlam.

In addition to his Provincetown debut in 2000–2001, Mac also began unofficially booking performances at several New York City gay bars, including the Marquis and the Slide. In performing these comic five-minute musical vignettes, Mac began to gain a celebrity status among the subcultural coteries of downtown New York. This early career approach to theater in a variety of redirected spaces also reflects Ludlam's origins, when he and the RTC precariously performed *Bluebeard* on reclaimed boards laid across the bar at the West Village watering hole Christopher's End.

Although Mac had lived in the East Village for several years, this was his first opportunity to perform in the unconventionally laissez-faire climate of downtown Manhattan. Mac jokes, "People much smarter than me called this performance art, which is just a fancy way of saying drag."[39] Mac's drag is a mélange of enlightened precision and a premeditated disarray. He created his at-odds aesthetic as a visual allegory drawn from the polemics and binaries that haunt the political themes and situations on which is work is primarily based. Furthermore, Mac thrived in the unique climate of the downtown theater scene because it provided room for both experimentation and failure. Of this he notes, "Uptown, failure is unacceptable, but suddenly downtown I found this access to a world that was just embracing of performance, and of difference, and of being in the moment, and kookiness, and failure. [Downtown] they'll clap more for you if you fail."[40] This quote can be read as an aesthetic failure to correctly perform a gender and aligns with Halberstam's notion failure as a choice of "style."[41] Halberstam goes on to state that "failure preserves some of the wondrous anarchy of childhood," thus disrupting formulaic constructs of maturity, family, and genealogy.[42]

Mac's initial foray into drag was motivated by his affinity for Camp aesthetics and kitsch culture as it has been absorbed and hyperbolized by the gay community. In metropolitan cities with large gay populations like San Francisco and New York, this aesthetic is highly visible within the confines of the gay ghetto as well as beyond in instances where it has been appropriated by the mainstream. Although at the genesis of his drag practice he was unaware of the works and unconventional genderfuck drag aesthetics of Smith, Ludlam, and Eichelberger, he had been unconsciously exposed to them via a prescriptive cultural transmission. Although he had not directly heard of nor seen the founding fathers of the Ridiculous movement, Mac was fully aware of his contemporary drag performers from the Wigstock generation.

Wigstock is an outdoor drag festival that was began in 1985 when performers from the Pyramid Club decided to hold a "dragstravaganza" in the band shell at Tompkins Square over Labor Day weekend. Led by the Lady Bunny, its premiere also featured performances by Ridiculous acolytes Eichelberger and John Kelly.[43] It was Kelly performing as his drag persona Dagmar Onassis who introduced a new version of Joni Mitchell's "Woodstock," leading the crowd's song in a grand finale:

DAGMAR: By the time we got to Wigstock we were several thousand falls . . .
    And I dreamed I saw the drag queens spraying hairspray in the sky and it made all the yuppies die.[44]

In 1995, *Wigstock: The Movie*, a documentary capturing the origins and history of the event, was released to celebrate its tenth anniversary.[45] By the time Mac came to New York in the late 1990s, Wigstock was a gay tradition that marked the end of summer. It gained notoriety for its ever-changing pantheon of drag stars, like RuPaul and Lypsinka, who were featured widely on the afternoon talk-show circuit. Wigstock has been revived contemporarily in the form of a themed cruise, still overseen by the Lady Bunny.

Mac also recalls finding early inspiration in the photography of Cindy Sherman. Sherman explores various marginalized identities by photographing herself as a diverse and often grotesque cast of characters. She rose to fame in the late 1970s New York art scene with a photographic series devoted to archetypes of women: the housewife, the prostitute, the woman in distress, the woman in tears, posing as all of the characters herself. More recent projects include self-portraits exploring themes of sex, death, and the grotesque. More specifically, Mac found inspiration in Sherman's chameleon-like ability to transform into a seemingly endless cast of characters without losing a sense of herself in the composition. This relates to Mac's approach to the development of characterization, in that he seeks to present stage-worthy representations of himself, made larger and more histrionic in the theatrical tradition.

Retroactive Tradition: Leigh Bowery

As Mac became more of a presence in the lower Manhattan art scene with his drag performance (not having a drag persona or a drag name, he is billed simply as "Taylor Mac"), several spectators recognized a similarity to performance artist, exhibitionist, and cult fashion designer Leigh Bowery (who also chose to be billed under his own name throughout his career). Mac considers Bowery to be one of his major aesthetic influences, and much of his makeup and costuming is drawn from Bowery's unique approach. Whereas Mac thrives in the creation and communality as the king of an inverted fool society, Bowery eventually perished as cultural deadwood when newer fads replaced his own brand of "fool," which was one of shallow imagery and shock-inducing antics. Bowery warrants more attention, in part because he was profoundly inspirational to the development of Mac's provocative aesthetic. Although Bowery and Mac are fundamentally different, Mac was often compared to Bowery in the press, which inspired him to explore his Ridiculous antecedents retroactively.[46] Starting with Bowery and moving backward, he immersed himself in the works of Eichelberger, Ludlam, and Smith. It was this intellectual pursuit that revealed the political satire that had been at the core of the early Ridiculous movement. This formulaically creates a sort of retroactive performance tradition, one imposed by the press and assumed later by Mac, who initially developed his practice with a full awareness of the tradition he now occupies and the torch he bears.

Bowery, a native Australian, migrated to London in 1980, where he became a figurehead of the avant-garde movement of the New Romantics. His childhood was comparable to Mac's in that he referred to his conservative hometown of Sunshine in Queensland, Australia, as "a cultural wasteland."[47] As an outsider coming to terms with his homosexuality, made apparent in his effeminate mannerisms, Bowery found solace in the pages of his mother's glossy fashion magazines imported from London, and hatched a plan to find solace and acceptance in England's capital city as quickly as possible. Upon arriving in London at the age of nineteen, Bowery became a staple of the gay club scene. He made one rule upon arriving in the capital city, "to wear makeup every day."[48] Bowery would stay true to his promise, appearing in drag whenever he left his apartment, whether going to the market, a department store, or a scheduled performance. One gallery's pamphlet described him as "peripheral in the notion of art practice by combining dandyism and body art, [he] reconstructed his image, [using] the expression of the 'other' to create a form of cultural lip-synching transvestitism."[49]

Bowery and his friends (including the painter Guy "Trojan" Barnes and designer David Walls) began to promote a serious of hedonistic underground parties including "Taboo," held on Thursdays at the Circus Maximus (on which the 2003 musical by Charles Busch is based). This period in London attempted to revive the decadence of Weimar-era Berlin. Bowery attracted the media spotlight with outrageous ensembles that transformed his body into the framework on which to build his performance art. Inspired by the haute couture that he had venerated since childhood, Bowery constructed an eccentric wardrobe out of everything from animal bone to inflatable Mylar. With these handcrafted sartorial confections, Bowery heightened the Ridiculous genderfuck sensibility to an entirely new level, projecting shock value with an extremist and grotesque polysexuality. For example, when Gary Glitter on his talk show *The Leader Speaks* inquired what Bowery's tits were made of, he coyly responded, "Will power more than anything."[50] His drag image became a metaphorical suit of armor, shielding the shy effete boy into any number of enigmatic characters (Mac on the other hand uses his drag to expose himself both physically and emotionally). Bowery achieved this in part by matching his larger-than-life-personality with costumes that physically exaggerated his already large frame, overpowering everyone else in the room. Using his image as the inspiration for his performance, Bowery began experimenting with dance, theater, music, tableaux vivants, and multi-media-based projects. These carnivalesque, grotesque, and often outré performances (such as his infamous enema-enabled *The Fountain*) were performed in nightclubs and galleries in London, Amsterdam, Tokyo, and New York. He also took on roles in the plays *Hey Luciano* (1986), *mmm* (1992), and *The Homosexual* (1993). In 1993 Bowery formed and fronted the band Minty, and continued to perform with the group until his death. Just as Bowery's fame reached its peak, marked by a series of Rubenesque nude portraits of the transvestite star by Lucien Freud, he succumbed to AIDS in 1994. On his deathbed he suggested that his friends tell the media he had "gone pig farming in Bolivia."[51] Bowery's colossal presence was arguably one of the most memorable in the fashion and art communities of the late 1980s and early 1990s. Vivienne Westwood, Alexander McQueen, David LaChapelle, Scissor Sisters, and Isabella Blow all acknowledge inspiration drawn from Bowery's unique aesthetic.

Beyond aesthetics the de rigueur comparison of Mac to Bowery lies primarily in their antinomian approaches. Bowery considered his routines to be political performance and described them as "quite violent and vulgar and yet beautiful and glamorous."[52] Senelick points out that Bowery's performances were in fact little more than "vestigial reminders"[53] of shock performance that spoke more to a generation of ecstasy-addicted Club Kids and ravers, not political activists.[54] Both Bowery's and Mac's early performances took place in club venues, but Bowery made it a point to headline in the techno-drenched clubs, while Mac's early performances were relegated to off-hours in basement bars. Bowery preached escapism by trying to create his own reality, whereas Mac, like Ludlam, hyperbolizes reality to extremes in order to expose the utter ridiculousness of what he declared injustice in the United States. Furthermore, Bowery's image was at the core of his performance, whereas Mac's is a well-thought-out component to accompany his sophisticated playwriting and classical performance skills.

As a performer, Mac began to carry the torch of the Ludlamesque Ridiculous tradition in spring 2001, just a few months before the terrorist attacks of 9/11. In the aftermath of the tragedy Mac found the motivation to make new work without the "crudeness of funding and producers" in the culture of fear and uncertainty that took a financial toll on theater artists and companies in New York City.[55] Tigger Ferguson, self-professed "actor, dancer, stripper, librarian," boylesque performer, and Mr. Exotic World 2006, recalls seeing Mac perform in drag for the first time at a going-away party that showcased him as "glamorously beaten." Ferguson recollects,

> [Mac] got up and sang "Nothing Compares to You," simply and gorgeously with his bald head, make-up bruises, and arm in a sling . . . by the time I'd seen a couple of his performances, I loudly began declaring him "the Future of Downtown." As time has shown, I was not alone in my assessment.[56]

Ferguson's observation points to the phenomenon of the fool as "trendsetter" whose vision and aesthetic choices ignite and define the performance of a certain time and place. Mac's drag aesthetic at this event set the stage for his practice of manifesting the emotional and emphasizing the topical through the physical as packaged in his glamorous down-at-heel style. While the practice of genderfuck was commonly practiced in the glam rock of the 1970s and metal bands of the 1980s, drag performers of the Wigstock generation largely constructed their images around luxurious custom-made garments awash in gemstones and glitter. As showcased in films such as *The Adventures of Priscilla, Queen of the Desert* (1994), and *To Wong Foo Thanks for Everything, Julie Newmar* (1995), the common goal of late twentieth-century male-to-female drag practice was to appear as feminine, glamorous, and over-the-top as possible to those unaware of the symbols and codes of gay Camp culture. This schmaltzy drag queen with a heart of gold who is hilariously mistaken for a real woman before being exposed to the community at large, which eventually accepts him for his differences, litters gay films of the era. This trend, supported by the programming of cable networks like MTV, launched the careers of performers like RuPaul (né Andre Charles) and Amanda Lepore (né Armand Lepore), who became cult icons in the fashion and music industries. Mac's constructed image abandons this approach, renouncing the excess and masquerade of high-profile drag in favor of his bare-bones approach. Through his carefully constructed drag Mac is responding to the feminist critique of glamour drag as a misogynistic act that mocks feminine stereotypes in contrast to the male performing body beneath. Mac discards the traditional/stereotypical drag queen aesthetic through genderfuck in order to act against what Judith Butler termed the "normal script" of normative expectations and patriarchal hierarchy.[57] For Mac, this drag is the omnipresent metaphor that steers his artistic practice. Of this, Neil Genzlinger wrote in the *New York Times*, "Mac wears something akin to rags when you first meet him [in performance], and before long he has made a mess of the stage as well. But the sloppier things get, the more you marvel at how assured and in control [he] is . . . working in drag, but not in drag clichés."[58] Thus, Mac's image is reflective of the uncertainty and frustration with the state of the war-driven American political climate post-9/11, attempting to radicalize and liberate preexistent glamour drag from its ties to capitalist excess and ignorance of current events in favor of shallow and often separatist amusements.

At Face Value

Mac's political performance is motivated by a purpose to reveal what he considers "the end of an American empire."[59] When the George W. Bush administration sought to reaffirm "moral values" in the 2004 reelection campaign, the president's advisers, led by Karl Rove, made certain that gay marriage referendums appeared on the ballot in conservative states. It was in these "red" states that anti-gay marriage supporters turned out in droves to reaffirm such "moral values." This significant action made members of the LGBT community the scapegoats of conservative Republican politics while also electing President Bush to his second term. This antigay/lesbian backlash began after the Supreme Court voted to overturn the so-called sodomy laws in 2003. A year later, the Bush administration capitalized on what the liberal press labeled jingoistic and zealous Christian fundamentalism that was spurred on, in part, by the fear of future terrorist attacks in the shadow of September 11, 2001.

In this mode, controversial gay activist and playwright Larry Kramer's cross-examination of the circumstances surrounding Bush's reelection verged on the hyperbolic when he delivered his emotionally charged lecture "The Tragedy of Today's Gays," on November 7, 2004. Employing the newly coined term "homo-hate," introduced by journalist Doug Ireland, Kramer lambasted the Bush administration:

> I hope we all realize that, as of November 2, 2004, gay rights in our country are officially dead. And that from here on we are going to be led even closer to the guillotine. The absoluteness of what has happened is terrifying. On the gay marriage initiatives alone: 2.6 million against us in Michigan, 3.2 million in Ohio, 1.1 million in Oklahoma, 2.2 million in Georgia, 1.2 million in Kentucky—George Bush won his presidency of our country by selling our futures. Almost 60 million people whom we live and work with every day think we are immoral. "Moral values" was at the top of many lists of why people supported George W. Bush. Not Iraq. Not the economy. Not terrorism. "Moral values." In case you need a translation that means us. It is hard to stand up to so much hate. Which is of course just the way they want it. "Moral values" is really a misnomer; it means just the reverse. It means they think we are immoral. And that we're dangerous and contaminated and dirty.[60]

Kramer's frustration and cynicism is derived from what he considered to be a giant step backward for the gay community. His involvement as a gay rights activist dates back to the mid-1980s, when at the start of the AIDS crisis Kramer wrote *The Normal Heart*, one of the first plays to consider the AIDS crisis seriously, and founded ACT UP, the first organization to bring media attention and funding to AIDS research and prevention. "The Tragedy of Today's Gays" polarized the gay community of New York City with its call for separatism from the heteronormative matrix, implying that the larger contemporary American identity is one of homophobic bias, if not hate. Furthermore, Kramer continued to stir up more controversy by pointing an accusatory finger at the gay community and blaming it for contributing to antigay sentiments with a conspicuous party culture, drug addiction, unsafe sexual practices, and self-centered detachment from civic responsibility. Kramer's gay audience was divided, with a supportive contingent figureheaded by iconic drag star Lady Bunny publicly praising him for his blatant honesty, and the contingent in opposition put off by what Richard Kim considered to be self-induced homophobia. Kim wrote, "[Kramer] recycles the kind of harangues about gay men (and young gay men in particular) that institutions like the *Times* love to print—that they are buffoonish, disengaged Peter Pans dancing, drugging, and fucking their lives away while the world and the disco burn down around them."[61]

Rather than taking sides in the mudslinging and vitriol spewing that Kramer's speech prompted, Mac approached the controversy as an objective observer. By collecting, patchworking, and parodying the controversy as a reflection of a publicly visible dysfunction that undermined gay identity in its struggle to be an accepted component of American society, Mac composed highly politicized work drawn from the headlines. The Bush juggernaut and its condemnation of nontraditional sexuality became the central and often repeated theme in his performances of this period, both directly and indirectly.

It is a politically driven pressure to conform that Mac combats, searching for a new national and personal identity in the post-9/11 era. Frustrated by the hegemonic rules of society, Mac strives to break them all with sequins, a ukulele, and an underlying humanistic message of fluid gender, race, and emotion: "We are not just men and women, not just black and white, old and young, rich [or] poor, but a combination of them all."[62] Mac's characterizations are polysexual and "embrace all pronouns," navigating the concrete boundaries that separate prescribed gender codes.[63] While Mac's aesthetic initially shocks, especially when presented unannounced and in public spaces, it demands the spectator peer more deeply into his own character or to reassess his own feelings of fear or discomfort that are promulgated by the juxtaposition of his hard and often shocking exterior with an earnest and gently delivered message. This celebration of his freakishness is especially poignant in the 2007 video for the song

"We've Nothing to Fear but Fear Itself." Mac ambles through urban London and rides the Underground in full-on genderfuck drag. He stresses that that this physical manifestation (like those in all of his performances) is not a character but rather "a heightened state of a stageworthy representation" of himself.[64] The video shows hundreds of people in Britain's capital as they completely ignore Mac in the midst of their commute. The message of apathy and fear of the commuters in the video is a poignant one as the they become a homogenized mass in contrast to Mac's jarring aesthetic, and people hide in their newspapers and MP3 players, never acknowledging that Mac exists.

The New York City theater community was hit especially hard by the events of 9/11 because shows that depended on tourists were suddenly empty. Mainstream and apolitical Broadway productions slowly bounced back, with the state of New York contributing $1 million for marketing the shows in the winter of 2001–2. Furthermore, the New York City tourism bureau began the "Spend Your Regards to Broadway" campaign that gave theater tickets to patrons who spent more than $500 in city stores. Mayor Giuliani also released a statement asking people to help their city by going to dinner and seeing a Broadway show. While the midtown theaters were able to remain open with the assistance of lobbyists, the downtown independent theater scene also did its part to survive in the aftermath of the attack. With a closer physical proximity to Ground Zero, theater companies located in lower Manhattan also bonded together to produce shows that honored the dead and consoled the living in the form of fundraisers and community-building events. One such show staged in 2002 was the series "Brave New World: American Theatre Responds to 9/11," which included pieces contributed by a variety of playwrights, actors, and theater artists. In her essay "New York's Visual Art World After 9/11," Julia Rothenberg observes that in the period following 9/11, New Yorkers were drawn to exhibits and shows that "touched on the devastating events," and she notes that "their keen interest in graphic representations of the horror and heroism was a vivid reminder of the importance of [the] arts in the cultural economic life of the city."[65] While the theater was a key element in the city's healing process, the period after the attack left artists whose work relied upon barefaced political commentary, like Mac, in an awkward position. The artistic and intellectual challenge became to broach the interrogation of American corruption in their work without appearing traitorous to their beloved city and its reputation as the innovator of American artistic culture?

In his essay "Cultural Criticism and Society," Theodor Adorno declares that "writing poetry after Auschwitz is barbaric."[66] If we are to take a new queerer reading of Adorno's statement as a warning against the solidarity of morally conscious art that is developed in response to the tragic, evil, and horrific, then perhaps Adorno is calling for art that is based on a critical honesty, not reverential memorializing. It is destructive to approach the memory of the violent past with only veneration, because the horrific event, whether the Holocaust or 9/11, becomes a lifeless facade of death, rather than the vital struggle of individual experience. In following Adorno's call for honest art that finds optimism in restorative power of its creativity, artists like Mac honor the dead by delivering works that unabashedly question, analyze, and criticize the normative value systems of the prevalent hegemony. By separating the political from the sacrifices of the deceased, Mac honors the dead by interrogating corruption and brainwashing in an effort to fight for what he sees as the core of American values, the right to life, liberty, and the pursuit of happiness. This is especially poignant, because as a gay performer reliant on gender-fluid performativity, Mac is representative of the marginalized American citizens who perished beside their more normative counterparts without equal constitutional rights.

In counterpoint to Ludlam, who never intended his Ridiculous Theatrical Company to produce agitprop theater, Mac delivers a leftist message with the exposure of his psyche and physical body, speaking through the often jarring and disturbing facade of his severe and intentionally messy transvestitism. Ferguson refers to Mac's work and drag:

> Taylor's work reflects the colliding worlds of art, politics, faggotry, frivolity, love, identity, and especially humanity. He is unique because he combines his fierce passion and intelligence and talent with more honest vulnerability than any performer I know. Oh yes, and his style. We offer many flavors of gender-fuck drag in our little family of freaks, but Taylor's style is one of my favorites.[67]

Mac's "style" as described by Ferguson stays true to his do-it-yourself aesthetic, using staples, safety pins, knots, and a hot-glue gun to "find an outfit in the trash."[68] His drag ensembles manifest the topic of an individual performance. For example, in a piece on the War on Terror Mac wears a dress made of dirty yellow latex gloves, ripped fishnets, and bits of trash haphazardly hanging off of him. In presenting himself to the audience Mac delivers the one-liner:

> MAC: This is an outfit that I made for the War on Terror—it's a meta-phor![69]

Although his appearance may initially cause discomfort, Mac's light-hearted, fool-driven, and often colloquial humor draws in the spectator, making him more comfortable with the journey that s/he is about to em-bark on. Furthermore, this convention becomes a performative represen-tation of the idiom "You can't judge a book by its cover," applying folk wisdom to a postmodern social climate.

In juxtaposing the subtle with the brash, Mac's approach to drag be-comes metaphoric for the moral that he attempts to convey in any given performance. His intention is to surprise the audience with the contradic-tion of his freakish physical appearance and gentle demeanor while also communicating responsibly:

> I read this in some science journal that human beings only feel emo-tion when they're surprised, the only time that you feel anything is because you're surprised—it can be a big surprise or a small surprise, it doesn't matter, but that's what triggers the emotion. That comes from wanting something, so I craft my shows and I adjust them depending on who my audience is going to be. You have to set up the rules. If you set up the rules and give people their expectations then it's okay to do whatever you want within the boundaries that you've created, and so I usually start off my stuff saying that there are no rules, and then people realize that the rules are there are no rules then that means that I can do anything that I want to do. In the first ten minutes of any show it's kind of about, I'm going to take you to lots of different places. This is a pastiche, you know?[70]

It is Mac's insistence on breaking rules and ignoring boundaries in a post-9/11 age defined by systematic regulations and "safeguards" that make his work as an artist so timely and insightful.

The terrorist attack on the World Trade Center prompted his one-man show *The Face of Liberalism*, where he played the role of a postmodern/post-9/11 Lord of Misrule. Performed from May to October 2003 in the basement of the Slide Bar, located in the Bowery in New York's East Village, the play was arguably the first theater piece to interrogate and satirize the "climate of fear" and resultant xenophobia that Mac suggests came from the Bush White House. Reinventing the Ridiculous genre as "in yer face"[71] Americana, Mac succeeded in subverting Ludlam's midcentury, nonpolitical gay theater and morphing it into its most socially conscious, extremist, and histrionic to date. This was the first of his solo projects to reflect both his performative and political agendas in a fully realized format and length. Referring to the plays as "a subversive jukebox musical," Mac relied upon the preferred Ridiculous practice of pastiche to formulate the highly politicized work. He advertised the show as "a mish-mash of original, songs, parodies, stories and mental illness" with the following description:

> There goes George W. Bitch Jr. playing up the machismo again. Pass the processed cracker and spread it thick. Faux Texan macho man battling with Middle Eastern hoopla; what is a revolutionary to do but don a pair of six-inch stilettos and walk the streets. Has all the US anti-intellectualism got you down? *The Face of Liberalism* may be just what you need.[72]

The format of the show was based around a set list of original songs, including "War Criminal Romp," a New Orleans–style jazz tune where the lyrics are a recitation of the names of supporters of the George W. Bush administration, and "Fear Itself," a thoughtful ballad that Mac sang without accompaniment to close the show:

> MAC: "I'm afraid of patriotism, and nationalism, and jingoism . . . we've nothing to fear but fear itself, fear itself, fear itself."[73]

Though the structure of the songs remained the same for each performance, Mac added to the transitional idiomatic and anecdotal monologues about a variety of themes affecting the American conscious. One, for example, explores tackiness through Mac as a disenfranchised teenage goth:

> MAC: (AS GOTH): People are selling baby American flags on the street for two dollars when you know they only cost like two cents and were made by some Taiwanese premi-baby [sic] in their makeshift bamboo incubator.[74]

In addition to such criticisms, Mac improvised dialogue rooted in the news of the day. Furthermore, in a postmodern riff on the Federal Theatre Project's Depression-era "living newspapers," Mac crafted a revealing Warholian newsprint ensemble each night that featured his favorite headline. For example, Mac recalls that one night his disposable garment prominently featured "Liza Beat Me," in boldfaced type, referring to the accusations of David Gest against his ex-wife, Liza Minnelli. It is this absurd recipe of pointed current events and wink-wink observations of pop culture that compose Mac's individual Ridiculous sensibility as an auteur.

Toward the end of its run, Mac developed distinctive antipatriotic makeup, painting his face with the stars and stripes of the American flag, applying thumbtacks to his jaw with spirit gum—points facing outward— and wearing a red, white, and blue wig made out of curling ribbons.[75] The deconstructed flag motif, created with drugstore cosmetics and stationery-aisle craft supplies, was a visceral expression of his agenda as a citizen/artist to "reveal the truth," his face a billboard for self-created graffiti, articulating his identity through its hyperbolized freakishness in a contemporary interpretation of the queer fool.[76] Although Mac continued to use the tricolor scheme as his guide, his makeup evolved and changed nightly, marking each aesthetic interpretation as unique and ephemeral, like the performance itself. His practice of employing his body as canvas marks him as a queer subject, his changing physical appearance a metaphor for performative gender. In a state of constant transformation, he creates a sense of agency that, in Victoria Pitts's words, "underscores the body's symbolic significance as a site of public identity and a resource for opposing (hetero) dominant culture."[77] In this vein, Mac offers his physical body as a corporeal representative of the liberal body politic, embodying the Foucauldian notion of the body as a text on which social reality is inscribed.[78]

In this sense, Mac's preparation becomes a rite in much the same way that a commedia dell'arte actor donned his mask as a catalyst for physical performance before going onstage. Mac physically transforms himself in order to "channel the spirit of Proteus."[79] Mac also adds that his aesthetic is aided by the mantra of "never erasing." He says, "If I'm doing my makeup and some eyeliner smudges—well, that night I'm going to compensate on the rest of my face to work with the smudge."[80]

The act of employing the body as a canvas is reminiscent of queer performance artist (and one of the NEA Four) Tim Miller. In his solo performance piece *My Queer Body* (1992) Miller disrobes onstage and then enters the audience on a psychosexual scavenger hunt in order to collect "parts" of his body from the audience (labels that read "head," "heart," "dick," "belly," etc.), before applying them to his anatomy. Each label represents a piece that when combined with others composes themes for the larger narrative of his biography. The literal and emotional exposure of his body supplies the raw material on which the piece is based. In the performance Miller says, "My skin is a map, a map of my world, my secret world."[81] In exposing himself at his most vulnerable, Miller invites the spectator to invest not only his own stories but also those that society has inscribed upon him. Nudity becomes the metaphor for society's discomfort with the "queer body" as representative of sex, fear, and disease. Perhaps the most poignant section of the piece comes when Miller reenters the audience, still nude, to sit on a stranger's lap. He says:

> This is the most nervous part of the performance. Here, feel my heart. I see my face reflected in your eyes. I am here with you. My body is right here. You are right there. Here, feel my heart. I still feel alone. A little afraid of all of you.[82]

This physical connection demands that the audience look beyond Miller's nudity in an attempt to connect with his humanity, represented by his racing heart and the admittance of fear. Whereas Miller asks that the spectator swathe his nude body by psychologically embracing and accepting it, Mac uses his painted body as a metaphoric shell, which must be chipped away to reveal his own state of vulnerability. In short, the spectator is convinced to forget Miller's nudity just as he is led to see beyond Mac's harsh exterior. Nudity is also being employed as a rite of intimacy and self-mediated martyrdom. As with the saints plays of late medieval Europe, the nude body is demonstrative of human vice in counterpoint to the transcendence of the soul achieved through sacrifice and suffering. In a postmodern context this highlights how Miller's and Mac's queer bodies become totems for queer pleasure and normative associations of taboo and perversion.

The Face of Liberalism provided a potential refuge for like-minded audience members who openly criticized the conservative political majority during a time of jingoistic fervor—the period directly following 9/11. Although audiences for the run of the show were admittedly limited, the performance space successfully doubled as a site of refuge and communion for urban Americans who harbored similar feelings of frustration with prevailing hegemonic ideologies that promoted xenophobia and absolutism. Mac embodied, hyperbolized, and performed this minority position through his carefully constructed image: a voluntary scapegoat, the traditional fool archetype reclaimed as a figurehead with a political agenda. In offering up his cosmeticized visage for consumption, he willingly became the unlikely "face" of liberalism. His continuing political stance as a self-proclaimed liberal is driven by his belief in a democratic society that supports the expression of individual freedoms across "a range of humanity."[83] When read in combination, themes discussed in *The Face of Liberalism*, including blind patriotism and subsequent threats to individualism, offer a subtle critique of neoliberalism and the social detachment that Mac sees as a destructive consequence of its global proliferation. *The Face of Liberalism* stands apart from Mac's later works because of its underground nature. Positioned as a piece of controversial antipatriotic art and located surreptitiously in an East Village basement with limited advertising or press, this foundational performance marked the materialization of his fresh take on the Ludlamesque tradition in a postmillennial context. This show and its distinctly deconstructed patriotic aesthetic would also inspire Mac's collaborative participation in the political cabaret *Live Patriot Acts: Patriots Gone Wiiild!* at Performance Space 122 with the Imagine Festival 2004. Taking place during the Republican National Convention, also in New York City, the show provided an alternative space for political protest through spoof and Ridiculous humor, including a "follow-the-bouncing-boobs-dressed-up-like-the-Bush-twins sing-along."[84] The show would also inspire a sequel, *Live Patriot Acts 2: Alien Nation* in 2007.

As Mac was performing *The Face of Liberalism* in 2003 he also completed a new one-act play titled *Okay*, relying on his invention of interlocked happenings. *Okay* premiered at the Spring Theatre in New York before transferring to the HERE Arts Center, where Mac continues to present new work.

Continuing to draw themes from newsworthy events, *Okay* is inspired by the story of a girl, Stephanie, who gives birth at her senior prom, struggling to hide her contractions in a bathroom stall while her friends discuss the shallow realities of early twenty-first-century adolescence. The title is derived from Stephanie's friend Jordan, who repeatedly asks if she's okay. Mac uses this situation as the sounding board to examine what it means to be "okay" in 2003 suburban America. Another character, Trish, a cocaine-addicted, angst-ridden, self-proclaimed intellectual, joins Stephanie in the restroom to deliver a diatribe criticizing the country at large. Her rant includes, among other things, attacks on prescription drugs, evangelical

fundamentalism, school violence, (as inspired by the Columbine High
School shooting in 1998), 9/11, and hate crimes:

> TRISH: I mean I could handle the idea of getting together and having a
> community, like that's a fucking valid desire right, to celebrate your
> community, but like why do we have to have themes in order to do
> it. Fucking mythology. Fucking Leda and the Swan. Zeus turns into
> some . . . heterogeneous group of animals and impregnates women.
> Like hello, what kind of fucked up information are we perpetuat-
> ing here. But then it's totally polytheistic which is like so much
> better than having some holy-roller derby for Christ or something,
> but like getting together to just have community isn't enough. But
> then you're supposed to be proud of being a part of a community
> and I'm like so not proud. It's like all those people waving all those
> American flags and I'm like okay, okay, okay, okay I get it we're all
> from the same country, I mean it's like such the thing to do, like
> suddenly there's this wave of fucking acrid bandwagon patriotism
> wafting through the country and people are selling baby American
> flags for like two dollars on the street when you know they only cost
> two cents and were made by some Taiwanese premi-baby in their
> makeshift bamboo incubator. And like people from New York, or
> not even from New York, are wearing T-shirts that say "I survived
> the Attack on America." . . . I mean I support the country and all it's
> just, I was reading in *The Nation* that basically we created the Tali-
> ban and like, what the fuck, then they came back to bite us in the ass
> and like all I ask of my president is that he be smarter than me right.
> I mean he's a fucking C student, I mean I'm a fucking coke head and
> I don't ever study, I mean like ever, and I still get A's, I mean how
> hard is it? And I was reading in *The Nation* that like there's this IQ
> test that some company does on all the presidents since like Frank-
> lin Roosevelt and George W. Bush Jr. was like one step up from like
> fucking retarded.[85]

Mac uses the character of Trish as the prophetic yet damaged soothsayer.
Like Aeschylus's Cassandra or the medieval fool, Trish's revelations are on
point with a critically liberal sensibility, but her credibility is diluted by the
fact that she is a cocaine addict with an affinity for sarcasm. Trish attempts
to fight against the "capitalist right-wing conspiracy," without realizing
that she is a cog in the machine of empire.

This monologue also demonstrates Mac's use of pastiche drawn not only from outside sources, but also from his own work. The "bamboo incubator" section was recycled from *The Face of Liberalism*. This practice, borrowed from Ludlam and the early Ridiculous, is comparable to the repetition of the *lazzi* in commedia dell'arte plays of sixteenth-century Italy: the actor becomes expert in a specific comic action that in turn becomes a signature of the performer and is liberally applied to multiple shows. In this case, Mac is using an anecdotal joke as a signature stamp. This supports Mac's self-proclaimed role as a "collagist."[86]

Before *Okay* concludes it is also revealed that the father of Stephanie's baby, Tommy, is struggling to come to terms with his homosexuality as he gives a hand job to his classmate, Mike, in another stall. The play, featuring a cast of postmodern stock characters, is a darker satirical take on teenage angst films of the 1980s, like John Hughes's cult classic *The Breakfast Club* (1985). Mac's reinterpretation of contemporary stereotypes also reinterprets the genre of a subtler postmodern *commedia americana*. Introduced in 1992 by Jules Tasca with his series of "*Commedia* plays for a modern audience," the concept of *commedia americana* retains traditional Renaissance Italian commedia dell'arte characteristics (like stock characters, and improvisational dialogue) and juxtaposes them with references that satirize contemporary American politics and culture.

In June 2004 Mac began performing a new solo performance piece entitled *Cardiac Arrest, or Venus on a Half-Clam*. It premiered at the HERE Arts Center for the annual Queer@HERE Fest (where contemporary neo-Ridiculous heir Bradford Louryk also frequently performs). Charles McNulty, critic for the *Village Voice*, referred to Mac as "a cross between Gene Simmons and a Vegas showgirl . . . wearing only what can be called Q-tip couture."[87] The allusion to Mac's Q-tip-laden dress not only metaphorically suggests a swabbing and disposal of waste, but also is in homage to his mother, who loved to employ Q-tips as the raw material for her children's art projects during Mac's youth.

Cardiac Arrest, like *The Face of Liberalism,* is a montage of original songs strung together with biting political criticism and humorous anecdotes concerning post-9/11 America. Mac creates a diegetic world, inviting the spectator to participate with imagistic prose and his highly symbolic costume. After the premiere, Mac continued to perform the piece at the Fez (inside Time Café) on Lafayette Street.

The same year Mac also participated as a guest performer in Karen Finley's *Make Love* at the Fez. The show was referred to in the *New York*

Times as "a messy, silly, upsetting, sometimes funny and surprisingly moving love poem to a place and its people in a time of crisis."[88] Finley, a member of the notorious NEA Four, portrayed a dragged-up version of the iconic Liza Minnelli as a personified metaphor for New York struggling to rise from beneath the ashes. For Mac, the thematic approach was complementary to his own work, though the "Liza drag" was in stark contrast to his definitive image. Nonetheless, for the run he became a festive part of Finley's message that "we can all be Lizas." Finley's invitation for this collaboration marks Mac's entrance as a brother in the inner circle of the exclusive world of NYC performance art. The practice of using drag versions of cult divas as the instrument for social critique and compassion first appeared in nineteenth-century minstrelsy before being appropriated by the early Ridiculous—from Smith's reverence for Maria Montez to Ludlam's portrayals of Gloria Swanson as Norma Desmond and his reinterpretation of Maria Callas as Galas.

Ebb and Flow

In 2005, as the winner of the first Ethyl Eichelberger Award sponsored by PS122 (where Eichelberger regularly performed and which she purportedly still haunts), Mac was invited to compose an original work. In homage to his Ridiculous forefathers Mac elected to create *Red Tide Blooming*, inspired by the early epic plays of Tavel and Ludlam in the genre of pastiche.

The plot of *RTB* is based on the gentrification of Coney Island's Mermaid Parade, where self-professed freaks dress up in outré costumes as marine creatures in a modern-day Feast of Fools. The capital-driven metamorphoses of the former bohemian enclaves of lower Manhattan has forced artists to seek new haunts beyond the city proper, among them Coney Island. This, along with Coney Island's colorful past as a nonstop carnival that provided escapist amusement away from the city, inspired the invention of the Mermaid Parade in 1983. As the parade grew in size and popularity, the once-exclusive celebration became a magnet for a wider audience.

As celebration for and of self-declared "freaks," the Coney Island Mermaid Parade took a cue from the tradition of gay pride parades. The concept of the gay pride parade was inspired by the Stonewall Riots of June 28, 1969. A year later the Gay Liberation Front of New York City (led by Connor Weir) organized a public march from Greenwich Village to Central Park to commemorate the one-year anniversary of Stonewall. That same weekend, tribute marches were also held in Los Angeles and San Francisco. Such marches and "gay-ins" continued through the 1970s.[89] In the 1980s as a younger generation took center stage and the primary social cause for gays shifted from liberation to the AIDS epidemic, the celebration dropped the politically radical title of *liberation* and replaced it with *pride*, intending to welcome a broader spectrum of the LGBT communities and their supporters. The popularity and carnival atmosphere of Gay Pride events led to large marketing campaigns and opportunities for the business-minded to capitalize on the crowds that gathered, though the overt sexual overtones of the event deterred a more conservative crowd. The Coney Island Mermaid Parade was created as an alternative by and for other disenfranchised members of society (both gay and heterosexual) who wanted a more inclusive event for "all artists" to show off and share their creativity in the form of homemade nautical costumes. It is less about sexual identity than about a subversion of labeling. Initially the Mermaid Parade was promoted by word of mouth, but a renewed interest in Coney Island has begun to attract a large and more diverse population of onlookers to the annual event.

Coney Island was chosen in part as the site for the Mermaid Parade because of its rich history of headlining "freaks." From 1880 to 1942 Coney Island was the largest amusement compound in the United States, with parks such Luna Park, Steeplechase Park, and Dreamland. In addition to rides and concessions, the parks also featured dime museums and a vibrant sideshow circuit featuring a rotating cast of "freaks." Freaks, or "human oddities," were either "natural" (conjoined twins, the bearded lady, the human torso) or "made freaks" (the tattooed man, the snake woman, the ventriloquist). The advent of television and a shift in human conscience put an end to the freak show after World War II. However, in 1985 the Coney Island Circus Sideshow reopened as "the world's first nonprofit theater dedicated to keeping alive the American sideshow."[90] Mac and his peers extend the fool by identifying as "made freaks," reflecting that every individual exhibits the characteristics of a "freak," and an attempt to conceal said characteristic in order to conform is equally "freakish." Mac's performative resistance to homogeneity and gentrification is a reaction to what David Savran refers to as a "nobrow" culture that erupted in the 1980s with the rise of MTV and Hollywood merchandizing extravaganzas.[91] *RTB* develops this theme a metatheatrical romp with characters as Mermaid Parade participants unknowingly presenting a play that seeks to answer the question "What happened to all of the freaks?" To highlight

this point, Mac composed a cast of "outsiders," including burlesque performers, performance artists, a transsexual, a couple of drag queens, radical fairies, a self-proclaimed slut, naked bodies of all shapes and sizes, four
generations of actors, all different kinds of sexual perversions, and even a
former Playhouse of the Ridiculous superstar, Ruby Lynn Reyner.

The cast constitutes a physical legacy of the Ridiculous tradition with
a histrionic family reunion of "divine freaks." The decision to construct
the play around contemporary stock characters is directly borrowed from
Ludlam, who, as a trained expert in commedia dell'arte, frequently built
texts around fool archetypes and situations drawn from the early modern
Italian genre.[92] Mac selected the varied cast members to showcase freakishness in both their dramatic characters and identities as artists and New
Yorkers. This reliance on a Brechtian gestic doubling was a favorite convention of Ludlam's, as when he played his signature Galas as an alter ego
of himself.[93]

The play is centered around Mac as Olokun, a hermaphrodite sea
creature who has secured his phallus to his posterior with duct tape. Appearing on stage on a desert island of discarded toys (which brings to
mind Smith's vision of a trash-heap metropolis combined with the 1960s
American Claymation classic *Rudolph the Red-Nosed Reindeer*), Olokun
opaquely elucidates his desire to find and commune with other freaks like
himself:

OLOKUN: All the freaks? Disappeared? They can't have disappeared.
Maybe they've gotten sad and have hidden away for a time.[94]

Mac's interpretation of the freak resonates with Michel Foucault's views on
insanity and how, as Chris Baldrick has summarized, "the freak must have
a purpose: to reveal the results of vice, folly and unreason as a warning to
erring humanity."[95] The "erring humanity" that Mac attempts to combat
in *Red Tide Blooming* is the conservative right wing. On a Candide-like
journey, Olokun encounters a cast of "citizens" who, declaring their dis-
taste for diversity, are led by the Collective Conscience, a sweater puppet
that condemns social subversion with Wizard of Oz–like brainwashing.
In short, the play warns of an impending Armageddon brought on by the
conformist agenda of the first decade of the twenty-first century.

Among the cast are the characters reveling in this satirical End of Days
are Lynne Cheney and Saddam Hussein. Cheney, who took part in the
construction of the Collective Conscience, has been thrown out of the
"upper echelons" because of her penchant for writing lesbian romance

novels and a secret love affair with Saddam Hussein. As expressed though the song "The Palace of the End," Hussein and Cheney rendezvous at his mythical execution, where they share a romantic moment through the viewing window of the poison gas chamber in which he is being executed. In opposition to the Bush regime's presentation of Hussein as the linchpin that holds together the "axis of evil,"[96] Mac controversially presents Hussein as tortured and misguided individual who is suffering from a psychosis brought on by repressed memories of child abuse. Furthermore, the character of Hussein is portrayed in Arabian Nights drag, another distinct reference to Smith's penchant for Middle Eastern glamour.[97] While the caricatures of Cheney and Hussein are extreme, Mac presents them with sympathy as two more uncomfortable freaks who are attempting to masquerade as normal.

This theme of the disenfranchised Other is reiterated toward the end of the play when the character of Constance Faubourg, an anxiety-ridden, germ-killing housewife who helps to manipulate the Collective Conscience (with Beep, a bearded lady as a male corporate cliché), exposes Olokun not as a hermaphrodite, but a transgendered nudist:

CONSTANCE FAUBOURG: (*To the audience and others.*) Don't let him fool you. He's not special. He's not different. He's not even a real hermaphrodite

BEEP: what?

CONSTANCE FAUBOURG: He just taped his dick to his ass so he could look like one.

COLIN: I knew it!

OLOKUN: Yes I did! (*Rips the duct tape off of his genitalia.*) I'm a freak *because* I did that! And what's more I'm not the only freak. (*Pointing to beep.*) That's a bearded lady. And it's not even a real beard. And you. Collin Clement. You. Come here. (*Slapping Collin's six-pack stomach.*)

That's not normal. (*To Constance.*) And you. You're a freak too. You're from the Bronx.

CONSTANCE FAUBOURG: (*With a heavy Bronx accent.*) Oh no he din't!

OLOKUN: I'm not the only freak. You're all freaks. (*Pointing to an audience member.*) You're a freak too! I slept with him. He's a freak. And you, look at you! I'm not the only freak. We're all—

(*Constance grabs a sword, the collective conscience holds Olokun's arms down, and Constance stabs Olokun.*)[98]

Olokun responds by ripping the duct tape from his genitals, disfigured through the act of fetishistic body modification as a symbolic expression of transidentity for the stage. This practice not only suggests an agency of choice, but also embodies a sort of physical deviance, what Michael Atkinson refers to as a "flesh journey: The process of intentionally constructing the corporeal in order to symbolically represent and physically chronicle changes in one's identity, thought, relationships or emotions."[99] After manifesting such a change in revealing his nude body (dyed an electric shade of green), a less-than-discreet metaphor for the baring of his soul, Olokun exposes the cast (as representative of the whole of society) for their own freakishness and for masking their individuality in an attempt to pass as normal.[100] Olokun specifically points to Colin Clement, a television weatherman-cum-celebrity whose overdeveloped muscular body suggests the gay subcultural aesthetic that developed in the late 1970s and early 1980s. Additionally, the comic bit concerning the exposure of Olokun's disfigured cock is drawn from Ludlam's *Bluebeard* (1970), in which the tortured title character struggles to create a third "gentler genital" representative of the third sex:

> BLUEBEARD: Love must be reinvented
> Sex to me is no longer mysterious
> And so I swear that while my beard is blue
> I'll twist some human flesh into a genital new.[101]

In the original production, the third genital is revealed at the end of the play, a chicken claw attached to an eggplant that protrudes from the crotch of the ingenue, Sybil. In a *New York Times* interview Ludlam explained that the third genital "means a synthesis of the sexes."[102] In the climate of post-Stonewall New York (*Bluebeard* premiered the year after the riots) the third genital was a less than subtle send-up of nontraditional sexual identity, gay, lesbian, and bisexual. Mac, on the other hand, uses his disfigured genital to represent role of transsexual and transgender identity in America, where these categories are still too often ignored in gay and lesbian politics. He carries through the trope of his signature fool as one who is at the same time natural and artificial, both born and made.

Unlike Ludlam, whose early works such as *Big Hotel* (1966) and *When Queen Collide* (1967) are rife with Hollywood stars, radio advertisements, and tongue-in-cheek product placement, in creating *RTB* as a neo-Ridiculous play, Mac avoided the use of pop-cultural references. Mac wanted to avoid this technique because of its inadvertent support of capitalist monopolies and institutions, exactly what he sees as the foundation for the Collective Conscience. In the opening scene a group of mermaids humorously discuss this exclusion:

> ATINA: We will redefine what a curse word is. Instead of a censored beep for words like fuck, fuck, fuck, and fuck—*corporations* and *pop cultural references* will be eradicated. For example:
> ALLANA: Hey Aquata what's your favorite pop star?
> AQUATA: Beep.[103]

The talents of choreographer Julie Atlas Muz and puppeteer Basil Twist supported the original frenetic production of *RTB*. Muz, a conceptual performer, burlesque artist, and choreographer, was awarded PS 122's Eichelberger prize the year following *Red Tide Blooming* in 2007. One of her most noted performance pieces is entitled *High Art at Low Tide*. The project features Muz dressed as a sea goddess named Julie La Sirena who swims in giant saltwater aquariums around the world, including a highly visible two-year run at the Coral Room in New York City. The mermaid continues to be a frequently used symbol for Mac's downtown family of freaks. The original Ridiculous appropriation of the mermaid into an iconic symbol can be traced to Jack Smith's *Normal Love* (1963), a film that opens with drag star Mario Montez in repose as the aquatic creature. Muz states that the purpose of her work is to "use humor, positive sexuality, and glamour to address serious topics."[104] The mermaid, a strangely contradictory figure that is associated with wanton sexuality without possessing genitalia, is an apt mascot for queer ambivalence, lending a mythic tone to nonnormative sexual desires, expressions, and performances.

Twist, on the other hand, is the first American ever to graduate from the Institut Internationel de la Marionnette in Charleville-Meizières, France. Drawing upon various forms and techniques of global puppetry, Twist introduces and advances new forms, including underwater puppetry. Mac and Twist's collaboration developed because they are both resident artists at HERE Arts Center.

Red Tide Blooming marked the first time that the media equated Mac with Ludlam's work. Phoebe Hoban of the *New York Times* noted that he "had taken a page from Charles Ludlam's Theatre of the Ridiculous,"[105] and Martin Denton credited him for turning the Ludlamesque "upside-down and inside-out."[106] The critical and popular success of *Red Tide*

Blooming secured Mac's identity as a contemporary Ridiculous performer, but it also gave him the confidence to bravely take his reinvention of the Ludlamesque beyond the site of its origin, attempting to expand his neo-Ridiculous community beyond New York City.

Best of the Be(a)st

Following the run of *RTB*, Mac returned to the format of a solo show with which he could tour widely and easily. Borrowing from the form of a traveling carnival, he transformed his fool into a wandering troubadour who was perhaps closest in character to Ludlam's Fool in *The Grand Tarot*. Mac's carnival world recalls Mikhail Bakhtin's theory of the carnivalesque, where participants are invited to live in a topsy-turvy world.[107] Through touring, Mac extended the queer world he created in *The Face of Liberalism* and *Red Tide Blooming*, expanding the boundaries of his fool society beyond New York City, where his earlier shows had taken place.

The Be(a)st of Taylor Mac, which premiered at Edinburgh's Fringe Festival in 2006, revolves around Mac with his ukulele, a trunk of costumes, and the war cry "The revolution will not be masculinized," (playing off of Gil Scott Heron's funk song-poem "The Revolution Will Not Be Televised" from 1971) which is also the title of the opening song.[108] At various times during its two-year run in over forty theaters around the globe, Mac dedicated performances of *The Be(a)st* to victims of hate crimes and violence spurred by their sexuality or sexual identity. For example, at the performance of the show on Valentine's Day of 2008 in San Francisco, Mac dedicated the show to Lawrence Fobes King, a transgender teenager who was shot in the head and killed in a classroom at his high school in Oxnard, California. This sympathetic and jarring technique sets the stage for an evening of life-affirming yet brutal honesty.

In exploring his role in the vast and complicated globalization of the world today, Mac discusses everything from past lovers to national security to masturbation to manatees in *The Be(a)st*. At one point, in attempting to express his own (poly)sexuality, Mac reveals:

I want to be a mermaid, merman, mermanaid.[109]

Not only does this intentionally connect back to Smith, the Coney Island Mermaid Parade, Muz, and *RTB*, it also expresses a chimerical identity that is nonhuman, nongendered, and physically without genitalia. The mermanmaid symbolically represents the anti-identitarian action of ungendering, allowing Mac a freedom of choice to dictate a fluid identity, rather than one based on a normative binary of cissexuality; he colloquially refers to this act as the radical process of "embracing all pronouns."[110] Although the show is filled with nods, winks, and pastiched reference like the mermaid, Mac challenges critics to review his show without making comparisons to other works (a bit of tongue-in-cheek queer ambivalence made manifest).

Mac traces the meandering and often episodic plot of the piece by quickly changing garments onstage, creating a metaphoric and physical presence. At the conclusion of the show the space is littered with the garments and accessories that Mac has thrown off, creating a multilayered art piece-cum-archive that records the evening's unique performance. In transforming the theater into a *Wunderkammer* adorned with strewn-about costumes, props, and errant sequins and glitter, Mac marks the audience as an extension of the carnival space. By the end of the performance, audience members are no longer merely observers, but belong to the world that has been created, a diasporic society of fools with Mac as its colonizer.

The Be(a)st is altered to varying degrees from performance to performance with the addition of local and timely references and discussion with the audience, Mac says:

> I like doing *Be(a)st* still because it's an ever-changing show and I can take numbers out and put new numbers in. I can do whatever I really want to. . . . It's a very political show, and I have to adjust a lot of things—so that's an ever-growing process. It's really fun to play it, 'cause there's a lot of freedom in the show, and it's this piece that kind of exploded for me where I got to go into the world and perform.[111]

Regardless of these alterations and additions, Mac closes each evening's performance of *The Be(a)st* with his communal-bonding, signature hymn, "Fear Itself," which has gained a larger audience since Mac granted Broadway veteran Mandy Patinkin permission to perform the song at his concerts. The nature of the song is to reveal Mac's own hang-ups in an uncertain world and is a presentational throwback to the folk songs of the Stonewall era. Just as folk music was immersed into mainstream culture, Patinkin's non-Ridiculous interpretation of the song gives it a broader context and scope, though it also paradoxically dissolves much of the subversive anti-commercialization behind Mac's original version. As the lights come up in the auditorium, the audience—now a chorus—is encouraged to view the attending others in a new light, as Mac attempts to ignite a spark of *communitas*. This act of transformation from distanced observer to engaged participant, which Jill Dolan describes as "moments in the perpetual present," marks the emergence of a new and fleetingly utopic community, while still encouraging autonomy and individuality among audience members.[112]

We Are Young

Beginning to explore both his individual experiences and emotions with *The Be(a)st*, Mac went one step farther and developed his most personal and autobiographical performance, *The Young Ladies of . . .* in 2007. Several boxes of letters that Mac's father, Lt. Robert Mac Bowyer, received while stationed in Vietnam inspired the play. The correspondence came from single women after Bowyer placed a singles advertisement in the back of the Australian *Daily Telegraph* in 1968. Bowyer died in a motorcycle accident when his son was four, and this play is Mac's lyrical attempt at creating a tangible interpretation of his father though the words and memories suspended in thousands of letters. Mac also revisits the hyper-masculine rites and traditions of his father's family (including losing one's virginity to a whore at the age of sixteen), which he was denied. In the play, which Leonard Jacobs referred to as "neo-Dada for Da Da,"[113] Mac desires to "discover some common ground" and "bridge the gap" between his deceased father and himself.[114]

The play takes place in a fantastical limbo of postmarked envelopes and stage fog where Mac's fool persona matures, trading youthful abandon for a self-awareness born of experience. Mac's transformation from Petit de Julleville's *jeunesse* into an adult is set in motion when he is isolated from the society that he created for himself to inhabit in his earlier plays. The play revolves around the theme of "The Carousel Waltz," from Rodgers and Hammerstein's *Carousel* (1945). *Carousel* was Bowyer's favorite film, which results in Mac equating his father with the rough-and-tumble character of Billy Bigelow:

> I imagine my father's favorite character in the movie musical *Carousel* was the central character of the wife beater. No, not the t-shirt but the

actual person. Bill, that's his name. And Bill was a tough macho kinda guy, as wife-beaters tend to be. . . . Through some deductive reasoning skills I have pieced together a few ideas as to the kind of man he was. For example: why I imagine Robert's favorite character was the central character of the wife beater is, well, he came from a tough, Texan, conservative, macho, military, farm family who would brag of their faggot bashing stampedes and who would use the biblical reference of Rib to refer to their wives: I quote, "Hey Rib, gimme a beer." And because of this I've come to assume, I've come to assume my father, like his father and brothers, was a bit rough trade. And not in a homoerotic way. And that perhaps we wouldn't have that much in common.[115]

The role of the absent father is a common one in the Ridiculous tradition. Ludlam's father constantly insulted his effeminate son and refused to see him perform on stage, even at the height of his success. Busch's father was also absent. As a widower he left his gay son to be raised by his sister-in-law, turning to alcohol and the company of women. Although the theme of the strained relationship between a hypermasculine father and gay son is a common theme in the shared American gay experience, Mac is the first Ridiculous artist to tackle it in performance, and Mac's refreshing approach is one of genuine curiosity rather than prescribed daddy bashing.

Mac brilliantly weaves together poignant soul-searching in the heartfelt quest to better understand his absent father with classic Ridiculous conventions. For example, after revealing his discovery of the letters to the audience, Mac performs a comic ballet where thousands of letters are thrown at him in gargantuan mailbags from all directions before pummeling him from the "sky." This bit requires him to emerge from a large pile to continue the performance, literally materializing from memories of the past. His immediate reaction is a dryly delivered:

MAC: My thong fell off.[116]

The scripted onstage adjustment of the bra he is wearing as a thong and the brief flash of his genitals plays into an improvisatory "anything can happen" recklessness while also reaffirming his male sexuality, in contrast to his sartorial deconstructed gender as represented in the dress, wig, makeup, and loads of glitter that he is wearing. Ironically the most poignant drag that Mac sports is found not in his feminine garments, but rather in his "trying on" of the identity of a son with a present father.

Mac continues to use the letters as the modus operandi better to understand the ghosts of his family. Rather than creating impromptu vignettes from the diverse content, Mac attempts to connect the similarities in the letters to paint a picture of his dad. To achieve this he channels the silent voices of the assorted Australian women who originally composed the letters. In transforming himself into these various women, Mac explores the desires, fears, needs, and loneliness in the faceless voices that are attempting to anxiously reach across time. This becomes a metaphor in Mac's final epistle to Bowyer—one in which the answer can only be extracted from the cultural artifacts of the past.

In another segment Mac incorporates one of Smith's favorite theatrical conventions: a Camp slide show to further demonstrate the schism between Mac and Bowyer. Mac shows a slide of "Dad with a boy toy" (an aged photograph of Bowyer holding a rifle) and then "Me with a boy toy" (where Mac calls upon an attractive young man from the audience to join him onstage). He continues to juxtapose pictures of his father in aggressively masculine situations with those of himself in drag and often in explicit poses. Mac playfully uses this segment to comment not only on his own feelings of disconnection with his father regarding sexuality and generational codes, but also wryly to reduce the battle of the definition of terms that plays so heavily into the debate for gay and lesbian rights. The slide show presents photographs that embody essentialist stereotypes around gender and masculinity for the audience to consider in relation to Mac's genderfuck aesthetic. In contrast to the stereotypical cissexual traits projected, he wears opaque-white Pierrot-like face paint, a Baby Jane wig, and a dirty and tattered dress, reminiscent of a unisexual christening gown, which suggests an androgynous and desexualized identity. The juxtaposition of this almost childlike aesthetic with the aforementioned weary experience of the displaced fool makes for a complex and inherently queer figure, as the ungendered Mac inhabits both his past and present in one body.

Finally, Mac reveals his goal for the project, which constitutes a performative letter to his father:

MAC: Dear Bob,

I am writing in response to your advertisement, which was in the Daily Telegraph dated May 6th, 1968 asking for Australian girls to write you. I am not an Australian but I am called "girl" by many people who know me. I'm thirty-four years old. The same age you were, when you crossed the yellow divider line and smashed head on into the on-coming traffic . . .

I just want us to be better. I have created this, for you, so that we could hate each other a little less. So that we could be better. So that you can have your one chance to come down and fix this. But what are you going to do with that chance? Hit me so hard I can't feel it at all? Write me a letter to make up for the lifetime of letters I've sent you, the 20,000 letters from lonely ladies . . .[117]

Though *TYLO* is Mac's very public search for his enigmatic father, in the end Mac begins to realize that as his stage persona he is as much an enigma himself. Mac begins to grasp that from his own vantage he is just as judgmental and opinionated as the larger-than-life oppressive masculinity that his gun-toting father symbolizes. This becomes a performative act of self-criticism, questioning his own intolerance for his father's beliefs that he marks as prejudiced and bigoted. This groundbreaking play is an opportunity for Mac to share generously and attempt to understand his own feelings of abandonment, disloyalty, and loss, and thus is also his metaphor for the state of the country under the Bush regime:

> MAC: Oh, by the way, for the two percent of the audience members who grew up with loving, stable, present fathers, you may be thinking, "Yet another father play that I can't relate to." If you could just do me a favor and every time I talk about dad, if you could just think of another conservative Texan, one in your life, who functions in a sort of absent father role—you're gonna relate just fine.[118]

In true Ridiculous form, Mac relies upon the letter not only for his concept, but also for his praxis: the letters become puppets, masks, and finally a dress that Mac gleefully sports in a grand dance to the "Carousel Waltz." This approach brings Ludlam's common practice of recycling trash into Camp-infused beauty to a more sophisticated level that is rich in symbolism and sentiment. During the course of the run, Mac used a program note to invite audience members to send in letters to the theater, a proposal that was successful in exponentially increasing the piles of mail onstage and physically representing a network of collective belonging. This technique of creative recycling also forms a queer archive, which Halberstam defines as "not simply a repository; [but] also a theory of cultural relevance, a construction of collective memory, and a complex record of queer activity."[119] Mac actualizes this notion by creating a physical legacy of the voices in the text, but also of many who attended the performance. As a continuation of this trope, the climactic gesture of donning the paper dress of letters revives Mac's spirit from his state of melancholy reflection; draped in the epistolary correspondence of his queer family in the form of a garment bearing the handwriting of dozens of contributors, he escapes from the limbo-like world of the play in this new suit of armor, dragging the train of letters behind and reciting the mantra, "I hope. I hope. I hope. I hope."[120]

The poignant coherency and quality of these works attracted the attention of New Dramatists, which awarded Mac a playwright residency (2007–14). This position ushered in a new artistic phase for Mac, providing an extended period of sustained funding that would allow him to subsist solely as a professional playwright and performer. It was at New Dramatists that Mac collaborated with librettist Edward Ficklin to create *The Holy Virgin Mary of Our Time*, a one-act musical comedy that parodies the Brooklyn Museum's controversial exhibit of Chris Ofili's *The Holy Virgin Mary*, a large mixed-media painting of Christ's mother that includes elephant dung in its composition. Although the play has never been produced outside of a workshop, the subject matter, parodying Catholic symbolism and iconography, was a favorite of Smith, Tavel, and Ludlam, who all professed to love the church's incense-infused liturgical pageantry but hated a doctrine that promoted an antigay, bigoted morality. This is another example of how the Ridiculous developed as arched version of tradition forms of ritual, performance, and theater.

Mac not only represents a distinct incarnation of the Ridiculous theater that first embodies frustrating and complex social issues connected to post-9/11 American identity, but also creates work that encourages audiences to dialogue and debate. Because Mac's public appearances are often in his signature and extreme drag, he highlights the normality and parallels of average citizens both gay and straight, in contrast to his consciously eccentric aesthetic. By taking on the persona and image of the fool, Mac becomes what Ludlam described as a "holy fool," one who refuses to be taken seriously, allowing room for individual spectatorship and analysis.[121] Though in his daily life Mac is a slight and handsome man in "boy drag," he checks his ego and donates his performances to an agenda of universal sympathy and egalitarianism. Mac's maxim "never [to] erase" allows him to examine honestly social injustices without judgment.[122]

Mac's fool persona has matured into a sophisticated cultural mouth-piece through practice, growing popular support, and recognition of its artistic value. The development of Mac as fool is fundamental to under-standing his revival of the Ridiculous sensibility by reshaping Ludlam's legacy as a reflection of the contemporary world. Although as a theatrical form the Ridiculous broke down the walls of concealment through the act of public performance, at its origin it constituted a safe space that al-lowed freedom of expression without fear of homophobic discrimination. For this reason, the Ridiculous legacy has not been broadly accessible, but has instead been disseminated and transformed through internal chan-nels of self-defined kinship.[123] Mac has extended such alternative chan-nels of transmission by bringing his fool society to new locations and audiences, inviting a more diverse group of queers and queer allies into the neo-Ridiculous fold. Rather than trying to reproduce the work of its originators, Mac has used the queer legacy of the Ridiculous to pick up from where they left off. This approach has allowed him to maintain and transform the past within the present via performance, avoiding revival-ism and upholding the Ridiculous as a genre with continued relevance as a mode for building a supportive community.

Epilogue

Since 2007, Mac's career has experienced a meteoric rise that resembles Ludlam's long-term reign of the West Village, but magnified to extend globally from Europe to Australia. Although Mac has always maintained his mission to make good art, his work has been embraced both popularly and critically, making him an undeniable commercial success. This has developed, in part, because Mac is incredibly productive, continuing to write and devise his own shows while also appearing in several produc-tions for other companies.

In 2009 Mac performed his postmodern Noh play titled *The Lily's Re-venge* with a cast of over 40. The production, more than four hours long, loosely follows the classical Japanese theater form's five-act structure, but is inspired thematically by Proposition 8, the 2008 California amendment that ruled gay marriage as illegal. As the title character of Lily, a flower that uproots itself to break free from the prison of the past, Mac takes a theatrical journey that challenges constructs of nostalgia, tradition, and time. *The Lily's Revenge* premiered at Manhattan's HERE Arts Center and won the 2010 Obie Award, before other productions were mounted in San Francisco, New Orleans, and Cambridge, Massachusetts, sponsored in part by a grant from the Massachusetts Council of Art. These various productions of *Lily* would take up a majority of Mac's time for the next four years.

As Mac continued to develop *Lily*, he simultaneously toured his solo concert: *Comparison Is Violence: The Ziggy Stardust meets Tiny Tim Songbook* (2010). The work, which allowed him to tour with minimal props, in contrast to the gigantic *Lily* production, was inspired by frequent comparisons of his performances to both Tiny Tim and David Bowie. Parallels had been drawn to Mac's use of the ukulele (Tiny Tim) and his glittered gender-bending appearance (Bowie as Ziggy Stardust). When I attended this performance in Brisbane, Australia, in February 2011, I was surprised to see that it had been falsely advertised as a drag review by the Australian press. As a result, the audiences were small and relegated to an older generation of queers, expecting a glamour drag cabaret of old standards. Instead Mac presented a pastiche of Tiny Tim and Bowie songs, recycled to highlight how vastly different he is in performance from his predecessors and structured around the theme of comparison as an act of violence. The same year Mac premiered his new play, *The Walk Across America for Mother Earth* (2011) through La MaMa at the Ellen Stewart Theatre in the East Village. Inspired by a nuclear protest walk in which Mac once took part, the play reimagines iconic, if not stereotypical, protesters as commedia dell'arte stock types and continuing the Ridiculous tradition of the clown through Mac's interpretation of the fool. *Walk Across America* was reviewed glowingly in the *New York Times,* with Charles Isherwood noting that this production marked Mac as "establish[ing] himself as a writer and artist of serious consequence."[124] I find this particularly interesting, because in a casual conversation Mac professed to me that he was lukewarm about the play, and was considerably more engaged in the continuation of *Lily,* which he considered his best work to date. I mention this only because it is the prime example of how an affective reaction can overpower a more traditional critical response when one tracks the development of his career as both an artist and a queer advocate.

In 2012 Mac was invited to play the dual-gender role of Shen Te / Shui Ta in the Foundry Theatre's production of Brecht's *The Goodperson of Szechwan* (completed in 1943), directed by Lear DeBessonet. This particular production originally opened at La MaMa before being transferred to the Public Theater, with perpetual Mac supporter Isherwood declaring it "a highlight of the theatre season."[125] Brecht's play, structured around the reconciliation of the sexes (the female as a metaphor for altruistic socialism and the masculine as a symbol for capitalist greed), provided the perfect opportunity for Mac to showcase his expertise at postmodern drag, and by playing a role originally intended for a woman Mac updates the performance to inherently comment on gender as a mode of performance as delinked from biological concepts of sexuality. Mac's period of artistic productivity capped off with a mainstream appearance with Mandy Patinkin in a cabaret titled *The Last Two People on Earth* (2013–15), as he garnered accolades including Future Legend of the New York Stage from *Time Out NYC* (2012) and Best Theater Actor of New York City from the *Village Voice* (2013).

Prolonging his miniature *age d'or*, Mac donned his hat as playwright when his original script of *Hir* (2014), a comic study of a suburban house where Maxine is transitioning to Max, a female-to-male transsexual. The play opened at San Francisco's Magic Theatre under the direction of Niegel Smith, receiving rave reviews and two sold-out extensions. The play also had a hugely successful run with a new cast at Manhattan's Playwrights Horizons in the fall of 2015. Never one to slow down, Mac's current project, *A 24-Decade History of Popular Music*, has replaced *Lily's Revenge* as his largest and most ambitious to date. Inspired by hope for a new, queerer America in the twenty-first century, Mac started to question the traditions and superstitions that have been woven together to form the cultural fabric of contemporary America since its founding in 1776. Working off this premise, Mac began to formulate a series of one-hour concerts that considered each of the twenty-four decades. The shows, performed separately, cleverly consider each period in a truly Ridiculous fashion. For example, the 1820s is a "Blind Show," with audience members blinded in homage to Louis Braille, who first developed his tactile writing system for the visually impaired in 1824. The 1900–1910 concert, on the other hand, considers Yiddish songs and monologues that were popular in New York's Jewish tenements at the turn of the century, and the 1990s hour is dedicated to queer butch lesbian anthems. Maintaining his stage-worthy fool character, Mac weaves together traditional period songs before critically unpacking their role in the cultural zeitgeist of the selected period. For example, in his 1980s concert, Mac sings Laura Branigan's 1982 anthem "Gloria," presenting it as the last song ever written that is completely without irony. He uses the concept of the unironic as a metaphor for the facade of propriety that the Reagan administration used to gild over social issues, like the

AIDS crisis. In performance, the song becomes an invocation to exorcise the conservative superstitions of the period, repeated throughout until the audience sings in unison with Mac at the conclusion. In January 2015 Mac premiered a six-hour version of the concert from 1900 to 1960 at New York Live Arts as part of the Under the Radar Festival. This was a precursor for October, 2016, when Mac performed an epic marathon concert of all twenty-four decades in twenty-four hours at St. Ann's Warehouse in Brooklyn, New York.

While Mac's career had been enveloped, elevated, and celebrated by the mainstream, his mission remains rooted in creating avant-garde, socially conscious art. After completing a new theater manifesto titled *I Believe* in 2013, inspired in part by Ludlam's original Ridiculous manifesto, Mac began using "judy" (lowercase) as a gender pronoun to describe his performative, stage-worthy fool character. judy states:

> I believe, as a theater artist, I'm not telling you anything you don't already know. Because I believe, as a theater artist, I'm not a teacher; I'm a reminder. I'm just trying to remind you of things you've dismissed, forgotten, or buried.[126]

This notion of returning to the past ties directly into Mac's Ludlamesque roots. It is demonstrative of queerness as a timeless method of being and doing that remains deeply hidden between normative and antinormative identities, until it is extracted and reshaped by artists like him. Mac has not changed the stage-worthy judy's mission to create meaningful art, but he continues to transition and has convinced an ever-growing cultish audience to change along with judy, eagerly anticipating what will come next, synonymously engaging in the past and future, Janus like, while firmly rooted to a queer present.

Epilogue

Paradigms of Queer Legacy, Heritage, and Influence

We're born naked, and the rest is drag.
—RuPaul

Wildely Influential

In his popular monograph *The Anxiety of Influence: A Theory of Poetry*, Harold Bloom reminds us that Oscar Wilde cheekily wrote of his inescapable bondage to influence in a letter to poet Richard Eberhart:

> I sympathize with your denial of any influence on my part. This sort of thing always jars me because, in my own case, I am not conscious of having been influenced by anybody and have purposely put off reading highly mannered people so that I should not absorb anything, even unconsciously.[1]

Here Wilde acknowledges the authoritative power of influence to affect the subconscious and thereafter impinge upon an individual's thinking or actions. Influence, Bloom suggests, is as old as the cosmos and the "divine afflatus" of the heavens, and is an inescapable force to be reckoned with.[2] In order to combat the magnitude of influence, Bloom endorses a misreading or *clinamen* of extant text and sources to germinate new and original ideas. While Bloom's sweeping theory takes into account the effects of knowledge, identity, and contemporary culture on the author, he completely ignores other affective, sensual, and psychological forces that may influence an artist, paying no heed to the biographical details of the poets in favor of reading the texts in a theoretical vacuum. In the

Figure 7. Charles Ludlam in his dressing room, probably before a production of *Salammbo* (c. 1985). Photographer: Sylvia Plachy. Courtesy of Laurence Senelick and the Laurence Senelick Collection.

model of queer legacy that I have proposed in the previous chapters, this canonical and unabashedly patriarchal approach just doesn't work. Taylor Mac, for example, discovered the Ridiculous aesthetic through the influence of media-generated images and references to the Ludlamesque without knowing at the time who Ludlam was or what he represented. It was only when Mac went in search of Ludlam and his work that he acknowledged this influence and self-consciously propelled himself to be a part of Ludlam's direct legacy. Legacies, like this one, are in a constant state of change. Busch, Louryk, and Mac all continue to develop as queer artists, not to mention all of the secondary artists that laterally intersect each of the narratives.

Queer legacies are the legacies of queers—genealogies of individuals who self-identify as openly queer (often LGBT) and live outside of normative binaries of gender and sexuality. Such self-defined queer legacies combat the mainstreaming and appropriation of queer culture by maintaining internal crisscrossing channels of transmission; however, due to this self-preservationist exclusivity, sanitized historical narratives too often subsume them. Though queer legacies may never achieve hegemonic dominance (nor is it their mission), they do offer alternative "model[s] of contestation [and] rupture" that are preserved through their self-generated inaccessibility.[3] Halberstam refers to such archives as "repressed," but I would argue that he overlooks the importance of the furtive, esoteric, and even occultic nature of this sort of queerness. It acts as a preservative that in turn allows for a complete subversion of the original form without erasing it, a sort philosophical palimpsest materialized—theoretical metaphors of rooms that remained locked, forgotten, and undisturbed for dozens of years. The creation of such spaces follow Foucault's notion of temporal heterotopia, spaces of otherness that allow for interplay and overlap, and I believe for a sort of leakage, by means of which a queer individual can inhabit several spaces at one time, both normative and antinormative, as well as the gap between.[4] Following this theme, Ahmed argues that it is sexual orientation that affectively creates bodies that "leak into worlds."[5] I read this across individual bodies, collective bodies, and bodies of work. I suggest that the droplets of memory potentially left by such "leakage," when painstakingly connected dot to dot in any number of complex patterns, form the frameworks of queer archives and resultant legacies. I love the metaphoric image of water droplets that preserve and cloud the past while also tacitly reflecting the present and future, necessitating careful examination and archiving before they evaporate and are lost forever. This method is also inspired by Ahmed's quest to investigate "what sticks," though, as demonstrated by the admittedly tangential exploration of this project, I am also equally interested in attempting to reparatively recover what didn't stick or was made obsolescent.[6] Muñoz suggests that such surreptitious archives are "fiction[s]" that have been produced as representative works to "cope with" and, I would add, manipulate or even retaliate against, modes of "socially prescribes straightness."[7] This approach, inclusive of all queer experiences and moreover perspectives (even if contradictory and objectivist), inadvertently recalls Edward Albee's statement that "fiction is fact distilled into truth."[8] Queer truths (often oral histories) and the archives that record them produce queer legacies that are self-selected, extended, and expanded, but are also often forgotten, hidden, or lost.

To understand legacy as a discourse it is also necessary to dissect the concept of heritage. A legacy is something that is passed down from ancestor to successor (whether an object or a tradition). It also bears the connotation of a gift. This is may be a gift of experience and skill that serves to inform the individuals to whom the legacy has been left. Thus Ludlam's heirs have been bequeathed a legacy that is both gay and theatrical. Heritage, on the other hand, denotes a piece of property or a tradition that is inherited through a birthright. The suggestions of ancestral inheritance speak to the gay community as "family," a slang term that developed within the urban gay community as both a mockery and an embrace of normative structures. The concept of "gay family" refers broadly to the entire community as well as the small family units originally developed in urban centers where newly arrived young gays were taken in and mentored by their peers, predecessors, and elders. Oftentimes these family units were formed around affinities, shared interests, or sexual tastes.[9] For example, Jennie Livingston's iconic (but also controversial) documentary film *Paris Is Burning* (1990) follows such gay families (therein termed "houses") that are built on African American and Latino roots and participation in the drag ball competitions and culture of New York City. Perhaps more importantly the drag balls and drag families of *Paris Is Burning* show remarkable similarities in their uses of artifice, fantasy, and reinvention of self (both corporeally and spiritually) to (re)create versions of the truth that trump the limitations of biological reproduction and socially normative decorum. Other films like Monika Treut's *Gendernauts* (1999) and Gabrielle Baur's *Venus Boyz* (2002) offer alternative queer families structured around performance in the style of Livingston's groundbreaking film.

The Ludlamesque Ridiculous and neo-Ridiculous family is, in fact, built on the same principle as other queer family units, and their mode of sharing and expressing gayness is through the medium of the theatrical process and performance, rich with tradition and connections to the past. Ater Ludlam's death and the end of the Ridiculous Theatrical Company, Ludlam's family legacy became conceptual rather than physical. Charles Busch reinvented himself as a "diva," whose reduction of the Ludlamesque in the 1980s provided escapism in a dire time and led to the premiere of a Ridiculous play on Broadway. Bradford Louryk is a "medium" that channels underrepresented queer voices of the midcentury (including Ludlam) as commentary on the paradigm of intellectualism and gentrification in contemporary New York. Taylor Mac is the "fool" who uses his body as the canvas to examine the role of art after 9/11 and, furthermore, the identity of gay Americans in a culture of contradictions and change. These three gay auteurs embody the Ludlamesque by criticizing their lives in the broader context of the twenty years after Ludlam's death. My attempt to cultivate a particular and admittedly minoritarian history that focuses on gay men living and working in the same area as Ludlam does not intend to exclude the universalizing possibility for future studies on Ridiculous offshoots by women, people of color, the differently abled, or other groups that have experienced oppression and/or disenfranchisement and unite under the banner of queer.

The role of the queer family and its inability to reproduce is, in fact, the central argument of Lee Edelman's controversial book *No Future: Queer Theory and the Death Drive*, and admittedly the specter that has haunted my work through the entire process of attempting to introduce the notion of a distinctly queer form of legacy.[10] Working against the notion of queer cultural production as a subversive act, Edelman suggests that it is the inability for queers to breed that gives them political agency and hence a heightened sort of self-awareness. This embrace of the negative forms a diametrical dichotomy through the process of severing, in turn driving a wedge between the normative and the antinormative, the practical and the theoretical, and the personal and the political. While I am supportive of such work that attempts to move us beyond the foundational but now old-fashioned if not essentialist "queer is singularly (fill in the blank) rhetoric," Edelman's notion of queer as defined by its biological limits completely ignores the productive gap between such binaries—what I have argued is the very center of ambivalent queer production and genealogy. Edelman's concept of the death drive is beautifully illustrated in his textual examples, but, as I hope this book corroborates, the inability to reproduce is, in fact, the spark for new, alternative, and queer modes of startling cultural productivity and subsequent approaches to ensure not only kinetic queer perpetuation but also regeneration.

The Ludlamesque Ridiculous sensibility has influenced many performers, but just because a performer is influenced consciously, subconsciously, or inadvertently by one or many Ridiculous tenets or characteristics does not necessarily make him part of a greater Ridiculous legacy. Kaufman points to Bette Midler, Buster Poindexter, Christopher Durang, Paul Rudnick, and Tony Kushner as all having acknowledged an influence from Ludlam. While the influence is clear, and all of these artists have produced distinct and undoubtedly queer works, their approaches have verged away from the Ludlamesque. Kenneth Yates Elliot dedicates an entire chapter of his dissertation to the Broadway production of *Hairspray* (2002) as a neo-Ridiculous work. While *Hairspray* includes Ridiculous conventions such as drag, Camp, and kitsch, it lacks a sense of encoded self-recognition and subversion to explore gay issues and themes at the time of its creation. It bears the influence of Ludlam because the tradition was passed through John Waters and the original film of *Hairspray* (1988). Thus, a sort of recessive gene exists in the Ridiculous legacy that allows for such inspired works to exist beyond Ludlam's direct lineage. While Ludlam's Ridiculous heirs branch out from him in the aforementioned model, "Ridiculous-like" works float around but are not connected to the web of gay sensibility.

The root of this modern gay sensibility begins with Wilde over a century ago. Of this Ludlam wrote:

> Wilde set the tragedy of woman's sexuality, which is synonymous with homosexuality. Both risk the possibility of rejection by the male. . . . Just as the male or female cells carry within them sexually determining factors, so too the individuals, regardless of sex, carry within them both sets of sexual characteristics, to pass on to their progeny or for their own use in self-realization. The ability to recognize opposites in ourselves is the basis of art, and definitely [my] drama. It is part of imagining and imitating. Few people dare to enact their fantasies in art; fewer dare to realize them in the flesh.[11]

According to Wilde's theory that "a true artist annexes everything," Ludlam used pastiche and Camp as his tools to create a revolutionary personal style that rejected the status quo and celebrated gayness. It was Ludlam who took the Ridiculous from its humble and often messy beginnings and perfected it into a form of American art that is on par with the major movements of modernist theater.

Revivals do not constitute legacy. Productions of or inspired by Ludlam's plays are fairly commonplace (particularly *Irma Vep*, which is a popular piece for repertory companies, like Quinton's 2014 revival in New York City), but they are merely imitations. Revivals or recreations of Ludlam's plays honor the memory of the auteur, but are completely averse to Ludlam's goal to create a theater that was representative of *his* time. By *his* time Ludlam was stressing that theater should reflect the sociocultural events of the period in which it was written, often using anachronistic historical periods and bizarre situations to magnify them. Furthermore, Ludlam reflected *his* time through his own lens, that of an openly gay man during the period of sexual liberation. He defined the purpose behind his mission in writing:

> [The Ridiculous theater] is a theatre that gives a forum to widely express unpopular nonconformist points of view, thereby preserving a spirit of independence and the importance of the individual.[12]

Ludlam's individualism is grounded in his homosexuality. His approach to gayness in both the aesthetic and concept of the theater was as a safe space: "Gay people have always found refuge in the arts, and the Ridiculous is notable for admitting it. The people in it never dream of hiding anything about themselves that they feel is honest and true."[13] Thus, the original RTC was a forum for gay expression without proselytizing or attempting to convert the audience. While Ludlam was hardly arguing for people to come out of the closet, his theater invited people into a closet of queer fantasy and performance. Gay became normalized at the RTC, and as raucous and wild as the early shows were, there was a sense of calm in contrast to the riots erupting on the streets. Though the basic form of the Ridiculous remains primarily the same, social changes and personal tastes alter its current (and ever changing) appearance. Because the sometimes sporadic and liberal nature of the independent artistic process may overlook its place in the family tree of a genre (like the Ridiculous), it is the responsibility of the theater historian to untangle the paradoxes and critically analyze this transcendence of time in order to make a concrete record of a given theatrical legacy. To watch a neo-Ridiculous play and grasp its Proustian subtext is to reconnect viscerally with origins of the gay liberation movement and the intricate connections between politics, queerness, and art.

Legacy usually appears as a theoretical model based on genealogy, implying a temporal and linear structure that passes influence from one generation to the next (through a variety of implicit and explicit sources). I argue that an Aristotelian web or an Adornean constellation provides a better model with which to trace and record queer legacy. While Busch, Louryk, and Mac all can be traced back to Ludlam's original sensibility (though they are not necessarily germinated from the original seed, but rather paper blossoms glued to the embryonic vine) and share an identity as creators of the neo-Ridiculous genre, each is unique in his artistic approach and independent mission. As the next generation of Ridiculous performers develop, subsets of Ridiculous sensibilities will continue to spread out and grow the web, both building on and subverting their predecessors, while still firmly rooted to Ludlamesque origins. Because, as I have suggested, queer legacies are ambivalently formed between the gaps of the seen and not seen, the obvious and the subtle, the sacred and the profane, and because queer time moves in all directions, I'm left to ponder if the discussion of queer legacies must be extended to consider alternate dimensions as sites of queer production. This process, which is reliant on that which cannot be seen, is clarified by Anna Henchman's quest to "imagine what other minds might be like."[14] I hope that this work serves as what Muñoz deems "an invitation, a performative provocation" for other scholars of queer theater and queer theory to explore and perhaps more importantly negotiate these unseen, unknown, and sometimes untenable sites between "sexual meaning and symbolic investment."[15] These are the very sites that make up the complex ambivalent structures on which I suggest we can start to build queer genealogies, using queer legacy as a methodological approach.[16] As this work continues I'm left to return to the concept of queer kinesis and ask: How, where, and when does queerness move, and how then do we trace such movement? How can the trace of queer migration shed light on different modes of queerness and queer performance in a globalizing and ever-changing world?

Notes

Prologue

Source of epigraph: Charles Ludlam, "Manifesto," in *Ridiculous Theatre: Scourge of Human Folly. The Essays and Opinions of Charles Ludlam*, ed. Steven Samuels (New York: Theatre Communications Group, 1992), 157. Hereafter cited as *Scourge of Human Folly.*

    1. Ludlam's other plays are *Big Hotel, Conquest of the Universe, The Grand Tarot, Eunuchs of the Forbidden City, Corn, Hot Ice, Stage Blood, Tabu Tableaux, Caprice, Jack and the Beanstalk, Der Ring Gott Farblonjet, The Ventriloquist's Wife, Utopia Incorporated, The Enchanted Pig, Elephant Woman, A Christmas Carol, Reverse Psychology, Love's Tangled Web, Secret Lives of the Sexists, Exquisite Torture, Le Bourgeois Avant-Garde, Salammbo, Galas, The Artificial Jungle,* and *How to Write a Play.* See *The Complete Plays of Charles Ludlam* (New York: HarperCollins, 1989).

    2. Many of these essays appear in Ludlam, *Scourge of Human Folly.*

    3. Diana Taylor, "Performance and/as History," *TDR* 50, no. 1 (2006): 67.

    4. Ann Pellegrini, "Touching the Past; or, Hanging Chad" *Journal of the History of Sexuality* 10, no. 2 (2001): 185.

    5. Martha Fleming, *Studiolo: The Collaborative Works of Martha Fleming and Lyne Lapointe* (Windsor: Artextes Editions and the Art Gallery of Windsor, 1997), 22.

    6. Arthur Evans, *Witchcraft and the Gay Counterculture* (Boston: Fag Rag Books, 2014), 14–15.

    7. Billy J. Harbin, Kim Marra, and Robert A. Schanke, *The Gay and Lesbian Theatrical Legacy: A Biographical Dictionary of Major Figures in American Stage History in the Pre-Stonewall Era* (Ann Arbor: University of Michigan Press, 2005), 1.

    8. Jennifer Moon, "Gay Shame and the Politics of Identity," in *Gay Shame*, ed. David M. Halperin and Valerie Traub (Chicago: University of Chicago Press, 2009), 368.

Introduction

Source of epigraph: Phillip Core, *Camp: The Lie That Tells the Truth* (London: Plexus, 1984), 1.

    1. Friend of Dorothy, or FOD for short, was common slang exchanged between

gay men in midcentury America, leading to encoded references around Oz, including dandy lions, ruby slippers, good witches, and heel clicking. The opening of this section is inspired by the stylish crafting of language by Ludlam in his plays, with "fuck-me pumps" originating in his *Conquest of the Universe / When Queens Collide* (1968). William Leap and Tom Boellstorf, *Speaking in Queer Tongues: Globalization and Gay Language* (Champaign: University of Illinois Press, 2003), 98.

2. David Kaufman, *Ridiculous! The Theatrical Life and Times of Charles Ludlam* (New York: Applause, 2002), 121.

3. While Mac's gender in performance is "judy," his day-to-day gender pronoun remains male or ambiguous, so I have used *he/him* throughout the manuscript unless referring specifically to "judy" in performance.

4. James M. Harding and Cindy Rosenthal, *Restaging the Sixties: Radical Theaters and Their Legacies* (Ann Arbor: University of Michigan Press, 2006).

5. Manny Farber coined the phrase *underground film* and introduced it in *Commentary* (November 1957). He describes it as "the hard bitten action film finds its natural home in caves; the murky, congested theatres, looking like glorified tattoo parlors on the outside and located near bus terminals in big cities." Parker Tyler, *Underground Film: A Critical History* (New York: DaCapo Press, 1995), vi. Smith referred to his loft as the "Plaster Foundation" because of a large pile of plaster of paris that he had spread in the midst of the space to act as an impromptu stage. For more on Smith see Edward Leffingwell, Carole Kismaric, and Marvin Heiferman, eds., *Flaming Creature: Jack Smith, His Amazing Life and Times* (London: Serpent's Tale, 1997).

6. While Ludlam is using "daddy" to infer influence, there is also a double entendre with the "daddy" as a fetishized sexual conquest. Stefan Brecht, *Queer Theatre* (Frankfurt am Main: Suhrkamp, 1978), 28.

7. Robert Thomas Wharton III, "The Working Dynamics of the Ridiculous Theatrical Company: An Analysis of Charles Ludlam's Relationship with His Ensemble from 1967–1981," Ph.D. diss., Florida State University, 1985, 186.

8. Sean Edgecomb, "A History of the Ridiculous, 1960–1987," *Gay and Lesbian Review Worldwide* 14, no. 3 (2007): 21–22.

9. José Esteban Muñoz, *Cruising Utopia: The Then and There of Queer Futurity* (New York: New York University Press, 2009), 171.

10. Although Jack Smith's theatrical work was arguably the first to introduce the genderfuck aesthetic as early as the late 1950s, the term was not introduced until 1974, in Christopher Lonc's article "Genderfuck and Its Delights," *Gay Sunshine* 21 (Spring 1974): 225 (quoted in David Bergman, *Camp Grounds: Style and Homosexuality* [Amherst: University of Massachusetts Press, 1993], 7). While the founders of the Ridiculous were experimenting with the aesthetic as introduced by Smith in mid-1960s New York, in San Francisco the Cockettes, a group of psychedelic, polysexual hippies who presented original performances in the city's North Beach neighborhood, were also engaging in public cross-gendered play. After the Cockettes completed a tour of New York City (in which they were critically panned), they influenced Jimmy Camicia and Ian Mckay to found the Hot Peaches, a genderfuck troupe in the East Village with a West Coast sensibility. See David Weber and David Weissman, *The Cockettes* (Culver City, CA: Strand, 2002), and "Centola, the Hot Peaches," in Brecht, *Queer Theatre*, 112–24.

11. David Román, *Acts of Intervention: Performance, Gay Culture and AIDS* (Bloomington: Indiana University Press, 1998), 136.

12. For a thorough historical biography of Ludlam (including his relationships and collaborators) see Kaufman, *Ridiculous!*.

13. Gautam Dasgupta, "Interview: Charles Ludlam," *Performing Arts Journal* 3, no. 1 (1978): 78.

14. Kaufman, *Ridiculous!*, xii.

15. Ludlam, *Scourge of Human Folly*, 261.

16. Hilton Als, "Freaks: The Characters of Charles Ludlam and John Steinbeck," *New Yorker*, April 28, 2014, 78–79.

17. Ludlam, *Scourge of Human Folly*, 228.

18. Bonnie Marranca and Gautam Dasgupta, preface to *Theatre of the Ridiculous* (Baltimore: Performing Arts Journal Publications, 1989), xiv.

19. Mel Gussow, "Ludlam's Consistently Amusing Linguistic Conceits," *New York Times*, May 5, 1970.

20. Kaufman, *Ridiculous!*, 277.

21. Ludlam, *Scourge of Human Folly*, 254.

22. Jordan Schildcrout, *Murder Most Queer* (Ann Arbor: University of Michigan Press, 2015), 80.

23. Schildcrout, *Murder Most Queer*, 256.

24. Jill Dolan, *Utopia in Performance* (Ann Arbor: University of Michigan Press, 2005), 11–15.

25. Lee Edelman, *No Future: Queer Theory and the Death Drive* (Durham, NC: Duke University Press Books, 2004), 17–25.

26. Muñoz, *Cruising Utopia*, 1.

27. For a critical review of Camp in relation to Ludlam's oeuvre see Rick Roemer, "Ridiculosity in Theory," in *Charles Ludlam and the Ridiculous Theatrical Company: Critical Analyses of 29 Plays* (Jefferson, NC: McFarland, 1998), 41–64.

28. Ludlam, *Scourge of Human Folly*, 225, 13.

29. Cynthia Morrill, "Revamping the Gay Sensibility: Queer Camp and Dyke Noir," in *The Politics and Poetics of Camp*, ed. Moe Meyer (New York: Routledge, 1993), 110–29.

30. Sigmund Freud, "The Uncanny," in *The Standard Edition of the Complete Psychological Works of Sigmund Freud*, vol. 17, trans. and ed. James Strachey (London: Hogarth Press, 1955), 243.

31. Core, *Camp*, 1.

32. Eve Kosofsky Sedgwick, *Epistemology of the Closet* (Berkeley: University of California Press, 2008), 155.

33. Isherwood's mention of Camp (albeit brief) is largely seen as the springboard for studies of Camp that followed, including Susan Sontag and Phillip Core. Christopher Isherwood, *The World in the Evening* (London, Methuen, 1954), 125.

34. Janet Staiger, "Finding Community in the Early 1960s," in *Queer Film Cinema: The Film Reader*, ed. Harry Benshoof and Sean Griffin (New York: Routledge, 2004), 167.

35. Martin P. Levine, *Gay Macho: The Life and Death of a Homosexual Clone* (New York: New York University Press, 1998), 70.

36. Muñoz, *Cruising Utopia*, 62.

37. "Gay is good" was one of the first widespread slogans of the gay liberation movement. It was introduced in 1968 Mattachine Society founder Frank Kameny as a riff on the popular "Black is beautiful."

38. Ludlam, *Scourge of Human Folly*, 226.

39. Kevin Kopelson, *Neatness Counts: Essays on the Writer's Desk* (Minneapolis: University of Minnesota Press, 2004), 19.

40. Margaret E. Gray, *Postmodern Proust* (Philadelphia: University of Pennsylvania Press, 1992), 152.

41. "Every reader finds himself. The writer's work is merely a kind of optical instrument that makes it possible for the reader to discern what, without this book, he would perhaps never have seen in himself." Marcel Proust, *Swann's Way*, trans. C. K. Scott Moncrieff (New York: Modern Library, 2004), 163–64.

42. Gray, *Postmodern Proust*, 9.

43. Wharton, "Working Dynamics," 285.

44. Marranca and Dasgupta, *Theatre of the Ridiculous*, viii.

45. Kate Davy, "Fe/male Impersonation: The Discourse of Camp," in *Critical Theory and Performance*, ed. Janelle G. Reinelt and Joseph R. Roach (Ann Arbor: University of Michigan Press, 1992), 364.

46. Jodie Taylor, *Playing It Queer: Popular Music, Identity and Queer World-Making* (Bern: Peter Lang, 2012), 73.

47. On didactic theater Bertolt Brecht suggested, "*The audience in the epic theatre says*: I wouldn't have thought that.—People shouldn't do things like that.—That's extremely odd, almost unbelievable.—This has to stop.—This person's suffering shocks me, because there might be a way out for him.—This is great art: nothing in it is self-evident. I laugh over the weeping, I weep over the laughing." From Bertolt Brecht, "Theatre for Learning," in *The Brecht Sourcebook*, ed. Henry Bial and Carol Martin (London: Routledge, 2000), 23.

48. "FUBU," an acronym meaning "for us / by us," was first introduced by African American scholar and activist W. E. B. DuBois. His original manifesto also included exhortations "about us" and "near us." "Krigwa Players Little Negro Theatre," *Crisis*, July 1926.

49. Kenneth Yates Elliott, "Beyond the Ridiculous: The Commercialization of an Alternative Theatre Movement from Jack Smith to *Hairspray*," Ph.D. diss., UCLA, 2004, 104.

50. Ludlam, *Scourge of Human Folly*, 234.

51. Judith Halberstam, *The Queer Art of Failure* (Durham, NC: Duke University Press, 2011), 19, 70.

52. Brecht, *Queer Theatre*, 77.

53. Core, *Camp*, 1.

54. Halberstam, *Queer Art of Failure*, 3.

55. Ludlam, *Scourge of Human Folly*, 98.

56. Michael Bronski, *Culture Clash* (Boston: South End Press, 1984), 191.

57. George Chauncey, *Gay New York* (New York: Basic Books, 1994), 229.

58. Jack Babuscio, "The Cinema of Camp," in *Gay Roots: Twenty Years of Gay Sunshine. An Anthology of Gay History, Sex, Politics and Culture*, ed. Winston Leyland (San Francisco: Gay Sunshine Press, 1991), 431.

59. Ludlam, *Scourge of Human Folly*, 148–50.

60. James Bidgood, interview by the author, November 20, 2006.

61. Román, *Acts of Intervention*, 99.

62. Fabio Cleto, ed., *Camp: Queer Aesthetics and the Performing Subject. A Reader* (Ann Arbor: University of Michigan Press, 1999), 90.

63. Richard Schechner, *Public Domain: Essays on the Theatre* (New York: Avon Books, 1969), 211.

64. Laurence Senelick, *The Changing Room: Sex, Drag and Theatre* (New York: Routledge, 2000), 427.

65. Calvin Tompkins, "Profiles: Ridiculous," *New Yorker*, November 15, 1976, 83.

66. Roemer, *Charles Ludlam*, 93.

67. Ludlam, *Complete Plays*, 121.

68. Richard Schechner, "Two Exemplary Productions," *Village Voice*, April 23, 1970.

69. Schechner, "Two Exemplary Productions."

70. Ludlam, *Scourge of Human Folly*, 221.

71. Gregory W. Bredbeck, "The Ridiculous Sound of One Hand Clapping: Placing Ludlam's 'Gay Theatre' in Space and Time," *Modern Drama* 39, no. 1 (1996): 64–83.

72. Bredbeck, "Ridiculous Sound," 65.

73. Ludlam, *Complete Plays*, 135.

74. I fully acknowledge the implications of queer fat politics that are inherent in Pashalinski's performance of Miss Cubbidge, but for the sake of focus, I will not investigate them in this particular study.

75. Ludlam, *Scourge of Human Folly*, 25.

76. Kaufman, *Ridiculous!*, 128.

77. One may refer to the documentary film *Gay Sex in the 70s* for an excellent introduction to the tie between gay liberation and promiscuity in 1970s New York. DVD, directed by Josh F. Lovett (New York: Wolfe Video, 2006).

78. Wharton, "Working Dynamics," 272.

79. Split Britches, "Beauty and the Beast," *Hemispheric Institute Digital Video Library—Split Britches video collection*, accessed May 13, 2013, http://hidvl.nyu. edu/video/000539386.html

80. Marranca and Dasgupta, *Theatre of the Ridiculous*, 78.

81. Elenore Lester, "Camille," *New York Times*, July 14, 1977.

82. Misha Berson, "A Moving and Funny Camille," *San Francisco Bay Guardian*, February 28, 1990.

83. Ludlam, *Complete Plays*, 246.

84. Senelick, *Changing Room*, 428.

85. Roemer, *Charles Ludlam*, 99.

86. Patricia Julian Smith, introduction to *The Queer Sixties* (New York: Routledge, 1999), xv.

87. Bidgood, Interview.

88. Daniel Harris, "The Death of Camp: Gay Men and Hollywood Diva Worship, from Reverence to Ridicule," *Salmagundi* 112 (1996): 166–91.

89. Ludlam passed away on May 28, 1987, at St. Vincent's Hospital, Manhattan, after suffering with AIDS-related pneumonia.

Chapter 1

Source of epigraph: Jean Cocteau, "Le paquet rouge," in *Opéra: Oeuvres Poétiques* (Paris: Delamain et Boutelleau, 1927), 540.

1. The Ridiculous theater should not be confused with the theater of the absurd. While absurdism grew out of existentialist disenchantment in post–World War II Europe, the Ridiculous was a distinctly American form responding to the cultural climate of 1960s New York City. As exhibited in works by Ionesco, Beckett, Genet, and Pinter, absurdism strives to expose the meaninglessness of human existence through the breakdown of language, whereas the Ridiculous is an extravagant, self-consciously chaotic celebration of excessive language originating in a theatrical gay sensibility. Edward Albee, whose distinctly American absurdism considers American consumerism and isolationism in the beatnik generation, may well be the link between the two forms.

2. Dennis Hevesi, "Ronald Tavel, Proudly Ridiculous Writer, Dies at 72," *New York Times*, March 27, 2009.

3. Erica Bentley, "The Ladies in Question: Drag Crosses Over," *TheatreWeek*, April 23, 1990.

4. Ludlam, *Scourge of Human Folly*, 242.

5. Sedgwick, *Epistemology of the Closet*, 1.

6. Deborah B. Gould, "The Shame of Gay Pride in Early AIDS Activism," in *Gay Shame*, ed. David M. Halperin and Valerie Traub (Chicago: University of Chicago Press, 2009), 221–55.

7. Muñoz, *Cruising Utopia*, 170.

8. Muñoz, *Cruising Utopia*, 118.

9. David Román, *Performance in America: Contemporary U.S. Culture and the Performing Arts* (Durham, NC: Duke University Press, 2005), 1.

10. Annamarie Jagose, *Queer Theory* (Melbourne: Melbourne University Press, 1996), 5.

11. Lee Edelman, *Homographesis: Essays in Gay Literary and Cultural Theory* (New York: Routledge, 1994), 114.

12. A distinct urban gay culture also developed in San Francisco synonymously with New York's queer renaissance. Though linked in spirit, they largely remained separate movements with distinct styles and aesthetics. See Susan Stryker, Jim Van Buskirk, and Armistead Maupin, *Gay by the Bay: A History of Queer Culture in the San Francisco Bay Area* (San Francisco: Chronicle Books, 1996); Jack Fristcher, *Gay San Francisco: Eyewitness Drummer* (Sebastopol, CA: Palm Drive Publishing, 2008), and the fictional *Tales of the City*, series also by Maupin (New York: Harper Perennial, 1978–2014).

13. Eve Kosofsky Sedgwick, *Between Men: English Literature and Male Homosexual Desire* (New York: Columbia University Press, 1992), x.

14. Jill Dolan, *Geographies of Learning: Theory and Practice, Activism and Performance* (Middletown, CT: Wesleyan University Press, 2001), 94; and Robin Bernstein, *Cast Out: Queer Lives in Theatre* (Ann Arbor: University of Michigan Press, 2006), 7.

15. Judith Halberstam, *In a Queer Time and Place: Transgender Bodies, Subcultural Lives* (New York: New York University Press, 2005), 10.

16. Feminist scholars who helped to formulate the critical mass of queer theory in-

clude Judith Butler, Eve Kosofsky Sedgwick, Lauren Berlant, Adrienne Rich, and Diana Fuss.

17. Harding and Rosenthal, *Restaging the Sixties*, 13.

18. Harding and Rosenthal, *Restaging the Sixties*, 16.

19. Jill Dolan, "Building a Theatrical Vernacular: Responsibility, Community, Ambivalence and Queer Theatre," *Modern Drama* 39, no. 1 (1996): 2.

20. Eve Kosofsky Sedgwick, *Tendencies* (Durham, NC: Duke University Press, 1993), 8.

21. This is an attempt that acknowledges that the ambiguous nature of queerness belies a singular practicable definition, and more than likely embodies a variety of possible definitions.

22. Taylor Mac's 2011 cabaret show *The Ziggy Stardust Meets Tiny Tim Songbook* is subtitled *Comparison Is Violence*.

23. Homi Bhabha, *The Location of Culture* (New York: Routledge, 2004), 85.

24. Ludlam, *Scourge of Human Folly*, 263.

25. Halberstam, *Queer Art of Failure*, 70.

26. Halberstam, *Queer Art of Failure*, 2.

27. Halberstam, *Queer Art of Failure*, 2–3.

28. Claude Lévi-Strauss, *The Elementary Structures of Kinship*, trans. James Harle Bell, John Richard von Sturmer, and Rodney Needham (Oxford: Eyre and Spottiswoode, 1969), 484.

29. David L. Eng, *The Feeling of Kinship: Queer Liberalism and the Racialization of Intimacy* (Durham, NC: Duke University Press, 2010).

30. Kath Weston, *Families We Choose: Lesbians, Gays, Kinship* (New York: Columbia University Press, 1997).

31. Gayle Rubin, *Deviations: A Gayle Rubin Reader* (Durham, NC: Duke University Press, 2011), 300.

32. Esther Newton, *Margaret Mead Made Me Gay: Personal Essays, Public Ideas* (Durham, NC: Duke University Press, 2000), 230.

33. Muñoz, *Cruising Utopia*, 123.

34. Corinne P. Hayden, "Gender, Genetics and Generation: Reformulating Biology in Lesbian Kinship," *Cultural Anthropology* 10, no. 1 (1995): 52.

35. Elizabeth Grosz, "Histories of a Feminist Future," *Signs* 25, no. 4 (2000): 1019.

36. For more on queer optimism see Michael D. Snediker, *Queer Optimism: Lyric Personhood and or Her Felicitous Persuasions* (Minneapolis: University of Minnesota Press, 2008), 3–15.

37. Joseph Roach, *Cities of the Dead: Circum-Atlantic Performance* (New York: Columbia University Press, 1996), 281.

38. Ramón H. Rivera-Servera, *Performing Queer Latinidad: Dance, Sexuality and Politics* (Ann Arbor: University of Michigan Press, 2012), 28.

39. Jacques Derrida, *Writing and Difference*, trans. Alan Bass, London, Routledge, 1978), 23.

40. Sara Ahmed, *The Cultural Politics of Emotion* (New York: Routledge, 2004), 11.

41. Michael Warner, *Public and Counterpublics* (Brooklyn: Zone Books, 2002).

42. Román, *Acts of Intervention*, 142.

43. Elizabeth Freeman, "Time Binds, or, Erotohistoriography," *Social Text* 23, nos. 3–4 (2005): 57–58.

44. Judith Butler, *Gender Trouble: Feminism and the Subversion of Identity* (New York: Routledge, 2006).

45. Carolyn Dinshaw, *Getting Medieval, Sexualities and Communities, Pre- and Postmodern* (Durham, NC: Duke University Press, 1999), I.

46. Erin O'Connell, *Heraclitus and Derrida: Presocratic Deconstruction* (New York: Peter Lang, 2005),75.

47. Roach, *Cities of the Dead*, xi.

48. Jacques Derrida, *Specters of Marx*, trans. Peggy Kamuf (New York: Routledge, 2006), 63.

49. Fredric Jameson, "Marx's Purloined Letter," in *Ghostly Demarcations: A Symposium on Jacques Derrida's "Spectres de Marx"*, ed. Michael Sprinkler (London: Verso, 1999), 39.

50. David Savran, *A Queer Sort of Materialism: Recontextuaizing American Theatre* (Ann Arbor: University of Michigan Press, 2003), 93.

51. Muñoz, *Cruising Utopia*, 169.

52. Harding and Rosenthal, *Restaging the Sixties*, 16.

53. Nayland Blake, "The Message from Atlantis," in Leffingwell, Kismaric, and Heiferman, *Flaming Creature*, 183.

54. Ahmed, *Cultural Politics of Emotion*, 11; Sara Warner, *Acts of Gaiety: LGBT Performance and the Politics of Pleasure* (Ann Arbor: University of Michigan Press 2012), 3.

55. Kathryn Bond Stockton, *The Queer Child, or Growing Sideways in the Twentieth Century* (Durham, NC: Duke University Press, 2009), 3.

Chapter 2

Source of epigraph: Charles Busch, *Whores of Lost Atlantis* (New York: Carroll and Graf, 2005), 2.

1. Dinshaw, *Getting Medieval*, i.

2. Halberstam, *Queer Time*, 10.

3. Dolan, *Geographies of Learning*, 94.

4. Halberstam, *Queer Art of Failure*, 70.

5. Muñoz, *Cruising Utopia*, 123.

6. Román, *Acts of Intervention*, xxix.

7. Ann Cvetkovich, *An Archive of Feelings: Trauma, Sexuality and Lesbian Public Cultures* (Durham, NC: Duke University Press, 2003) 1.

8. Ernst Bloch, *The Spirit of Utopia* (Stanford, CA: Stanford University Press, 2000), 11.

9. Ronald Tavel, "Maria Montez: Anima of an Antediluvian World," in Leffingwell, Kismaric, and Heiferman, *Flaming Creature*, 92.

10. Ronald Sullivan, "In City, AIDS Affecting Drug Users More Often," *New York Times*, October 1, 1984.

11. Elliott, "Beyond the Ridiculous," 196.

12. Román, *Acts of Intervention*, 1–21.

13. I am using the lowercase c for "camp" because this is in reference to Tavel and Vaccaro's approach, previous to Ludlam.

14. Marranca and Dasgupta, *Theatre of the Ridiculous*, 20.

15. Benedict Anderson, *Imagined Communities: Reflections on the Origin and Spread of Nationalism* (New York: Verso, 2006), 224.

16. Mary Bernstein, "Celebration and Suppression: The Strategic Uses of Identity by the Lesbian and Gay Movement," *American Journal of Sociology* 103, no. 3 (1997): 531.

17. Verta Taylor and Nancy E. Whittier, "Collective Identity in Social Movement Communities," in *Frontiers in Social Movement Theory*, ed. A. D. Morris and C. McClurg (New Haven: Yale University Press, 1992), 105.

18. Gregg Bordowitz, *The AIDS Crisis Is Ridiculous and Other Writings, 1986–2003* (Cambridge: MIT Press, 2006), 2.

19. Ludlam, *Scourge of Human Folly*, 248.

20. Bronski, *Culture Clash*, 42.

21. Andrew Holleran, "The Spectacle at the Bottom of the Shaft," *New York Native*, May 23, 1983.

22. Charles Busch, *The Tale of the Allergist's Wife and Other Plays* (New York: Grove Press, 2001), xi.

23. Elliott, "Beyond the Ridiculous," 150.

24. Senelick, *Changing Room*, 432.

25. Elliott, "Beyond the Ridiculous," 185.

26. Artist Keith Haring rose to prominence in this period for his fluid, socially conscious, and often-homoerotic line drawings just as countertenor Klaus Nomi became the rising star of the East Village neovaudeville scene. Both gay men like Busch, Haring and Nomi epitomize the sort of contemporary artists that rose to fame during the period due to the gentrification of the neighborhood. Both would succumb to AIDS before the end of the decade.

27. Cynthia Carr, "The Hot Bottom: Art and Artifice in the East Village," in *On Edge: Performance at the End of the Twentieth Century* (Middletown, CT: Wesleyan University Press, 1993), 51.

28. Elliott, "Beyond the Ridiculous," 173.

29. Charles Busch, interview by the author, July 8, 2008.

30. Busch, interview.

31. John Kelly, email to author, May 2, 2008.

32. Kelly, email to author, May 2, 2008.

33. *The Cockettes*, DVD, directed by David Weissman and Bill Webber (New York: Strand Releasing, 2003).

34. The Pyramid Club first opened on Avenue A in the West Village and quickly became the center of the performance-art drag scene of the period. *Village Voice* columnist Michael Musto described the Pyramid Club as "a ramshackle place where struggling artists could take chances, make fools of themselves, and create beautiful work . . . a springboard for some talent that eventually went more mainstream, as well as just a place where anyone with some nerve could nab a spotlight and some onlookers." Patrick Hedlund, "Push to Make Pyramid Club City's First Drag Landmark," *Villager*, last accessed July 16, 2014, http://thevillager.com/villager_241/pushtomake.html

35. The biography reads as follows: "John Kelly is Dagmar Onassis, the Greek Ameri-

can contralto who graced the stages of clubs and cabarets from New York City to Berlin in the early 1980s. Ms. Onassis has been hailed as a 'singer of endless depths who spins a web of magic, allowing it to hang in the air for those few precious and tense moments before it pierces our hearts and leaves its imprints on our souls.' Dagmar is the daughter of a diva from our past, the great niece of Marcel Duchamp's Rose Selavy. A long-time fan of the singer describes Dagmar's performance as 'a visceral dream, a manifestation of emotion crystallized through sound.' Her repertoire includes arias and songs by Scarlatti, Cavalli, Monteverdi, Bellini, Boito, Purcell, Schumann, Mahler, Weill, and Negro Spirituals." Donn Russell, *Avant-Guardian, 1965–1990: A Theater Foundation Director's Twenty-Five Years Off Broadway* (Pittsburgh: Dorrance, 1996), 428.

36. Russell, *Avant-Guardian*, 428.

37. Senelick, *Changing Room*, 434.

38. Stephen Whittle, "Gender Fucking or Fucking Gender," in *Queer Theory*, ed. I. Morland and A. Wilcox (New York: Palgrave Macmillan, 2005), 117.

39. Kelly, email to author, May 2, 2008.

40. Kelly, email to author, May 2, 2008.

41. Kelly, email to author, May 2, 2008.

42. John Kelly, "John Kelly Performance," last accessed June 23, 2013, http://johnkellyperformance.org/wp2/?page_id=59

43. Kelly, email to author, May 2, 2008.

44. Busch, *Tale of the Allergist's Wife*, ix.

45. On watching Ludlam's *Camille* Busch remembers: "I saw that and it was just the end—or rather the beginning. I just knew the Garbo film so well and suddenly there he was doing this and with so little effort with physicality making us believe that he was this dazzling creature." Busch, interview.

46. Busch, interview.

47. Busch, interview.

48. Kaufman, *Ridiculous!*, 241.

49. J. Hoberman and Jonathan Rosenbaum, eds., *Midnight Movies* (New York: Harper and Row, 1983), 37.

50. Tavel, "Maria Montez," 92.

51. *The Lady in Question Is Charles Busch: A Drag to Riches Story*, DVD, directed by John Cantania and Charles Ignacio (New York: Docurama, 2006).

52. Busch, interview.

53. Busch, interview.

54. The Chicago chapter of the Ridiculous theater is largely ignored in theater scholarship and demands more work. Busch, interview.

55. Busch, interview.

56. Busch, interview.

57. Busch, interview.

58. Busch, interview.

59. Busch, interview.

60. Kaufman, *Ridiculous!*, 98–99.

61. Busch, interview.

62. Busch, interview.

63. Busch, interview.

64. Senelick, *Changing Room*, 410.

65. Richard Niles, "Charles Busch and Theatre-in-Limbo," Ph.D. diss., City University of New York, 1993, 162.

66. Tompkins, "Profiles: Ridiculous."

67. Pashalinski would perform in *Vampire Lesbians* only for the first weekend; she would be replaced by Julie Halston, a longtime member of Theatre-in-Limbo who continues to work with Busch in theater and film today.

68. Busch, interview.

69. Busch, interview.

70. Many of Smith's fantastical and exotic landscapes were inspired by the B movies of the 1930s and 1940s, and particularly those featuring his idol, Maria Montez.

71. David Wilkerson, *The Vision* (Old Tappan, NJ: Fleming H. Revell, 1974), 50–51.

72. Mary Fink, "AIDS Vampires: Reimagining Illness in Octavia Butler's 'Fledgling,'" *Science Fiction Studies* 37, no. 3 (November 2010): 416.

73. Thomas L. Long, *AIDS and American Apocalypticism: The Cultural Semiotics of an Epidemic* (Albany: State University of New York Press, 2005), 21.

74. Charles Busch, *Vampire Lesbians of Sodom*, in *Tale of the Allergist's Wife and Other Plays*, 7.

75. Busch, *Vampire Lesbians of Sodom*, 10.

76. Nowhere was this more evident than when Calvin Klein in Times Square in 1983 unveiled a huge billboard of the nearly naked Brazilian Olympic pole-vaulter Tom Hintnaus, who had been photographed by noted gay photographer Bruce Weber. Clad only in white briefs and leaning against a white phallic tower, the sexually charged homoerotic image of Hintnaus became an instant icon, something to strive for. Gay pornographic films followed suit, and soon the actors who had once been cast primarily for their endowments had to sport ripped abdominals and pumped-up pectorals and biceps to stay employed.

77. Taylor, *Playing It Queer*, 55.

78. Admittedly the desirability of the vampire as a gay cult figure comes to the fore long after Busch's reign in the East Village in postmillennial works across different forms of media. Entire panels have been dedicated to the topic at the Popular Studies Association Conference, focusing on works including (but not limited to) Stephanie Meyer's *Twilight* series and the resultant film adaptations; HBO's homoerotic *True Blood*, based on *The Southern Vampire Mysteries* by Charlaine Harris; and gay icon Buffy the Vampire Slayer.

79. Kaufman, *Ridiculous!*, 407.

80. Ludlam, *Scourge of Human Folly*, 19.

81. Ludlam, *Scourge of Human Folly*, 254.

82. Laurence Senelick, "The Word Made Flesh: Staging Pornography in Eighteenth-Century Paris," *Theatre Research International* 33, no. 2 (2008): 194.

83. Busch, *Vampire Lesbians of Sodom*, 23.

84. Busch, interview.

85. Busch, *Vampire Lesbians of Sodom*, 32.

86. Elliott, "Beyond the Ridiculous," 192.

87. Cleto, *Camp*, 92.

88. William Leap, ed., *Beyond the Lavender Lexicon: Authenticity, Imagination and Appropriation in Lesbian and Gay Language* (Buffalo: Gordon and Breach, 1995), 1.

89. Don Kulick, "Gay and Lesbian Language," *Annual Review of Anthropology* 9 (2000): 246.

90. Busch, *Vampire Lesbians of Sodom*, 32.

91. D. J. R. Bruckner, "Stage: *Vampire Lesbians of Sodom*," *New York Times*, June 20, 1985.

92. Kaufman, *Ridiculous!*, 361.

93. Ben Brantley, "Charles Busch Takes on a Trouser Role," *New York Times*, November 3, 1994.

94. Brantley, "Charles Busch."

95. Busch, interview.

96. Busch, interview.

97. Busch, interview.

98. Busch, interview.

99. See Daniel Boyarin, Daniel Itzkovitz, and Ann Pellegrini, *Queer Theory and the Jewish Question* (New York: Columbia University Press, 2003).

100. Nicole Neroulias, "Gay Jews Connect Their Experience to Story of Purim," *Washington Post*, February 24, 2007.

101. Neroulias, "Gay Jews."

102. Neroulias, "Gay Jews," B08.

103. "Linda Richman Sketches," *Saturday Night Live*, last accessed June 12, 2014, http://www.nbc.com/saturday-night-live/cast/mike-myers-15006/character/linda-richman-16071

104. Ben Brantley, "A Woman on the Verge of Another Breakdown," *New York Times*, March 1, 2000.

105. Busch, interview.

106. Busch, *Tale of the Allergist's Wife*, 52.

107. "Coffee Talk," *Wikipedia*, last accessed June 12, 2014, https://en.wikipedia.org/wiki/Coffee_Talk

108. Charles Busch, *Die Mommie, Die!* (New York: Samuel French, 2010), 22.

109. Busch, *Die Mommie, Die!*, 31.

110. Busch, interview.

111. Busch, *Psycho Beach Party*, in *Tale of the Allergist's Wife*, 47.

112. Busch, interview.

113. Busch, interview.

114. Don Shewey, "Review: Our Leading Lady," *Advocate*, May 2007.

115. Shewey, "Review: Our Leading Lady."

Chapter 3

An earlier book chapter that helped to inspire this chapter was published in 2009: *"We Will Be Citizens": New Essays on Gay and Lesbian Theatre*, ed. James Fisher (Jefferson, NC: McFarland, 2008).

1. Grosz, "Feminist Future," 1019.

2. Román, *Performance in America*, 1.

3. Jagose, *Queer Theory*, 5.

4. Davy, 361.

5. Savran, *Queer Sort of Materialism*, 93.

6. Bradford Louryk, interview by the author, February 22, 2006.

7. Ray Cashman, "Critical Nostalgia and Material Culture in Northern Ireland," *Journal of American Folklore* 119, no. 472 (2006): 137–60.

8. Cashman, "Critical Nostalgia," 138.

9. Although Louryk often plays women in his work, his interpretation of drag is not uniquely dependent on female impersonation (as is more traditional cabaret drag performance). Louryk's use of drag is closer to Esther Newton's description in her essay "Mother Camp: Female Impersonators in America." Judith Butler reiterates this in her essay "Imitation and Gender Insubordination," writing: "drag is not an imitation or copy of some prior and true gender; according to Newton, drag enacts the very structure of impersonation by which *any gender* is assumed. Drag is not the putting on of a gender that belongs to some other group, i.e. an act of expropriation or appropriation that assumes gender is the rightful property of sex . . . it implies that all gendering is a kind of impersonation and approximation." *The Judith Butler Reader*, ed. Sarah Salih with Judith Butler (Malden, MA: Blackwell, 2004), 127.

10. Davy, 361.

11. Ludlam, *Scourge of Human Folly*, 221–24.

12. Ludlam, *Scourge of Human Folly*, 65.

13. Louryk, interview.

14. Kenneth Yates Elliott offers an excellent definition of the Ridiculous theater in the context of this purpose: "[The Ridiculous] expos[ed] the ridiculousness of dominant culture. It often did so by parodying high and/or low literary and theatrical forms of the past, especially pop culture. It was a non-illusionistic, self-conscious performance style marked by camp, cheap theatrics, the grotesque, sexual ambiguity and drag performances. Its founders were gay men, and the theatre they created was a direct assault on the mainstream values of the time." Elliott, "Beyond the Ridiculous," vii–viii.

15. Charles Ludlam wrote, "The Ridiculous is really about rugged individualism. It didn't come out of any communal, left-wing, sentimental, folksy thing." *Scourge of Human Folly*, 14.

16. Louryk, interview.

17. Marranca and Dasgupta, *Theatre of the Ridiculous*, 79.

18. Søren Kierkegaard, "Journals 1835," last accessed May 4, 2010, http://www.age-of-the-sage.org/philosophy/kierkegaard.html

19. Warner, *Acts of Gaiety*, 2.

20. Norman Bryson, "Todd Haynes' *Poison* and Queer Cinema," *In[]visible Culture: An Electric Journal for Visual Studies*, last accessed April 12, 2013, http://www.rochester.edu/in_visible_culture/issue1/bryson/bryson.html. Bryson derives the concept of minoritarian thinking in part from Whitney Davis's groundbreaking *Studies in Gay and Lesbian Art History* (New York: Haworth Press, 1994).

21. Bryson, "Todd Haynes' *Poison*," 2.

22. Bryson, "Todd Haynes' *Poison*," 2.

23. Michael Warner, ed., *Fear of a Queer Planet: Queer Politics and Social Theory* (Minneapolis: University of Minnesota Press, 1993), xi.

24. Louryk, interview.

25. Gabrielle Cody, email to the author, October 18, 2007.

26. Cody, email to the author, October 18, 2007.

27. Louryk, interview.

28. Rob Grace, email to the author, September 14, 2007.

29. Ludlam, *Scourge of Human Folly*, 64.

30. Louryk, interview.

31. Louryk, interview.

32. Rob Grace and Bradford Louryk, *The Tragedy of Hamlet, Prince of Denmark*, unpublished manuscript, 1999 (available directly through the authors).

33. This also may be read as an homage to one of Ludlam's earliest Dada-type plays titled *Southern Fried Chekhov*.

34. Marranca and Dasgupta, *Theatre of the Ridiculous*, 82.

35. Ludlam, *Scourge of Human Folly*, 19.

36. Joe E. Jeffreys, "Ethyl Eichelberger," in *Extreme Exposure: An Anthology of Solo Performance Texts from the Twentieth Century*, ed. Jo Bonney (New York: Theatre Communications Group, 2000), 72.

37. Louryk, interview.

38. Helene Foley, "Bad Women: Gender Politics in Late Twentieth-Century Performance and Revision of Greek Tragedy," in *Dionysus since 69: Greek Tragedy at the Dawn of the Third Millennium*, ed. Edith Hall (Oxford: Oxford University Press, 2004), 97.

39. Joe E. Jeffreys, "An Outre Entrée into the Para-Ridiculous Histrionics of Drag Diva Ethyl Eichelberger: A True Story," Ph.D. diss., New York University, 1993, 85.

40. Foley, "Bad Women," 96.

41. Rob Grace and Bradford Louryk, *Klytaemnestra's Unmentionables*, original unpublished manuscript (available directly through the authors).

42. Roemer, *Charles Ludlam*, 101.

43. Grace and Louryk, *Klytaemnestra's Unmentionables*, 13.

44. Grace and Louryk, *Klytaemnestra's Unmentionables*, 13.

45. "Ethyl Eichelberger," *PS122.org*, last accessed June 12, 2013, http://www.ps122.org/eichelberger/

46. Louryk, interview.

47. Marvin Carlson, *The Haunted Stage: The Theatre as Memory Machine* (Ann Arbor: University of Michigan Press, 2001), 1.

48. Ludlam, *Scourge of Human Folly*, 68.

49. Foley, "Bad Women," 96.

50. Senelick, *Changing Room*, 398–99.

51. Roemer, *Charles Ludlam*, 101.

52. Louryk, interview.

53. Maureen Connor, "Review: *Fashion and Fetishism: A Social History of the Corset, Tight-Lacing and Other Forms of Body Sculpture in the West* by David Kunzle," *Art Journal* 42, no. 2 (1982): 166.

54. David Kunzle, *Fashion and Fetishism: A Social History of the Corset, Tight-Lacing*

and Other Forms of Body Sculpture in the West (Totowa, NJ: Rowman and Littlefield, 1982), 2.

55. Cody, email to the author, October 18, 2007.

56. This claim was untrue. In 1931 pioneering German sex doctor Magnus Hirschfeld oversaw sexual reassignment surgery on the Danish artist Lili Elbe through his Institute of Sexual Science in Berlin. Jorgensen differed because her reassignment process included the prescription of artificial hormones.

57. Louryk, interview.

58. Christopher Wallenberg, "A Man Playing a Woman Who Used to Be a Man: Actor Channels a Sex-Change Pioneer on Stage," *Boston Globe*, April 2, 2006.

59. Wallenberg, "Man Playing a Woman."

60. Ludlam, *Scourge of Human Folly*, 221.

61. Though Russell was also a pioneer of sorts as a pre-civil rights African American actor, his race is not mentioned in *Christine Jorgensen Reveals*.

62. Louryk and Grace appeared briefly in a production of *First Year Born*, sharing only half a scene and exchanging one line of dialogue.

63. Wallenberg, "Man Playing a Woman."

64. Henry James, *The Art of Fiction* (New York: Oxford University Press, 1948), 13.

65. Rob Grace and Bradford Louryk, *Christine Jorgensen Reveals*, original unpublished manuscript (available directly through the authors).

66. Grace and Louryk, *Christine Jorgensen Reveals*.

67. Louryk, interview.

68. Foley, "Bad Women," 96.

69. Wallenberg, "Man Playing a Woman."

70. Ludlam uses Jorgensen as the tagline for a joke about hermaphrodites in act 2 of *The Grand Tarot* (1960).

71. Wallenberg, "Man Playing a Woman."

72. Linda Rapp, "Epperson, John," *GLBTQ: An Encyclopedia on Gay, Lesbian, Bisexual, Transgender, and Queer Culture*, last accessed June 12, 2014, http://www.glbtq.com/arts/epperson_j,2.html

73. Joe E. Jeffreys, "The Soundplay's the Thing: A Formal Analysis of John (aka Lypsinka) Epperson's Queer Performance Texts," in Fisher, *We Will Be Citizens*, 177.

74. Jeffreys, "The Soundplay's the Thing," 177.

75. Senelick, *Changing Room*, 385.

76. Jeffreys, "The Soundplay's the Thing," 177.

77. An op-ed article on this topic: Gary Giddins, "Put Your Voice Where Your Mouth Is," *New York Times*, December 29, 2004.

78. Rapp, "Epperson, John," 2.

79. Deni Kasrel, "Lypsinka: Grandes Dames," *City Paper* (Philadelphia), September 14, 1995.

80. Román, *Acts of Intervention*, 99.

81. Wallenberg, "Man Playing a Woman."

82. Simi Horwitz, "Self-Starter: Bradford Louryk," *Backstage.com*, last accessed April 11, 2010, http://www.backstage.com/news/self-starter-bradford-louryk/

83. Horwitz, "Self-Starter."

84. This is a topic that resonates within the often underrepresented politics of the trans community as an extension of the LGB community in contemporary America.

85. Foley, "Bad Women," 95.

86. Barbara Siegel and Scott Siegel, "Read Her Lips," *Theatremania.com*, last accessed October 12, 2012, http://bradford.com/pop/theatermania_cjr_feature.html

87. This term was coined by B. Ruby Rich in the *Village Voice* in 1992 to describe a renaissance of gay and lesbian filmmakers. The list also included Jennie Livingston, Gus Van Sant, Tom Kalin, Gregg Araki, and Laurie Lynd. Justin Wyatt, "Cinematic/Sexual: An Interview," *Film Quarterly* 6, no. 3 (1993): 7.

88. Rich, "Cinematic/Sexual," 7.

89. Teresa Theophano, "Christine Jorgensen (1926–1989)," *glbtqarts.com*, last accessed May 12, 2012, http://www.glbtq.com/arts/jorgensen_c.html

90. Leslie Feinberg, "Transgender Liberation: A Movement Whose Time Has Come," in *The Transgender Studies Reader*, ed. Susan Stryker and Stephen Whittle (New York: Routledge, 2006), 219.

91. Bill Schenley, "Obituary: Christine Jorgensen, *Newsday*, May 3, 1989.

92. Louryk, interview.

93. Rapp, "Epperson, John," 2.

94. Jackie McGlone, "From GI to Glamour Girl," *Scotsman* (Edinburgh), July 14, 2005.

95. Bradford Louryk, "The Lucrezia Borgia Project," *vimeo.com*, last accessed June 20, 2014, http://vimeo.com/15849389

96. Louryk, interview.

97. Bradford Louryk, "Profile: Bradford Louryk," *facebook.com*, last accessed June 20, 2014, https://www.facebook.com/brahdfjord?fref=ts

98. Bradford Louryk, "Bradford Louryk: Quotes," *wikipedia.org*, last accessed June 15, 2008, http://en.wikipedia.org/wiki/Bradford_Louryk

Chapter 4

An early and very brief version of this chapter was published in 2012: Sean F. Edgecomb, "The Ridiculous Performance of Taylor Mac," *Theatre Journal* 64, no. 4 (2012): 549–63.

1. Taylor Mac, interview by the author, March 13, 2008.

2. Savran, *Queer Sort of Materialism*, 3–10.

3. Halberstam, *Queer Art of Failure*, 2–3.

4. Ahmed, *Cultural Politics of Emotion*, 11.

5. Román, *Acts of Intervention*, 142.

6. Rivera-Servera, *Performing Queer Latinidad*, 28.

7. Taylor Mac, "Quotes," *taylormac.net*, last accessed July 12, 2012, http://www.taylor-mac.net/TaylorMac.net/Press%20Quotes.html

8. Caridad Svich, "Glamming It Up with Taylor Mac," *American Theatre* 25, no. 10 (2008): 36.

9. Ludlam, *Scourge of Human Folly*, 30.

10. Ludlam, *Scourge of Human Folly*, 225.

11. Enid Welsford, *The Fool: His Social and Literary History* (New York: Doubleday, 1961), 76,

12. Louis Petit de Julleville, *La comédie et les moeurs en France au Moyen Âge* (Paris: Adamant Media Corp. 2001), 282.

13. The extended tradition of the neo-Romantics of the 1980s is epitomized by the London performances of Lee Bowery, who is discussed later in this chapter.

14. Mac, interview..

15. Svich, "Glamming It Up," 36.

16. Jack Smith, *Wait for Me at the Bottom of the Pool: The Writing of Jack Smith*, ed. J. Hoberman and Edward Leffingwell (New York: Serpent's Tail, 1997), 56.

17. Smith, *Wait for Me*, 56.

18. Smith, *Wait for Me*, 5.

19. Smith, *Wait for Me*, 18.

20. Wayne Koestenbaum, *The Queen's Throat: Opera, Homosexuality, and the Mystery of Desire* (New York: Poseidon, 1993), 62.

21. Michael Feingold, "The Bold Soprano," *Village Voice*, February 27, 1983.

22. Mac, interview.

23. As previously mentioned, so called because of the mound of plaster that Smith crafted in the middle of the apartment and sometimes used as a stage in his queer midnight revels.

24. Ludlam, *Scourge of Human Folly*, 243–44.

25. Taylor Mac, "I Believe: A Theatre Manifesto by Taylor Mac," *taylormac. net*, last accessed June 16, 2014, http://taylormac.net/TaylorMac.net/Thoughts/Entries/2013/1/10_I_Believe:__A_Theater_Manifesto_by_Taylor_Mac.html

26. Ludlam, *Scourge of Human Folly*, 257.

27. Ludlam, *Scourge of Human Folly*.

28. Mac, *Red Tide Blooming*, 1.

29. Mac, interview.

30. Mac, interview.

31. Mac, interview.

32. Mac, interview.

33. Jeffreys, "Ethyl Eichelberger," 73.

34. Mac, interview.

35. Mac, interview.

36. Mac, interview.

37. Mac, interview.

38. Mac, interview.

39. Mac, interview.

40. Mac, interview.

41. Halberstam, *Queer Art of Failure*, 3.

42. Mac, interview.

43. See chapter 2.

44. "Wigstock: History," *wigstock.nu.history*, last accessed June 11, 2013, http://www.wigstock.nu/history

45. *Wigstock: The Movie*, DVD, directed by Barry Shils (Los Angeles: MGM, 2003).

46. See "Taylor Mac," *The List/Edinburgh Festival,* last accessed June 12, 2013, https://edinburghfestival.list.co.uk/article/3266-taylor-mac/

47. Sue Tilley, *Leigh Bowery: The Life and Times of an Icon* (London: Hodder and Stoughton, 1999), 4.

48. *The Legend of Leigh Bowery,* DVD, directed by Charles Atlas (1999; London: BBC, 2004).

49. Nicola Bowery / Estate of Leigh Bowery, "Leigh Bowery," *migratingidentity.net,* last accessed July 12, 2012, http://migratingidentity.net/tr/artists.html#detaile113

50. Gary Glitter and Leigh Bowery, "Leigh Bowery Interview [*sic*] Gary Glitter," *youtube.com,* last accessed July 12, 2012, https://www.youtube.com/watch?v=uZlf-5OeVO0

51. Tilley, *Leigh Bowery,* 5.

52. Senelick, *Changing Room,* 418.

53. Senelick, *Changing Room,* 419.

54. The "Club Kids" were a group of trust-fund-supported twenty-somethings who took the Manhattan club scene by storm in the late 1980s and 1990s. Led by Michael Alig and James St. James, the Club Kids preached a message of reckless abandon, outrageous costumes, and severe drug use. Employed by club owner Peter Gatien, the Club Kids were hired simply to show up in order to attract business with their wild antics. Leigh Bowery often appeared with them while in New York, and also jointly appeared on several television talk shows. The era of the Club Kids came to a screeching halt when Gatien was arrested for drug peddling and tax evasion and Alig was convicted of brutally murdering and dismembering his drug dealer, Angel Melendez, in 1996. The rise and fall of the Club Kids is documented in James St. James, *Disco Bloodbath* (London: Sceptre Books, 1999).

55. Mac, interview.

56. Tigger Ferguson, email to the author, April 1, 2008.

57. Judith Butler, "Performative Acts and Gender Constitution: An Essay in Phenomenology and Feminist Theory," *www.mariabuszeck.com,* last accessed June 11, 2012, http://www.mariabuszek.com/kcai/PoMoSeminar/Readings/BtlrPerfActs.pdf

58. Neil Genzlinger, "A Stand-Up Comic in Drag, Bursting Protective Bubbles," *New York Times,* July 11, 2008.

59. Mac, interview.

60. Larry Kramer, *The Tragedy of Today's Gays* (New York: Jeremy P. Tarcher / Penguin, 2005), 36–37.

61. Richard Kim, "Sex Panic," *salon.com,* last accessed July 12, 2012, http://www.salon.com/2005/05/07/kramer_6/

62. The *Voice* Best of Awards "Best be(a)st New York 2007," *Village Voice,* 2007.

63. Mac, interview.

64. Mac, interview.

65. Julia Rothenberg, "New York's Visual World After 9/11," *allacademic.com,* last accessed June 15, 2011, http://www.allacademic.com/meta/p_mla_apa_research_citation/1/0/8/2/6/p108260_index.html

66. Theodor Adorno, "Cultural Criticism and Society," in *Prisms,* trans. Samuel Weber and Shierry Weber (Cambridge: MIT Press, 1967), 34.

67. Ferguson, email to the author, April 1, 2008.

68. Mac, interview.

69. Taylor Mac, *The Face of Liberalism*, unpublished manuscript, 2003 (accessible through Morgan Jenness, Abrams Artists Agency, New York City).

70. Mac, *The Face of Liberalism*.

71. The genre of "in yer face," which developed in the United Kingdom in the late 1980s and 1990s, is an evocative and confrontational drama that seeks to reach its audience by causing viewers discomfort, using severe language and images.

72. Taylor Mac, "The Face of Liberalism," *taylormac.net*, last accessed June 15, 2013, http://www.taylormac.net/TaylorMac.net/The%20Face%20of%20Liberalism.html

73. Mac, *The Face of Liberalism*.

74. Mac, *The Face of Liberalism*.

75. This makeup scheme was applied to his cabaret-style show entitled *Live Patriot Acts!* (2002).

76. Mac, interview.

77. Victoria Pitts, "Visibly Queer: Body Technologies and Sexual Politics," *Sociological Quarterly* 41, no. 3 (2000): 443.

78. Thomas J. Csordas, *Embodiment and Experience: The Existential Ground of Culture and Self* (Cambridge: Cambridge University Press, 1994), 12.

79. Mac, interview.

80. Svich, "Glamming It Up," 36.

81. Tim Miller, "My Queer Body," in *Body Blows: Six Performances* (Madison: University of Wisconsin Press, 2002), 79.

82. Miller, "My Queer Body," 107–8.

83. Mac, interview.

84. Taylor Mac, "Live Patriot Acts," *taylormac.net*, last accessed July 5, 2015, http://www.taylormac.net/TaylorMac.net/Live_Patriot_Acts.html

85. Taylor Mac, "Okay," *newdramatisst.org*, last accessed April 4, 2013, http://newdramatists.org/taylor-mac/okay

86. Svich, "Glamming It Up," 36.

87. Charles McNulty, "Tears of a Clown," *Village Voice*, June 15, 2004.

88. Ben Brantley, "Riffs on 9/11 and City Life and Lots of Liza Minnellis," *New York Times*, July 18, 2003.

89. One of the largest of such marches took place in San Francisco in 1978, when 25,000 people marched in vigil to honor the assassinated Harvey Milk, the first openly gay man elected to a public office in the United States.

90. "Coney Island Circus Sideshow," *coneyisland.com*, last accessed June 12, 2013, http://www.coneyisland.com/sideshow.shtml

91. Savran, *Queer Sort of Materialism*, ix.

92. Ludlam, who offered public commedia dell'arte workshops at the Evergreen Theatre in 1974, noted that the Italian genre also influenced his casting process within the RTC: "Actors were chosen for their personalities, almost like 'found objects'; the character fell somewhere between the intention of the script and the personality of the actor" (Ludlam, *Scourge of Human Folly*, 17).

93. In the Vatican scene of *Galas* Ludlam commented on his own views of Catholicism through the title character. First he (as Galas) questions the pope about his bias toward women and homosexuals, and then uses a rosary to lasso his hand and take control of the situation.

94. Taylor Mac, *Red Tide Blooming*, in *Plays and Playwrights 2007*, ed. Martin Denton (New York: New York Theatre Experience, 2007), 54.

95. Chris Baldrick, *In Frankenstein's Shadow: Myth, Monstrosity, and Nineteenth-Century Writing* (Oxford: Oxford University Press, 1987), 10.

96. The phrase "axis of evil" was coined for President George W. Bush's State of the Union Address delivered on January 29, 2002, in Washington, DC.

97. Performance artist Ron Vawter also appeared as Jack Smith in Arabian drag for his solo piece *What's Underground about Marshmallows* (1996).

98. Mac, *Red Tide Blooming*, 64.

99. Michael Atkinson, "Flesh Journeys: Neo Primitives and the Contemporary Rediscovery of Radical Body Modification," *Deviant Behavior* 22, no. 2 (2001): 118.

100. Hermaphrodites were common attractions in carnival sideshows in the latter half of the nineteenth and beginning of the twentieth centuries. Mac's portrayal of Olokun is a riff on the "half-and-half trick," which promised a figure whose gender was split down the middle.

101. Ludlam, *Bluebeard*, in *Complete Plays*, 119.

102. Tompkins, "Profiles: Ridiculous."

103. Mac, *Red Tide Blooming*, 66.

104. Julie Atlas Muz, "Artist's Statement," *julieatlasmuz.com*, last accessed November 24, 2012, http://www.julieatlasmuz.com/bio.shtml

105. Phoebe Hoban, "Sea Creatures Spare Nothing, Especially Not the Glitter, in 'Red Tide Blooming,'" *New York Times*, April 19, 2006.

106. Martin Denton, "Red Tide Blooming," *nytheatre.com*, last accessed July 11, 2013, http://www.nytheatre.com/Show/Review/5006355

107. David Bergman notes that "because camp likes to stand the world on its head, it is comparable to Mikhail Bakhtin's notion of the *carnivalesque*, a style noted for its gay relativity and its mocking and deriding tone. The carnivalesque, like camp, is characterized by a licensed release of anarchic forces that tend to invert standard social hierarchies." See "Camp," *GLBTQ: An Encyclopedia of Gay, Lesbian, Bisexual, Transgender and Queer Culture, glbtq.com*, last accessed July 21, 2012, http://www.glbtq.com/literature/camp,2.html

108. Taylor Mac, *The Be(a)st of Taylor Mac*, unpublished manuscript, 2006 (accessible through Morgan Jenness, Abrams Artists Agency, New York City).

109. Mac, *Be(a)st of Taylor Mac*.

110. Mac, interview.

111. Mac, interview.

112. Dolan, *Utopia in Performance*, 65.

113. Leonard Jacobs, "Papa Don't Preach: *The Young Ladies of* Channels Big Daddy," *NY Press Review*, October 3–9, 2007.

114. Mac, interview.

115. Taylor Mac, *The Young Ladies of* (New York: Black Wave Press, 2009), 5.

116. Mac, The Young Ladies of, 8.

117. Mac, The Young Ladies of, 43.

118. Mac, The Young Ladies of, 13.

119. Halberstam, *Queer Time*, 169.

120. Halberstam, *Queer Time*.

121. Ludlam, *Scourge of Human Folly*, 22.

122. Mac, interview.

123. In recent years, a critical mass of scholarship has developed that explores notions of queer kinship. See, for example, Dinshaw, *Getting Medieval*; Eng, *Feeling of Kinship*; Weston, *Families We Choose*; Freeman, "Time Binds, or, Erotohistoriography"; and Newton, *Margaret Mead Made Me Gay*.

124. Charles Isherwood, "Protesters Armed with Wigs and Sequins," *New York Times*, January 20, 2011.

125. Charles Isherwood, "Among the Huddles Masses," *New York Times*, October 29, 2013.

126. Taylor Mac, "Manifesto," *taylormac.net*, last accessed June 15, 2014, http://taylor-mac.net/TaylorMac.net/Thoughts/Entries/2013/1/10

Epilogue

Source of epigraph: RuPaul, *Lettin' It All Hang Out: An Autobiography* (New York: Hyperion, 1995), 2.

1. Harold Bloom, *The Anxiety of Influence: A Theory of Poetry* (Oxford: Oxford University Press, 1997), 7.

2. Bloom, *The Anxiety of Influence*, 1.

3. Halberstam, *Queer Art of Failure*, 19.

4. See Michel Foucault, *The Order of Things* (New York: Vintage, 1971).

5. Ahmed, *Cultural Politics of Emotion*, 145.

6. Ahmed, *Cultural Politics of Emotion*, 11.

7. Muñoz, *Cruising Utopia*, 121.

8. Edward Albee in James Beasely Simpson, *Simpson's Contemporary Quotations* (Boston: Houghton Mifflin, 1998), 398.

9. The sexually driven subcultures of the gay community, including "hanky codes," also developed from this same principle, probably beginning with the post–World War II leather/biker culture in the late 1940s.

10. Edelman, *No Future*, 1–33.

11. Kaufman, *Ridiculous!*, 391.

12. Ludlam, *Scourge of Human Folly*, 250.

13. Ludlam, *Scourge of Human Folly*, 228.

14. Anna Henchman, "Bookworms, Earthworms and the Sense of Space," 2013, unpublished paper. Made available through an email to the author, January 22, 2013.

15. Muñoz, *Cruising Utopia*, 189.

16. Richard Meyer and Catherine Lord, *Art and Queer Culture* (London: Phaidon, 2013), 9.

Bibliography

Books, Articles, and Other Sources

Adorno, Theodor. "Cultural Criticism and Society." *Prisms*. Cambridge: MIT Press, 1967.

Ahmed, Sara. *The Cultural Politics of Emotion*. New York: Routledge, 2004.

Anderson, Benedict. *Imagined Communities: Reflections on the Origin and Spread of Nationalism*. New York: Verso, 2006.

Atkinson, Michael. "Flesh Journeys: Neo Primitives and the Contemporary Rediscovery of Radical Body Modification." *Deviant Behavior* 22, no. 2 (2001): 117–46.

Babuscio, Jack. "The Cinema of Camp." *Gay Roots: Twenty Years of Gay Sunshine. An Anthology of Gay History, Sex, Politics and Culture*. Edited by Winston Leyland. San Francisco: Gay Sunshine Press, 1991.

Baldrick, Chris. *In Frankenstein's Shadow: Myth, Monstrosity, and Nineteenth-Century Writing*. Oxford: Oxford University Press, 1987.

Bergman, David. "Camp." *GLBTQ: An Encyclopedia of Gay, Lesbian, Bisexual, Transgender and Queer Culture*. *glbtq.com*. http://www.glbtq.com/literature/camp,2.html

Bergman, David. *Camp Grounds: Style and Homosexuality*. Amherst: University of Massachusetts Press, 1993.

Bernstein, Mary. "Celebration and Suppression: The Strategic Uses of Identity by the Lesbian and Gay Movement." *American Journal of Sociology* 103, no. 3 (1997): 531.

Bernstein, Robin. *Cast Out: Queer Lives in Theatre*. Ann Arbor: University of Michigan Press, 2006.

Bhabha, Homi. *The Location of Culture*. New York: Routledge, 2004.

Blake, Nayland. "The Message from Atlantis." In *Flaming Creatures, Jack Smith: His Amazing Life and Times*. London: Serpent's Tail Press, 1997.

Bloch, Ernst. *The Spirit of Utopia*. Stanford, CA: Stanford University Press, 2000.

Bloom, Harold. *The Anxiety of Influence: A Theory of Poetry*. Oxford: Oxford University Press, 1997.

Bordowitz, Gregg. *The AIDS Crisis Is Ridiculous and Other Writings, 1986–2003*. Cambridge: MIT Press, 2006.

Bowery, Nicola / Estate of Leigh Bowery. "Leigh Bowery." *migratingidentity.net*. http://migratingidentity.net/tr/artists.html#detaile113

Boyarin, Daniel, Daniel Itzkovitz, and Ann Pellegrini. *Queer Theory and the Jewish Question*. New York: Columbia University Press, 2003.

Brecht, Berthold. "Theatre for Learning." In *The Brecht Sourcebook*. Edited by Henry Bial and Carol Martin. London: Routledge, 2000.

Brecht, Stefan. *Queer Theatre*. Frankfurt am Main: Suhrkamp, 1978.

Bredbeck, Gregory W. "The Ridiculous Sound of One Hand Clapping: Placing Ludlam's 'Gay Theatre' in Space and Time." *Modern Drama* 39, no. 1 (1996): 64–83.

Bronski, Michael. *Culture Clash: The Making of a Gay Sensibility*. Boston: South End Press, 1984.

Bryson, Norman. "Todd Haynes' *Poison* and Queer Cinema." *In[]visible Culture: An Electric Journal for Visual Studies*. http://www.rochester.edu/in_visible_culture/issue1/bryson/bryson.html

Busch, Charles. *Die Mommie, Die!* New York: Samuel French, 2010.

Busch, Charles. *The Tale of the Allergists Wife and Other Plays*. New York: Grove Press, 2001.

Busch, Charles. *Whores of Lost Atlantis*. New York: Carroll and Graf, 2005.

Butler, Judith. *Gender Trouble: Feminism and the Subversion of Identity*. New York: Routledge, 2006.

Butler, Judith. "Performative Acts and Gender Constitution: An Essay in Phenomenology and Feminist Theory." *www.mariabuszek.com*. http://www.mariabuszek.com/kcai/PoMoSeminar/Readings/BtlrPerfActs.pdf

Carlson, Marvin. *The Haunted Stage: The Theatre as Memory Machine*. Ann Arbor: University of Michigan Press, 2001.

Carr, Cynthia. "The Hot Bottom: Art and Artifice in the East Village." In *On Edge: Performance at the End of the Twentieth Century*." Middletown, CT: Wesleyan University Press, 1993.

Cashman, Ray. "Critical Nostalgia and Material Culture in Northern Ireland." *Journal of American Folklore* 119, no. 472 (2006): 137–60.

Chauncey, George. *Gay New York*. New York: Basic Books, 1994.

Cleto, Fabio. *Camp, Queer Aesthetics and the Performing Subject. A Reader*. Ann Arbor: University of Michigan Press, 1999.

Cocteau, Jean. "Le paquet rouge." In *Opéra, Oeuvres Poétiques*. Paris: Delamain et Boutelleau, 1927.

"Coffee Talk." *Wikipedia*. https://en.wikipedia.org/wiki/Coffee_Talk

Connor, Maureen. "Review: *Fashion and Fetishism: A Social History of the Corset, Tight-Lacing and Other Forms of Body Sculpture in the West* by David Kunzle." *Art Journal* 42, no. 2 (1982): 165–71.

Core, Phillip. *Camp: The Lie That Tells the Truth*. London: Plexus, 1984.

Csordas, Thomas J. *Embodiment and Experience: The Existential Ground of Culture and Self*. Cambridge: Cambridge University Press, 1994.

Cvetkovich, Ann. *An Archive of Feelings: Trauma, Sexuality and Lesbian Public Cultures*. Durham, NC: Duke University Press, 2003.

Dasgupta, Gautam. "Interview: Charles Ludlam." *Performing Arts Journal* 3, no. 1 (1978): 69–80.

Davis, Whitney, ed. *Studies in Gay and Lesbian Art History*. New York: Haworth Press, 1994.

Davy, Kate. "Fe/male Impersonation: The Discourse of Camp." In *Critical Theory and Performance*. Edited by Janelle G. Reinelt and Joseph R. Roach. Ann Arbor: University of Michigan Press, 1992.

Derrida, Jacques. *Specters of Marx*. New York: Routledge, 2006.

Derrida, Jacques. *Writing and Difference*. Translated by Alan Bass. London: Routledge, 1978.

Dinshaw, Carolyn. *Getting Medieval: Sexualities and Communities, Pre- and Postmodern*. Durham, NC: Duke University Press, 1999.

Dolan, Jill. "Building a Theatrical Vernacular: Responsibility, Community, Ambivalence and Queer Theatre." *Modern Drama* 39, no. 1 (1996): 1–15.

Dolan, Jill. *Geographies of Learning: Theory and Practice, Activism and Performance*. Middletown, CT: Wesleyan University Press, 2001.

Dolan, Jill. *Utopia in Performance*. Ann Arbor: University of Michigan Press, 2005.

Du Bois, W. E. B. "Krigwa Players Little Negro Theatre." *Crisis*, July 1926.

Edelman, Lee. *Homographesis: Essays in Gay Literary and Cultural Theory*. New York: Routledge, 1994.

Edelman, Lee. *No Future: Queer Theory and the Death Drive*. Durham, NC: Duke University Press, 2004.

Edgecomb, Sean. "A History of the Ridiculous, 1960–1987." *Gay and Lesbian Review Worldwide* 14, no. 3 (2007): 21–22.

Edgecomb, Sean. "'Not Just Any Woman': Bradford Louryk, a Legacy of Charles Ludlam and the Ridiculous Theatre for the Twenty-First Century." In *We Will Be Citizens: New Essays on Gay and Lesbian Theatre*. Edited by James Fisher. Jefferson, NC: McFarland, 2008.

Edgecomb, Sean. "The Ridiculous Performance of Taylor Mac." *Theatre Journal* 64, no. 4 (2012): 549–63.

Eng, David L. *The Feeling of Kinship: Queer Liberalism and the Racialization of Intimacy*. Durham, NC: Duke University Press, 2010.

"Ethyl Eichelberger." *PS122.org*. http://www.ps122.org/eichelberger/

Evans, Arthur. *Witchcraft and the Gay Counterculture*. Boston: Fag Rag Books, 2014.

Feinberg, Leslie. "Transgender Liberation: A Movement Whose Time Has Come." In *The Transgender Studies Reader*. Edited by Susan Stryker and Stephen Whittle. New York: Routledge, 2006.

Fink, Mary. "AIDS Vampires: Reimagining Illness in Octavia Butler's 'Fledgling.'" *Science Fiction Studies* 37, no. 3 (2010): 416–32.

Fleming, Martha. *Studiolo: The Collaborative Works of Martha Fleming and Lyne Lapointe*. Windsor: Artextes Editions and the Art Gallery of Windsor, 1997.

Foley, Helene. "Bad Women: Gender Politics in Late Twentieth-Century Performance and Revision of Greek Tragedy." In *Dionysus since 69: Greek Tragedy at the Dawn of the Third Millennium*. Edited by Edith Hall. Oxford: Oxford University Press, 2004.

Freeman, Elizabeth. "Time Binds, or, Erotohistoriography." *Social Text* 23, nos. 3–4 (2005): 57–68.

Freud, Sigmund. "The Uncanny." In *Standard Edition*. Translated by James Strachey. London: Hogarth Press, 1955.

Fristcher, Jack. *Gay San Francisco: Eyewitness Drummer*. Sebastopol, CA: Palm Drive, 2008–.

Glitter, Gary, and Leigh Bowery, "Leigh Bowery interview Gary Glitter." *youtube.com*. https://www.youtube.com/watch?v=uZlf-5OeVO0.

Gould, Deborah B. "The Shame of Gay Pride in Early AIDS Activism." In *Gay Shame*. Edited by David M. Halperin and Valerie Traub. Chicago: University of Chicago Press, 2009.

Gray, Margaret E. *Postmodern Proust*. Philadelphia: University of Pennsylvania Press, 1992.

Grosz, Elizabeth. "Histories of a Feminist Future." *Signs* 25, no. 4 (2000): 1017–21.

Halberstam, Judith. *In a Queer Time and Place: Transgender Bodies, Subcultural Lives*. New York: New York University Press, 2005.

Halberstam, Judith. *The Queer Art of Failure*. Durham, NC: Duke University Press, 2011.

Harbin, Billy J., Kim Marra, and Robert A. Schanke. *The Gay and Lesbian Theatrical Legacy: A Biographical Dictionary of Major Figures in American Stage History in the Pre-Stonewall Era*. Ann Arbor: University of Michigan Press, 2005.

Harding, James M., and Cindy Rosenthal. *Restaging the Sixties: Radical Theaters and Their Legacies*. Ann Arbor: University of Michigan Press, 2006.

Harris, Daniel. "The Death of Camp: Gay Men and Hollywood Diva Worship, from Reverence to Ridicule." *Salmagundi* 112 (1996): 166–91.

Hayden, Corinne P. "Gender, Genetics and Generation: Reformulating Biology in Lesbian Kinship." *Cultural Anthropology* 10, no. 1 (1995): 41–63.

Hoberman, J., and Jonathan Rosenbaum, eds. *Midnight Movies*. New York: Harper and Row, 1983.

Isherwood, Christopher. *The World in the Evening*. London: Methuen, 1954.

James, Henry. *The Art of Fiction*. New York: Oxford University Press, 1948.

Jameson, Fredric. "Marx's Purloined Letter." In *Ghostly Demarcations: A Symposium on Jacques Derrida's "Spectres de Marx"*. Edited by Michael Sprinkler. London: Verso, 1999.

Jeffreys, Joe E. "Ethyl Eichelberger." In *Extreme Exposure: An Anthology of Solo Performance Texts from the Twentieth Century*. Edited by Jo Bonney. New York: Theatre Communications Group, 2000.

Jeffreys, Joe E. "The Soundplay's the Thing: A Formal Analysis of John (aka Lypsinka) Epperson's Queer Performance Texts." In *We Will Be Citizens: New Essays on Gay and Lesbian Drama*. Edited by James Fisher. Jefferson, NC: McFarland, 2008.

Jagose, Annamarie. *Queer Theory*. Melbourne: Melbourne University Press, 1996.

Kaufman, David. *Ridiculous! The Theatrical Life and Times of Charles Ludlam*. New York: Applause, 2002.

Kelly, John. "John Kelly Performance." http://johnkellyperformance.org/wp2/?page_id=59

Kierkegaard, Søren. "Journals 1835." http://www.age-of-the-sage.org/philosophy/kierkegaard.html

Kim, Richard. "Sex Panic." *salon.com*. http://www.salon.com/2005/05/07/kramer_6/

Koestenbaum, Wayne. *The Queen's Throat: Opera, Homosexuality, and the Mystery of Desire*. New York: Poseidon, 1993.

Kopelson, Kevin. *Neatness Counts: Essays on the Writer's Desk*. Minneapolis: University of Minnesota Press, 2004.

Kramer, Larry. *The Tragedy of Today's Gays*. New York: Jeremy P. Tarcher / Penguin, 2005.

Kulick, Don. "Gay and Lesbian Language." *Annual Review of Anthropology* 9 (2000): 243–85.

Kunzle, David. *Fashion and Fetishism: A Social History of the Corset, Tight-Lacing and Other Forms of Body Sculpture in the West.* Totowa, NJ: Rowman and Littlefield, 1982.

Leap, William, ed. *Beyond the Lavender Lexicon: Authenticity, Imagination and Appropriation in Lesbian and Gay Language.* Buffalo: Gordon and Breach, 1995.

Leap, William, and Tom Boellstorf. *Speaking in Queer Tongues: Globalization and Gay Language.* Urbana: University of Illinois Press, 2003.

Leffingwell, Edward, Carole Kismeric, and Marvin Heiferman, eds. *Flaming Creature: Jack Smith, His Amazing Life and Times.* London: Serpent's Tale, 1997.

Lévi-Strauss, Claude. *The Elementary Structures of Kinship.* Oxford: Eyre and Spottiswoode, 1969.

Levine, Martin P. *Gay Macho: The Life and Death of a Homosexual Clone.* New York: New York University Press, 1998.

"Linda Richman Sketches." *Saturday Night Live.* http://www.nbc.com/saturday-night-live/cast/mike-myers-15006/character/linda-richman-16071

Lonc, Christopher. "Genderfuck and Its Delights." *Gay Sunshine* 21 (Spring 1974): 225.

Long, Thomas L. *AIDS and American Apocalypticism: The Cultural Semiotics of an Epidemic.* Albany: State University of New York Press, 2005.

Louryk, Bradford. "Bradford Louryk: Quotes." *wikipedia.org.* http://en.wikipedia.org/wiki/Bradford_Louryk

Louryk, Bradford. "The Lucrezia Borgia Project." *vimeo.com.* http://vimeo.com/15849389

Louryk, Bradford. "Profile: Bradford Louryk." *facebook.com.* https://www.facebook.com/brahdfjord?fref=ts

Ludlam, Charles. *The Complete Plays of Charles Ludlam.* New York: Harper Collins, 1989.

Ludlam, Charles. *Ridiculous Theatre: Scourge of Human Folly. The Essays and Opinions of Charles Ludlam.* Edited by Steven Samuels. New York: Theatre Communications Group, 1992.

Marranca, Bonnie, and Gautam Dasgupta. *Theatre of the Ridiculous.* Baltimore: Performing Arts Journal Publications, 1989.

Mac, Taylor. "The Face of Liberalism." *taylormac.net.* http://www.taylormac.net/Taylor-Mac.net/The%20Face%20of%20Liberalism.html

Mac, Taylor. "I Believe: A Theatre Manifesto by Taylor Mac." *taylormac.net.* http://taylormac.net/TaylorMac.net/Thoughts/Entries/2013/1/10_I_Believe:__A_Theater_Manifesto_by_Taylor_Mac.html

Mac, Taylor. "Live Patriot Acts." *taylormac.net.* http://www.taylormac.net/TaylorMac.net/Live_Patriot_Acts.html

Mac, Taylor. "Manifesto." *taylormac.net.* http://taylormac.net/TaylorMac.net/Thoughts/Entries/2013/1/10_

Mac, Taylor. "Okay." *newdramatisst.org.* http://newdramatists.org/taylor-mac/okay

Mac, Taylor. "Quotes." *taylormac.net.* http://www.taylormac.net/TaylorMac.net/Press%20Quotes.html

Mac, Taylor. "Red Tide Blooming." In *Plays and Playwrights 2007.* Edited by Martin Denton. New York: New York Theatre Experience, 2007.

Mac, Taylor. *The Young Ladies of . . . .* New York: Black Wave Press, 2009.

Meyer, Richard, and Catherine Lord. *Art and Queer Culture*. London: Phaidon, 2013.

Moon, Jennifer. "Gay Shame and the Politics of Identity." In *Gay Shame*. Edited by David M. Halperin and Valerie Traub. Chicago: University of Chicago Press, 2009.

Morrill, Cynthia. "Revamping the Gay Sensibility: Queer Camp and Dyke Noir." In *The Politics and Poetics of Camp*. Edited by Moe Meyer. New York: Routledge, 1993.

Muñoz, José Esteban. *Cruising Utopia: The Then and There of Queer Futurity*. New York: New York University Press, 2009.

Muz, Julie Atlas. "Artist's Statement." *julieatlasmuz.com*. http://www.julieatlasmuz.com/bio.shtml

Newton, Esther. *Margaret Mead Made Me Gay: Personal Essays, Public Ideas*. Durham, NC: Duke University Press, 2000.

O'Connell, Erin. *Heraclitus and Derrida: Presocratic Deconstruction*. New York: Peter Lang, 2005.

Pellegrini, Ann. "Touching the Past; or, Hanging Chad." *Journal of the History of Sexuality* 10, no. 2 (2001): 185–94.

Petit de Julleville, Louis. *La comédie et les moeurs en France au Moyen-Âge*. Paris: Adamant Media Corp. 2001.

Pitts, Victoria. "Visibly Queer: Body Technologies and Sexual Politics." *Sociological Quarterly* 41, no. 3 (2000): 443–63.

Proust, Marcel. *Swann's Way*. Translated by C. K. Scott Moncrieff. New York: Modern Library, 2004.

Rapp, Linda. "Epperson, John." *GLBTQ: An Encyclopedia on Gay, Lesbian, Bisexual, Transgender, and Queer Culture*. http://www.glbtq.com/arts/epperson_j,2.html

Rivera-Servera, Ramón H. *Performing Queer Latinidad: Dance, Sexuality and Politics*. Ann Arbor: University of Michigan Press, 2012.

Roach, Joseph. *Cities of the Dead: Circum-Atlantic Performance*. New York: Columbia University Press, 1996.

Roemer, Rick. *Charles Ludlam and the Ridiculous Theatrical Company: Critical Analyses of 29 Plays*. Jefferson, NC: McFarland, 1998.

Román, David. *Acts of Intervention: Performance, Gay Culture and AIDS*. Bloomington: Indiana University Press, 1998.

Román, David. *Performance in America; Contemporary U.S. Culture and the Performing Arts*. Durham, NC: Duke University Press, 2005.

Rothenberg, Julia. "New York's Visual World after 9/11." http://www.allacademic.com/meta/p_mla_apa_research_citation/1/0/8/2/6/p108260_index.html

Rubin, Gayle. *Deviations: A Gayle Rubin Reader*. Durham, NC: Duke University Press, 2011.

RuPaul. *Lettin' It All Hang Out: An Autobiography*. New York: Hyperion, 1995.

Russell, Donn. *Avant-Guardian, 1965–1990: A Theater Foundation Director's Twenty-Five Years Off Broadway*. Pittsburgh: Dorrance, 1996.

Salih, Sara, ed., with Judith Butler. *The Judith Butler Reader*. Malden, MA: Blackwell, 2004.

Savran, David. *A Queer Sort of Materialism: Recontextualizing American Theatre*. Ann Arbor: University of Michigan Press, 2003.

Schechner, Richard. *Public Domain: Essays on the Theatre*. New York: Avon Books, 1969.

Schildcrout, Jordan. *Murder Most Queer*. Ann Arbor: University of Michigan Press, 2015.

Sedgwick, Eve Kosofsky. *Between Men: English Literature and Male Homosexual Desire.* New York: Columbia University Press, 1992.

Sedgwick, Eve Kosofsky. *Epistemology of the Closet.* Berkeley: University of California Press, 2008.

Sedgwick, Eve Kosofsky. *Tendencies.* Durham, NC: Duke University Press, 1993.

Senelick, Laurence. *The Changing Room: Sex, Drag and Theatre.* New York: Routledge, 2000.

Senelick, Laurence. "The Word Made Flesh: Staging Pornography in Eighteenth-Century Paris." *Theatre Research International* 33, no. 2 (2008): 191–203.

Simpson, James Beasely. *Simpson's Contemporary Quotations.* Boston: Houghton Mifflin, 1998.

Smith, Jack. *Wait for Me at the Bottom of the Pool: The Writing of Jack Smith.* Edited by J. Hoberman and Edward Leffingwell. New York: Serpent's Tail, 1997.

Smith, Patricia Julian. *The Queer Sixties.* New York: Routledge, 1999.

Snediker, Michael D. *Queer Optimism: Lyric Personhood and or Her Felicitous Persuasions.* Minneapolis: University of Minnesota Press, 2008.

Split Britches. "Beauty and the Beast." *Hemispheric Institute Digital Video Library—Split Britches Video Collection.* http://hidvl.nyu.edu/video/000539386.html

St. James, James. *Disco Bloodbath.* London: Sceptre Books, 1999.

Staiger, Janet. "Finding Community in the Early 1960s." In *Queer Film Cinema: The Film Reader.* Edited by Harry Benshoof and Sean Griffin. New York: Routledge, 2004.

Stockton, Kathryn Bond. *The Queer Child, or Growing Sideways in the Twentieth Century.* Durham, NC: Duke University Press, 2009.

Stryker, Susan, Jim Van Buskirk, and Armistead Maupin. *Gay by the Bay: A History of Queer Culture in the San Francisco Bay Area.* San Francisco: Chronicle Books, 1996.

Svich, Caridad. "Glamming It Up with Taylor Mac." *American Theatre* 25, no. 10 (2008): 34–36.

Tavel, Ronald. "Maria Montez: Anima of an Antediluvian World." In *Flaming Creature: Jack Smith and His Amazing Life and Times.* Edited by Edward Leffingwell, Carole Kismaric, Marvin Heiferman. London: Serpent's Tail, 2007.

Taylor, Diana. "Performance and/as History." *TDR* 50.1, no. 189 (2006): 67–86.

Taylor, Jodie. *Playing It Queer: Popular Music, Identity and Queer World-Making.* Bern: Peter Lang, 2012.

Taylor, Verta, and Nancy E. Whittier. "Collective Identity in Social Movement Communities." In *Frontiers in Social Movement Theory.* Edited by A. D. Morris and C. McClurg. New Haven: Yale University Press, 1992.

Theophano, Teresa. "Christine Jorgensen (1926–1989)." *glbtqarts.com.* http://www.glbtq.com/arts/jorgensen_c.html

Tilley, Sue. *Leigh Bowery: The Life and Times of an Icon.* London: Hodder and Stoughton, 1999.

Tyler, Parker. *Underground Film: A Critical History.* New York: DaCapo Press, 1995.

Warner, Michael, ed. *Fear of a Queer Planet: Queer Politics and Social Theory.* Minneapolis: University of Minnesota Press, 1993.

Warner, Michael. *Public and Counterpublics.* Brooklyn: Zone Books, 2002.

Warner, Sara. *Acts of Gaiety: LGBT Performance and the Politics of Pleasure.* Ann Arbor: University of Michigan Press, 2012.

Welsford, Enid. *The Fool: His Social and Literary History.* New York: Doubleday, 1961.
Weston, Kath. *Families We Choose: Lesbians, Gays, Kinship.* New York: Columbia University Press, 1997.
Whittle, Stephen. "Gender Fucking or Fucking Gender." In *Queer Theory.* Edited by I. Morland and A. Wilcox. New York: Palgrave Macmillan, 2005.
"Wigstock: History." *wigstock.nu.history.* http://www.wigstock.nu/history
Wilkerson, David. *The Vision.* Old Tappan, NJ: Fleming H. Revell, 1974.
Wyatt, Justin. "Cinematic/Sexual: An Interview." *Film Quarterly* 6, no. 3 (1993): 7–8.

Dissertations

Elliott, Kenneth Yates. "Beyond the Ridiculous: The Commercialization of an Alternative Theatre Movement from Jack Smith to Hairspray." Ph.D. dissertation, UCLA, 2004.
Jeffreys, Joe E. "An Outre Entrée into the Para-Ridiculous Histrionics of Drag Diva Ethyl Eichelberger: A True Story." Ph.D. dissertation, New York University, 1993.
Niles, Richard. "Charles Busch and Theatre-in-Limbo." Ph.D. dissertation, City University of New York, 1993.
Wharton, Robert Thomas III. "The Working Dynamics of the Ridiculous Theatrical Company: An Analysis of Charles Ludlam's Relationship with His Ensemble from 1967–1981." Ph.D. dissertation, Florida State University, 1985.

Films and Videos

The Cockettes. Directed by David Weissman and Bill Webber. Culver City CA: Strand Releasing, 2002.
Gay Sex in the 70s. Directed by Josh F. Lovett. New York: Wolfe Video, 2006.
The Lady in Question Is Charles Busch: A Drag to Riches Story. Directed by John Cantania and Charles Ignacio. New York: Docurama, 2006.
The Legend of Leigh Bowery. Directed by Charles Atlas. 1999; London: BBC, 2004.
Wigstock: The Movie. Directed by Barry Shils. Los Angeles: MGM, 2003.

Newspaper and Periodical Articles and Reviews

Als, Hilton. "Freaks: The Characters of Charles Ludlam and John Steinbeck." *New Yorker*, April 28, 2014.
Bentley, Erica. "The Ladies in Question: Drag Crosses Over." *Theatre Week*, April 23, 1990.
Berson, Misha. "A Moving and Funny Camille." *San Francisco Bay Guardian*, February 28, 1990.
Brantley, Ben. "Charles Busch Takes on a Trouser Role." *New York Times*, November 3, 1994.

Brantley, Ben. "Riffs on 9/11 and City Life and Lots of Liza Minnellis." *New York Times*, July 18, 2003.

Brantley, Ben. "A Woman on the Verge of Another Breakdown." *New York Times*, March 1, 2000.

Bruckner, D. J. R. "Stage: *Vampire Lesbians of Sodom*." *New York Times*, June 20, 1985.

Denton, Martin. "Red Tide Blooming." *nytheatre.com*. http://www.nytheatre.com/Show/Review/5006355

Feingold, Michael. "The Bold Soprano." *Village Voice*, February 27, 1983.

Genzlinger, Neil. "A Stand-Up Comic in Drag, Bursting Protective Bubbles." *New York Times*, July 11, 2008.

Giddins, Gary. "Put Your Voice Where Your Mouth Is." *New York Times*, December 29, 2004.

Gussow, Mel. "Ludlam's Consistently Amusing Linguistic Conceits." *New York Times*, May 5, 1970.

Hedlund, Patrick. "Push to Make Pyramid Club City's First Drag Landmark." *Villager*, December 5, 2007. http://thevillager.com/villager_241/pushtomake.html

Hevesi, Dennis. "Ronald Tavel, Proudly Ridiculous Writer, Dies at 72." *New York Times*, March 27, 2009.

Hoban, Phoebe. "Sea Creatures Spare Nothing, Especially Not the Glitter, in 'Red Tide Blooming.'" *New York Times*, April 19, 2006.

Holleran, Andrew. "The Spectacle at the Bottom of the Shaft." *New York Native*, May 23, 1983.

Horwitz, Simi. "Self-Starter: Bradford Louryk." *Backstage.com*. http://www.backstage.com/news/self-starter-bradford-louryk/

Isherwood, Charles. "Among the Huddles Masses." *New York Times*, October 29, 2013.

Isherwood, Charles. "Protesters Armed with Wigs and Sequins." *New York Times*, January 20, 2011.

Jacobs, Leonard. "Papa Don't Preach: *The Young Ladies of* Channels Big Daddy." *NY Press Review*, October 3–9, 2007.

Kasrel, Deni. "Lypsinka: Grandes Dames." *City Paper*, September 14, 1995.

Lester, Elenore. "Camille." *New York Times*, July 14, 1977.

McGlone, Jackie. "From GI to Glamour Girl." *Scotsman*, July 14, 2005.

Neroulias, Nicole. "Gay Jews Connect Their Experience to Story of Purim." *Washington Post*, February 24, 2007.

Schechner, Richard. "Two Exemplary Productions." *Village Voice*, April 23, 1970.

Schenley, Bill. "Obituary: Christine Jorgensen." *Newsday*, May 3, 1989.

Shewey, Don. "Review: Our Leading Lady." *Advocate*, May 2007.

Siegel, Barbara, and Scott Siegel. "Read Her Lips." *Theatremania.com*. http://bradford.com/pop/theatermania_cjr_feature.html

Sullivan, Ronald. "In City, AIDS Affecting Drug Users More Often." *New York Times*, October 1, 1984.

Tompkins, Calvin. "Profiles: Ridiculous." *New Yorker*, November 15, 1976.

Wallenberg, Christopher. "A Man Playing a Woman Who Used to Be a Man: Actor Channels a Sex-Change Pioneer on Stage." *Boston Globe*, April 2, 2006.

Index

Printed and bound by CPI Group (UK) Ltd, Croydon, CR0 4YY

13/04/2025

14656530-0002